*for
friend
. Campbell
with love,
Barbara
1986*

STARHAWK

The Spiral Dance

A Rebirth of
the Ancient Religion
of the Great Goddess

Published in San Francisco by
HARPER & ROW, PUBLISHERS
New York, Hagerstown, San Francisco, London

Thanks and Acknowledgments

This book could not have come into being without the love and support of my husband, Ed Rahsman, and my mother, Dr. Bertha Simos.

For the opportunity to explore and strive to understand the Mysteries, I thank the members of my covens: in Compost, Guidot, Quest, Diane, Beth, Arden, Mother Moth, Amber, Valerie and Paul; in Honeysuckle, Laurel, Brook, Susan, Zenobia, Diane, and especially Kevyn, for the added inspiration of her drawing.

I would also like to acknowledge those who have taught me the Craft: Victor and Cora Anderson, Ruth, Z. Budapest, and the others.

I am also grateful for the support and encouragement of the Bay Area pagan community and Witches of the Covenant of the Goddess, and for friends and companions too numerous to be listed here. In particular, I want to thank my brother-in-spirit, Alan Acacia, and my brother-in-flesh, Mark Simos, for their contributions; Patty and Nada, for being there in the beginning; Ann, for her inspiration; and Carol Christ and Naomi Goldenberg, for their help in reaching a wider community.

Finally, I want to express my appreciation to my editor, Marie Cantlon, for her sensitivity and courage in taking on this subject, and to Sarah Rush, for all her help.

To all of you, to She Who Sings in The Heart, and He Who Dances, this work is dedicated.

THE SPIRAL DANCE: A Rebirth of the Ancient Religion of the Great Goddess.

Designed by Leigh McLellan

Library of Congress Cataloging in Publication Data

Starhawk.
    The spiral dance.

    Bibliography: p. 214.
    1. Witchcraft.   I.   Title.
BF1566.S77 1979   299   79-1775
ISBN 0-06-067535-7

86 18 17 16 15 14

Contents

EXERCISES

INVOCATIONS, CHANTS, AND BLESSINGS

SPELLS

MYTHS

1 *Witchcraft as Goddess Religion*

Between the Worlds

The moon is full. We meet on a hilltop that looks out over the bay. Below us, lights spread out like a field of jewels, and faraway skyscrapers pierce the swirling fog like the spires of fairytale towers. The night is enchanted.

Our candles have been blown out, and our makeshift altar cannot stand up under the force of the wind, as it sings through the branches of tall eucalyptus. We hold up our arms and let it hurl against our faces. We are exhilarated, hair and eyes streaming. The tools are unimportant; we have all we need to make magic: our bodies, our breath, our voices, each other.

The circle has been cast. The invocations begin:

> All-dewy, sky-sailing pregnant moon,
> Who shines for all.
> Who flows through all . . .
> Aradia, Diana, Cybele, Mah . . .
>
> Sailor of the last sea,
> Guardian of the gate,
> Ever-dying, ever-living radiance . . .
> Dionysus, Osiris, Pan, Arthur, Hu . . .

The moon clears the treetops and shines on the circle. We huddle closer for warmth. A woman moves into the center of the circle. We begin to chant her name:

"Diana ..."

"Dee-ah-nah ..."

"Aaaah ..."

The chant builds, spiraling upward. Voices merge into one endlessly modulated harmony. The circle is enveloped in a cone of light.

Then, in a breath—silence.

"You are Goddess," we say to Diane, and kiss her as she steps back into the outer ring. She is smiling.

She remembers who she is.

One by one, we will step into the center of the circle. We will hear our names chanted, feel the cone rise around us. We will receive the gift, and remember:

"I am Goddess. You are God, Goddess. All that lives, breathes, loves, sings in the unending harmony of being is divine."

In the circle, we will take hands and dance under the moon.

> "To disbelieve in witchcraft is the greatest of all heresies."
> *Malleus Maleficarum* (1486)

On every full moon, rituals such as the one described above take place on hilltops, beaches, in open fields and in ordinary houses. Writers, teachers, nurses, computer programmers, artists, lawyers, poets, plumbers, and auto mechanics—women and men from many backgrounds come together to celebrate the mysteries of the Triple Goddess of birth, love, and death, and of her Consort, the Hunter, who is Lord of the Dance of life. The religion they practice is called *Witchcraft.*

Witchcraft is a word that frightens many people and confuses many others. In the popular imagination, Witches are ugly old hags riding broomsticks, or evil Satanists performing obscene rites. Modern Witches are thought to be members of a kooky cult, primarily concerned with cursing enemies by jabbing wax images with pins, and lacking the depth, the dignity and seriousness of purpose of a true religion.

But Witchcraft is a religion, perhaps the oldest religion extant in the West. Its origins go back before Christianity, Judaism, Islam—before Buddhism and Hinduism, as well, and it is very different from all the so-called great religions. The Old Religion, as we call it, is closer in spirit to Native American traditions or to the shamanism of the Arctic. It is not based on dogma or a set of beliefs, nor on scriptures or a sacred book revealed by a great man. Witchcraft takes its teachings from nature, and reads inspiration in the movements of the sun, moon, and stars, the flight of birds, the slow growth of trees, and the cycles of the seasons.

According to our legends, Witchcraft began more than 35 thousand years ago, when the temperature of Europe began to drop and the great sheets of ice crept slowly south in their last advance. Across the rich tundra, teeming with animal life, small groups of hunters followed the free-running reindeer and the thundering bison. They were armed with only the most primitive of weapons, but some among the clans were gifted, could "call" the herds to a cliffside or a pit, where a few beasts, in willing sacrifice, would let themselves be trapped. These gifted shamans could attune themselves to the spirits of the herds, and in so doing they became aware of the pulsating rhythm that infuses all life, the dance of the double spiral, of whirling into being, and whirling out again. They did not phrase this insight intellectually, but in images: the Mother Goddess, the birthgiver, who brings into existence all life; and the Horned God, hunter and hunted, who eternally passes through the gates of death that new life may go on.

Male shamans dressed in skins and horns in identification with the God and the herds; but female priestesses presided naked, embodying the fertility of the Goddess.[1] Life and death were a continuous stream; the dead were buried as if sleeping in a womb, surrounded by their tools and ornaments, so that they might awaken to a new life.[2] In the caves of the Alps, skulls of the great bears were mounted in niches, where they pronounced oracles that guided the clans to game.[3] In lowland pools, reindeer does, their bellies filled with stones that embodied the souls of deer, were submerged in the waters of the Mother's womb, so that victims of the hunt would be reborn.[4]

In the East—Siberia and the Ukraine—the Goddess was Lady of the Mammoths; She was carved from stone in great swelling curves that embodied her gifts of abundance.[5] In the West, in the great cave temples of southern France and Spain, her rites were performed deep in the secret wombs of the earth, where the great polar forces were painted as bison and horses, superimposed, emerging from the cave walls like spirits out of a dream.[6]

The spiral dance was seen also in the sky: in the moon, who monthly dies and is reborn; in the sun, whose waxing light brings summer's warmth and whose waning brings the chill of winter. Records of the moon's passing were scratched on bone,[7] and the Goddess was shown holding the bison horn, which is also the crescent moon.[8]

The ice retreated. Some clans followed the bison and the reindeer into the far north. Some passed over the Alaskan land bridge to the Americas. Those who remained in Europe turned to fishing and gathering wild plants and shellfish. Dogs guarded their campsites, and new tools were refined.

Those who had the inner power learned that it increased when they worked together. As isolated settlements grew into villages, shamans and priestesses linked forces and shared knowledge. The first covens were formed. Deeply attuned to plant and animal life, they tamed where once they had hunted, and they bred sheep, goats, cows, and pigs from their wild cousins. Seeds were no longer only gathered; they were planted, to grow where they were set. The Hunter became Lord of the Grain, sacrificed when it is cut in autumn, buried in the womb of the Goddess and reborn in the spring. The Lady of the Wild Things became the Barley Mother, and the cycles of moon and sun marked the times for sowing and reaping and letting out to pasture.

Villages grew into the first towns and cities. The Goddess was painted on the plastered walls of shrines, giving birth to the Divine Child—her consort, son, and seed.[9]

In the lands once covered with ice, a new power was discovered, a force that runs like springs of water through the earth Herself. Barefoot priestesses trace out "ley" lines on the new grass. It was found that certain stones increase the flow of power. They were set at the proper points in great marching rows and circles that mark the cycles of time. The year became a great wheel divided into eight parts: the solstices and equinoxes and the cross-quarter days between, when great feasts were held and fires lit. With each ritual, with each ray of the sun and beam of the moon that struck the stones at the times of power, the force increased. They became great reservoirs of subtle energy, gateways between the worlds of the seen and the unseen. Within the circles, beside the menhirs and dolmens and passage graves, priestesses could probe the secrets of time, and the hidden structure of the cosmos. Mathematics, astronomy, poetry, music, medicine, and the understanding of the workings of the human mind developed side by side with the lore of the deeper mysteries.[10]

But in other lands, cultures developed that devoted themselves to the arts of war. Wave after wave of invasion swept over Europe from the Bronze Age on. Warrior gods drove the Goddess peoples out from the fertile lowlands and fine temples, into the hills and high mountains where they became known as the Sidhe, the Picts or Pixies, the Fair Folk or Faeries.[11] The mythological cycle of Goddess and Consort, Mother and Divine Child, which had held sway for 30 thousand years, was changed to conform to the values of the conquering patriarchies. In Greece, the Goddess, in her many guises, "married" the new gods—the result was the Olympian Pantheon. In the British Isles, the victorious Celts adopted many features of the Old Religion, incorporating them into the Druidic mysteries.

The Faeries, breeding cattle in the stony hills and living in turf-covered, round huts, preserved the Old Religion. Clan mothers, called

"Queen of Elphame," which means Elfland, led the covens, together with the priest, the Sacred King, who embodied the dying God, and underwent a ritualized mock death at the end of his term of office. They celebrated the eight feasts of the Wheel with wild processions on horseback, singing, chanting, and the lighting of ritual fires. The invading people often joined in; there was mingling and intermarriage, and many rural families were said to have "Faery blood." The Colleges of the Druids, and the Poetic Colleges of Ireland and Wales, preserved many of the old mysteries.

Christianity, at first, brought little change. Peasants saw in the story of Christ only a new version of their own ancient tales of the Mother Goddess and her Divine Child who is sacrificed and reborn. Country priests often led the dance at the Sabbats, or great festivals.[12] The covens, who preserved the knowledge of the subtle forces, were called *Wicca* or *Wicce,* from the Anglo-Saxon root word meaning "to bend or shape." They were those who could shape the unseen to their will. Healers, teachers, poets, and midwives, they were central figures in every community.

Persecution began slowly. The twelfth and thirteenth centuries saw a revival of aspects of the Old Religion by the troubadours, who wrote love poems to the Goddess under the guise of living noble ladies of their times. The magnificent cathedrals were built in honor of Mary, who had taken over many of the aspects of the ancient Goddess. Witchcraft was declared a heretical act, and in 1324 an Irish coven led by Dame Alice Kyteler was tried by the Bishop of Ossory for worshipping a non-Christian god. Dame Kyteler was saved by her rank, but her followers were burned.

Wars, Crusades, plagues, and peasant revolts raged over Europe in the next centuries. Joan of Arc, the "Maid of Orleans," led the armies of France to victory, but was burned as a Witch by the English. "Maiden" is a term of high respect in Witchcraft, and it has been suggested that the French peasantry loved Joan so greatly because she was, in truth, a leader of the Old Religion.[13] The stability of the medieval Church was shaken, and the feudal system began to break down. The Christian world was swept by messianic movements and religious revolts, and the Church could no longer calmly tolerate rivals.

In 1484, the Papal Bull of Innocent VIII unleashed the power of the Inquisition against the Old Religion. With the publication of the *Malleus Malleficarum,* "The Hammer of the Witches," by the Dominicans Kramer and Sprenger in 1486, the groundwork was laid for a reign of terror that was to hold all of Europe in its grip until well into the eighteenth century. The persecution was most strongly directed against women: Of an estimated 9 million Witches executed, 80 percent were women, including children and young girls, who were believed to inherit the "evil" from their mothers. The ascetism of early Christianity, which turned its back on the world of the flesh, had degenerated, in some quarters of the

Church, into hatred of those who brought that flesh into being. Misogyny, the hatred of women, had become a strong element in medieval Christianity. Women, who menstruate and give birth, were identified with sexuality and therefore with evil. "All witchcraft stems from carnal lust, which is in women insatiable," stated the *Malleus Maleficarum.*

The terror was indescribable. Once denounced, by anyone from a spiteful neighbor to a fretful child, a suspected Witch was arrested suddenly, without warning, and not allowed to return home again. She* was considered guilty until proven innocent. Common practice was to strip the suspect naked, shave her completely in hopes of finding the Devil's "marks," which might be moles or freckles. Often the accused were pricked all over their bodies with long, sharp needles; spots the Devil had touched were said to feel no pain. In England, "legal torture" was not allowed, but suspects were deprived of sleep and subjected to slow starvation, before hanging. On the continent, every imaginable atrocity was practiced—the rack, the thumbscrew, "boots" that broke the bones in the legs, vicious beatings—the full roster of the Inquisition's horrors. The accused were tortured until they signed confessions prepared by the Inquisitors, until they admitted to consorting with Satan, to dark and obscene practices that were never part of true Witchcraft. Most cruelly, they were tortured until they named others, until a full coven quota of thirteen were taken. Confession earned a merciful death: strangulation before the stake. Recalcitrant suspects, who maintained their innocence, were burned alive.

Witch hunters and informers were paid for convictions, and many found it a profitable career. The rising male medical establishment welcomed the chance to stamp out midwives and village herbalists, their major economic competitors. For others, the Witch trials offered opportunities to rid themselves of "uppity women" and disliked neighbors. Witches themselves say that few of those tried during the Burning Times actually belonged to covens or were members of the Craft. The victims were the elderly, the senile, the mentally ill, women whose looks weren't pleasing or who suffered from some handicap, village beauties who bruised the wrong egos by rejecting advances, or who had roused lust in a celibate priest or married man. Homosexuals and freethinkers were caught in the same net. At times, hundreds of victims were put to death in a day. In the Bishopric of Trier, in Germany, two villages were left with only a single female inhabitant apiece after the trials of 1585.

The Witches and Faeries who could do so, escaped to lands where the Inquisition did not reach. Some may have come to America. It is possible

---

*Generically, Witches are female—this usage is meant to include males, not to exclude them.

that a genuine coven was meeting in the woods of Salem before the trials, which actually marked the end of active persecution in this country. Some scholars believe that the family of Samuel and John Quincy Adams were members of the megalithic "Dragon" cult, which kept alive the knowledge of the power of the stone circles.[14] Certainly, the independent spirit of Witchcraft is very much akin to many of the ideals of the "Founding Fathers": for example, freedom of speech and worship, decentralized government, and the rights of the individual rather than the divine right of kings.

In America, as in Europe, the Craft went underground, and became the most secret of religions. Traditions were passed down only to those who could be trusted absolutely, usually to members of the same family. Communications between covens were severed; no longer could they meet on the Great Festivals to share knowledge and exchange the results of spells or rituals. Parts of the tradition became lost or forgotten. Yet somehow, in secret, in silence, over glowing coals, behind closed shutters, encoded as fairytales and folksongs, or hidden in subconscious memories, the seed was passed on.

After the persecutions ended, in the eighteenth century, came the age of disbelief. Memory of the true Craft had faded; the hideous stereotypes that remained seemed ludicrous, laughable, or tragic. Only in this century have Witches been able to "come out of the broom closet," so to speak, and counter the imagery of evil with truth. The word "Witch" carries so many negative connotations that many people wonder why we use the word at all. Yet to reclaim the word "Witch" is to reclaim our right, as women, to be powerful; as men, to know the feminine within as divine. To be a Witch is to identify with 9 million victims of bigotry and hatred and to take responsibility for shaping a world in which prejudice claims no more victims. A Witch is a "shaper," a creator who bends the unseen into form, and so becomes one of the Wise, one whose life is infused with magic.

Witchcraft has always been a religion of poetry, not theology. The myths, legends, and teachings are recognized as metaphors for "That-Which-Cannot-Be-Told," the absolute reality our limited minds can never completely know. The mysteries of the absolute can never be explained —only felt or intuited. Symbols and ritual acts are used to trigger altered states of awareness, in which insights that go beyond words are revealed. When we speak of "the secrets that cannot be told," we do not mean merely that rules prevent us from speaking freely. We mean that the inner knowledge literally *cannot* be expressed in words. It can only be conveyed by experience, and no one can legislate what insight another person may draw from any given experience. For example, after the ritual described at the opening of this chapter, one woman said, "As we were chanting, I felt that we blended together and became one voice; I sensed the oneness of everybody." Another woman said, "I became aware of how different the chant sounded for each of us, of how unique each person is." A man said simply, "I felt loved." To a Witch, all of these statements are equally true and valid. They are no more contradictory than the statements, "Your eyes are as bright as stars" and "Your eyes are as blue as the sea."

The primary symbol for "That-Which-Cannot-Be-Told" is the Goddess. The Goddess has infinite aspects and thousands of names—She is the reality behind many metaphors. She *is* reality, the manifest deity, omnipresent in all of life, in each of us. The Goddess is not separate from the world—She *is* the world, and all things in it: moon, sun, earth, star, stone, seed, flowing river, wind, wave, leaf and branch, bud and blossom, fang and claw, woman and man. In Witchcraft, flesh and spirit are one.

As we have seen, Goddess religion is unimaginably old, but contemporary Witchcraft could just as accurately be called the New Religion. The Craft, today, is undergoing more than a revival, it is experiencing a renaissance, a re-creation. Women are spurring this renewal, and actively reawakening the Goddess, the image of "the legitimacy and beneficence of female power."[15]

Since the decline of the Goddess religions, women have lacked religious models and spiritual systems that speak to female needs and experience. Male images of divinity characterize both western and eastern Religions. Regardless of how abstract the underlying concept of God may be, the symbols, avatars, preachers, prophets, gurus, and Buddhas are overwhelmingly male. Women are not encouraged to explore their own strengths and realizations; they are taught to submit to male authority, to identify masculine perceptions as their spiritual ideals, to deny their bodies and sexuality, to fit their insights into a male mold.

Mary Daly, author of *Beyond God The Father,* points out that the model of the universe in which a male God rules the cosmos from outside serves to legitimize male control of social institutions. "The symbol of the Father God, spawned in the human imagination and sustained as plausible by patriarchy, has in turn rendered service to this type of society by making its mechanisms for the oppression of women appear right and fitting."[16] The unconscious model continues to shape the perceptions even of those who have consciously rejected religious teachings. The details of one dogma are rejected, but the underlying structure of belief is imbibed at so deep a level it is rarely questioned. Instead, a new dogma, a parallel structure, replaces the old. For example, many people have rejected the "revealed truth" of Christianity without ever questioning the underlying concept that truth is a set of beliefs revealed through the agency of a "Great Man," possessed of powers or intelligence beyond the ordinary human scope. Christ, as the "Great Man," may be replaced by Buddha, Freud, Marx, Jung, Werner Erhard, or the Maharaj Ji in their theology, but truth is always seen as coming from someone else, as only knowable secondhand. As feminist scholar Carol Christ points out, "Symbol systems cannot simply be rejected, they must be replaced. Where there is no replacement, the mind will revert to familiar structures at times of crisis, bafflement, or defeat."[17]

The symbolism of the Goddess is not a parallel structure to the symbolism of God the Father. The Goddess does not rule the world; She *is* the world. Manifest in each of us, She can be known internally by every individual, in all her magnificent diversity. She does not legitimize the rule of either sex by the other and lends no authority to rulers of temporal hierarchies. In Witchcraft, each of us must reveal our own truth. Deity is seen in our own forms, whether female or male, because the Goddess has her male aspect. Sexuality is a sacrament. Religion is a matter of relinking, with the divine within and with her outer manifestations in all of the human and natural world.

The symbol of the Goddess is *poemagogic,* a term coined by Anton Ehrenzweig to "describe its special function of inducing and symbolizing the ego's creativity."[18] It has a dreamlike, "slippery" quality. One aspect slips into another: She is constantly changing form and changing face. Her images do not define or pin down a set of attributes; they spark inspiration, creation, fertility of mind and spirit: "One thing becomes another,/ In the Mother . . . In the Mother . . . " (ritual chant for the Winter Solstice).

The importance of the Goddess symbol for women cannot be overstressed. The image of the Goddess inspires women to see ourselves as divine, our bodies as sacred, the changing phases of our lives as holy, our aggression as healthy, our anger as purifying, and our power to nurture and create, but also to limit and destroy when necessary, as the very force that sustains all life. Through the Goddess, we can discover our strength, enlighten our minds, own our bodies, and celebrate our emotions. We can move beyond narrow, constricting roles and become whole.

The Goddess is also important for men. The oppression of men in Father God-ruled patriarchy is perhaps less obvious but no less tragic than that of women. Men are encouraged to identify with a model no human being can successfully emulate: to be minirulers of narrow universes. They are internally split, into a "spiritual" self that is supposed to conquer their baser animal and emotional natures. They are at war with themselves: in the West, to "conquer" sin; in the East, to "conquer" desire or ego. Few escape from these wars undamaged. Men lose touch with their feelings and their bodies, becoming the "successful male zombies" described by Herb Goldberg in *The Hazards of Being Male*: "Oppressed by the cultural pressures that have denied him his feelings, by the mythology of the woman and the distorted and self-destructive way he sees and relates to her, by the urgency for him to "act like a man," which blocks his ability to respond to his inner promptings both emotionally and physiologically, and by a generalized self-hate that causes him to feel comfortable only when he is functioning well in harness, not when he lives for joy and personal growth."[19]

Because women give birth to males, nurture them at the breast, and in our culture are primarily responsible for their care as children, "every male brought up in a traditional home develops an intense early identification with his mother and therefore carries within him a strong feminine imprint."[20] The symbol of the Goddess allows men to experience and integrate the feminine side of their nature, which is often felt to be the deepest and most sensitive aspect of self. The Goddess does not exclude the male; She contains him, as a pregnant woman contains a male child. Her own male aspect embodies both the solar light of the intellect and wild, untamed animal energy.

Our relationship to the earth and the other species that share it has also been conditioned by our religious models. The image of God as outside of nature has given us a rationale for our own destruction of the natural order, and justified our plunder of the earth's resources. We have attempted to "conquer" nature as we have tried to conquer sin. Only as the results of pollution and ecological destruction become severe enough to threaten even urban humanity's adaptability have we come to recognize the importance of ecological balance and the interdependence of all life. The model of the Goddess, who is immanent in nature, fosters respect for the sacredness of all living things. Witchcraft can be seen as a religion of ecology. Its goal is harmony with nature, so that life may not just survive, but thrive.

The rise of Goddess religion makes some politically oriented feminists uneasy. They fear it will sidetrack energy away from direct action to bring about social change. But in areas as deeply rooted as the relations between the sexes, true social change can only come about when the myths and symbols of our culture are themselves changed. The symbol of the Goddess conveys the spiritual power both to challenge systems of oppression and to create new, life-oriented cultures.

Modern Witchcraft is a rich kaleidoscope of traditions and orientations. Covens, the small, closely knit groups that form the congregations of Witchcraft, are autonomous; there is no central authority that determines liturgy or rites. Some covens follow practices that have been handed down in an unbroken line since before the Burning Times. Others derive their rituals from leaders of modern revivals of the Craft—the two whose followers are most widespread are Gerald Gardner and Alex Sanders, both British. Feminist covens are probably the fastest-growing arm of the Craft.

Many are Dianic: a sect of Witchcraft that gives far more prominence to the female principle than the male. Other covens are openly eclectic, creating their own traditions from many sources. My own covens are based on the Faery Tradition, which goes back to the Little People of Stone Age Britain, but we believe in creating our own rituals, which reflect our needs and insights of today.

The myths underlying philosophy and "thealogy" (a word coined by religious scholar Naomi Goldenburg from "thea," the Greek word for Goddess) in this book are based on the Faery Tradition. Other Witches may disagree with details, but the overall values and attitudes expressed are common to all of the Craft. Much of the Faery material is still held secret, so many of the rituals, chants, and invocations come from our creative tradition. In Witchcraft, a chant is not necessarily better because it is older. The Goddess is continually revealing Herself, and each of us is potentially capable of writing our own liturgy.

In spite of diversity, there are ethics and values that are common to all traditions of Witchcraft. They are based on the concept of the Goddess as immanent in the world and in all forms of life, including human beings.

Theologians familiar with Judeo-Christian concepts sometimes have trouble understanding how a religion such as Witchcraft can develop a system of ethics and a concept of justice. If there is no split between spirit and nature, no concept of sin, no covenant or commandments against which one can sin, how can people be ethical? By what standards can they judge their actions, when the external judge is removed from his place as ruler of the cosmos? And if the Goddess is immanent in the world, why work for change or strive toward an ideal? Why not bask in the perfection of divinity?

Love for life in all its forms is the basic ethic of Witchcraft. Witches are bound to honor and respect all living things, and to serve the life force. While the Craft recognizes that life feeds on life and that we must kill in order to survive, life is never taken needlessly, never squandered or wasted. Serving the life force means working to preserve the diversity of natural life, to prevent the poisoning of the environment and the destruction of species.

The world is the manifestation of the Goddess, but nothing in that concept need foster passivity. Many Eastern religions encourage quietism not because they believe the divine is truly immanent, but because they believe She/He is not. For them, the world is Maya, Illusion, masking the perfection of the Divine Reality. What happens in such a world is not really important; it is only a shadow play obscuring the Infinite Light. In Witchcraft, however, what happens in the world is vitally important. The Goddess is immanent, but She needs human help to realize her fullest beauty. The harmonious balance of plant/animal/human/divine awareness is not automatic; it must constantly be renewed, and this is the true function of Craft rituals. Inner work, spiritual work, is most effective when it proceeds hand in hand with outer work. Meditation on the balance of nature might be considered a spiritual act in Witchcraft, but not as much as would cleaning up garbage left at a campsite or marching to protest an unsafe nuclear plant.

Witches do not see justice as administered by some external authority, based on a written code or set of rules imposed from without. Instead, justice is an inner sense that each act brings about consequences that must be faced responsibly. The Craft does not foster guilt, the stern, admonishing, self-hating inner voice that cripples action. Instead, it demands responsibility. "What you send, returns three times over" is the saying— an amplified version of "Do unto others as you would have them do unto you." For example, a Witch does not steal, not because of an admonition in a sacred book, but because the threefold harm far outweighs any small material gain. Stealing diminishes the thief's self-respect and sense of honor; it is an admission that one is incapable of providing honestly for one's own needs and desires. Stealing creates a climate of suspicion and fear, in which even thieves have to live. And, because we are all linked in the same social fabric, those who steal also pay higher prices for groceries, insurance, taxes. Witchcraft strongly imbues the view that all things are interdependent and interrelated and therefore mutually responsible. An act that harms anyone harms us all.

Honor is a guiding principle in the Craft. This is not a "macho" need to take offense at imagined slights against one's virility—it is an inner sense of pride and self-respect. The Goddess is honored in oneself, and in others. Women, who embody the Goddess, are respected, not placed on pedestals or etherealized but valued for all their human qualities. The self, one's individuality and unique way of being in the world, is highly valued. The Goddess, like nature, loves diversity. Oneness is attained not through losing the self, but through realizing it fully. "Honor the Goddess in yourself, celebrate your self, and you will see that Self is everywhere."

In Witchcraft, "All acts of love and pleasure are My rituals." Sexuality, as a direct expression of the life force, is seen as numinous and sacred. It can be expressed freely, so long as the guiding principle is love. Marriage is a deep commitment, a magical, spiritual, and psychic bond. But it is only one possibility out of many for loving, sexual expression.

Misuse of sexuality, however, is heinous. Rape, for example, is an intolerable crime because it dishonors the life force by turning sexuality to the expression of violence and hostility instead of love. A woman has the sacred right to control her own body, as does a man. No one has the right to force or coerce another.

Life is valued in Witchcraft, and it is approached with an attitude of joy and wonder, as well as a sense of humor. Life is seen as the gift of the Goddess. If suffering exists, it is not our task to reconcile ourselves to it, but to work for change.

Magic, the art of sensing and shaping the subtle, unseen forces that flow through the world, of awakening deeper levels of consciousness beyond the rational, is an element common to all traditions of Witchraft. Craft rituals are magical rites: they stimulate an awareness of the hidden side of reality, and awaken long-forgotten powers of the human mind.

The magical element in Witchcraft is disconcerting to many people. Much of this book is devoted to a deep exploration of the real meaning of magic, but here I would like to speak to the fear I have heard expressed that Witchcraft and occultism are in some way a revival of Nazism. There does seem to be evidence that Hitler and other Nazis were occultists—that is, they may have practiced some of the same techniques as others who seek to expand the horizons of the minds. Magic, like chemistry, is a set of techniques that can be put to the service of any philosophy. The rise of the Third Reich played on the civilized Germans' disillusionment with rationalism and tapped a deep longing to recover modes of experience Western culture had too long ignored. It is as if we had been trained, since infancy, never to use our left arms: The muscles have partly atrophied, but they cry out to be used. But Hitler perverted this longing and twisted it into cruelty and horror. The Nazis were not Goddess worshippers; they denigrated women, relegating them to the position of breeding animals whose role was to produce more Aryan warriors. They were the perfect patriarchy, the ultimate warrior cult—not servants of the life force. Witchcraft has no ideal of a "superman" to be created at the expense of inferior races. In the Craft, all people are already seen as manifest gods, and differences in color, race, and customs are welcomed as signs of the myriad beauty of the Goddess. To equate Witches with Nazis because neither are Judeo-Christians and both share magical elements is like saying that swans are really scorpions because neither are horses and both have tails.

Witchcraft is not a religion of masses—of any sort. Its structure is cellular, based on covens, small groups of up to thirteen members that allow for both communal sharing and individual independence. "Solitaries," Witches who prefer to worship alone, are the exception. Covens are autonomous, free to use whatever rituals, chants and invocations they prefer. There is no set prayer book or liturgy.

Elements may change, but Craft rituals inevitably follow the same underlying patterns. The techniques of magic, which has been termed by occultist Dion Fortune "the art of changing consciousness at will," are used to create states of ecstasy, of union with the divine. They may also be used to achieve material results, such as healings, since in the Craft there is no split between spirit and matter.

Each ritual begins with the creation of a sacred space, the "casting of a circle," which establishes a temple in the heart of the forest or the center of a covener's living room. Goddess and God are then invoked or awakened within each participant and are considered to be physically present within the circle and the bodies of the worshippers. Power, the subtle force that shapes reality, is raised through chanting or dancing and may be directed through a symbol or visualization. With the raising of the cone of power comes ecstasy, which may then lead to a trance state in which visions are seen and insights gained. Food and drink are shared, and coveners "earth the power" and relax, enjoying a time of socializing. At the end, the powers invoked are dismissed, the circle is opened, and a formal return to ordinary consciousness is made.

Entrance to a coven is through an initiation, a ritual experience in which teachings are transmitted and personal growth takes place. Every initiate is considered a priestess or priest; Witchcraft is a religion of clergy.

This book is structured around those elements that I feel are constants among all the varied traditions of the Craft. Interest in Witchcraft is growing rapidly. Colleges and universities are beginning to feature courses in the Craft in their religious studies departments. Women in ever greater numbers are turning to the Goddess. There is a desperate need for material that will intelligently explain Witchcraft to non-Witches in enough depth so that both the practices and philosophy can be understood. Because entrance to a coven is a slow and delicate process, there are many more people who want to practice the Craft than there are covens to accommodate them. So this book also contains exercises and practical suggestions that can lead to a personal Craft practice. A person blessed with imagination and a moderate amount of daring could also use it as a manual to start her or his own coven. It is not, however, meant to be followed slavishly; it is more like a basic musical score, on which you can improvise.

Mother Goddess is reawakening, and we can begin to recover our primal birthright, the sheer, intoxicating joy of being alive. We can open new eyes and see that there is nothing to be saved *from*, no struggle of life *against* the universe, no God outside the world to be feared and obeyed; only the Goddess, the Mother, the turning spiral that whirls us in and out of existence, whose winking eye is the pulse of being—birth, death, rebirth—whose laughter bubbles and courses through all things and who is found only through love: love of trees, of stones, of sky and clouds, of scented blossoms and thundering waves; of all that runs and flies and swims and crawls on her face; through love of ourselves; life-dissolving world-creating orgasmic love of each other; each of us unique and natural as a snowflake, each of us our own star, her Child, her lover, her beloved, her Self.

Notes

1. The female figure is almost always shown naked in Paleolithic art. Examples include: The bas-reliefs of Laussel, Dordogne, France—see Johannes Maringer and Hans-George Bandi, *Art in the Ice Age* (New York: Frederick A. Praeger, 1953), pp. 84–85 for photograph; nude figures in La Magdaleine and Angles-Sur-Anglin, Dordogne, France, described by Philip Van Doren Stern in *Prehistoric Europe: From Stone Age Man to the Early Greeks* (New York: W. W. Norton, 1969) p. 162; engraved figures in the underground sanctuary of Pech-Merle, France, described by Stern, pp. 174–175; and the Aurignacian sculptured "fat Venuses" such as that of Willendorf, shown by Maringer and Bandi on p. 28 and Lespugue, see Maringer and Bandi, p. 29.

   Examples of male "sorcerors" are found painted in the cave of Le Trois Freres, Dordogne, France, (Stern, p.115) and the chamois-headed figures of Abu Mege, Teyjat, France, (Stern, p.166) among many other examples.

   References are given for the purpose of indicating descriptions and illustrations of archaeological and anthropological finds that corroborate Craft oral tradition. The interpretations given here of the meanings of finds and customs illustrate Craft traditions of our history, and are by no means meant to be taken as academically accepted or proven. If scholars agree on anything, it is that they don't know what many of these figures meant, or how they were used.

2. See descriptions of La Ferassie, Dordogne, France in Stern, pp. 85, 95; also La Barma Grande, France in Grahame Clark and Stuart Piggott, *Prehistoric Societies* (London: Hutchinson & Co., 1967) pp. 77–79, and Grimaldi, Calabria, Italy, in Clark and Piggott, pp. 77–79.

3. As at Drachenloch, Switzerland, described by Stern, p. 89.

4. At Meindorf and Stellmoor, Germany; see Alberto C. Blanc, "Some Evidence for the Ideologies of Early Man," in Sherwood L. Washburn, ed., *The Social Life of Early Man*, (Chicago, Aldine Publications, 1961), p. 124.

5. Finds of the Mammoth Goddess near the Desna River in the Ukraine are described by Joseph Campbell, *The Masks of God: Primitive Mythology* (New York: Viking Press, 1959) p. 327.

6. Annette Laming, *Lascaux*, trans. by Eleanor Frances Armstrong, (Harmondsworth, Middlesex: Penguin Books, 1959); André Leroi-Gourhan, "The Evolution of Paleolithic Art," in *Scientific American*, Vol. 218, No. 17, 1958, pp. 58–68.

7. Gerald S. Hawkins, *Beyond Stonehenge* (New York, Harper & Row, 1973), see descriptions of engraved mammoth tusks (15,000 B.C.) from Gontzi in the Ukraine, Russia, pp. 236–237; red ochre markings at Abri de las Vinas, Spain (8000—6000 B.C.), pp. 232–233; and wall paintings at Canchal de Mahoma, Spain (7000 B.C.), pp. 230–231.

8. Laussel, Dordogne, France: see Maringer and Bandi, pp. 84–85.

9. James Mellaart, *Catal Hüyük, a Neolithic Town in Anatolia*, (New York: McGraw-Hill, 1967).

10. Alexander Thom, "Megaliths and Mathematics," *Antiquity*, 1966, *40*, 121–8.

11. Margaret A. Murray, *The Witch-Cult in Western Europe*, (Oxford, England: Oxford University Press, 1971), pp. 238–246.

12. Murray, p. 49.

13. Murray, pp. 270–276.

14. Andrew E. Rothovius, "The Adams Family and the Grail Tradition: The Untold Story of the Dragon Persecution," *East-West 1977, 7* (5), 24–30; Andrew E. Rothovius, "The Dragon Tradition in the New World," *East-West* 1977, *7* (8), 43–54.

15. Carol P. Christ, "Why Women Need The Goddess" in Carol P. Christ and Judith Plaskow, *Womanspirit Rising: A Feminist Reader in Religion*, (San Francisco: Harper & Row, 1979), p. 278.

16. Mary Daly, *Beyond God the Father* (Boston: Beacon Press, 1973), p. 13.
17. Christ, p. 275.
18. Anton Ehrenzweig, *The Hidden Order of Art* (London: Paladin, 1967), p. 190.
19. Herb Goldberg, *The Hazards of Being Male* (New York: Signet, 1977), p. 4.
20. Goldberg, p. 39.

2 *The World View of Witchcraft*

Between the Worlds

CREATION[1]

Alone, awesome, complete within Herself, the Goddess, She whose name cannot be spoken, floated in the abyss of the outer darkness, before the beginning of all things. And as She looked into the curved mirror of black space, She saw by her own light her radiant reflection, and fell in love with it. She drew it forth by the power that was in Her and made love to Herself, and called Her "Miria, the Wonderful."

Their ecstasy burst forth in the single song of all that is, was, or ever shall be, and with the song came motion, waves that poured outward and became all the spheres and circles of the worlds. The Goddess became filled with love, swollen with love, and She gave birth to a rain of bright spirits that filled the worlds and became all beings.

But in that great movement, Miria was swept away, and as She moved out from the Goddess She became more masculine. First She became the Blue God, the gentle, laughing God of love. Then She became the Green One, vine-covered, rooted in the earth, the spirit of all growing things. At last She became the Horned God, the Hunter whose face is the ruddy sun and yet dark as Death. But always desire draws Him back toward the Goddess, so that He circles Her eternally, seeking to return in love.

All began in love; all seeks to return to love. Love is the law, the teacher of wisdom, and the great revealer of mysteries.

> "The Sioux idea of living creatures is that trees, buffalo and men are temporary energy swirls, turbulence patterns. . .that's an early intuitive recognition of energy as a quality of matter. But that's an old insight, you know, extremely old—probably a Paleolithic shaman's insight. You find that perception registered so many ways in archaic and primitive lore. I would say that it is probably the most basic insight into the nature of things, and that our more common, recent Occidental view of the universe as consisting of fixed things is out of the main stream, a deviation from basic human perception."
>
> Gary Snyder[2]

The mythology and cosmology of Witchcraft are rooted in that "Paleolithic shaman's insight": that all things are swirls of energy, vortexes of moving forces, currents in an ever-changing sea. Underlying the appearance of separateness, of fixed objects within a linear stream of time, reality is a field of energies that congeal, temporarily, into forms. In time, all "fixed" things dissolve, only to coalesce again into new forms, new vehicles.

This view of the universe as an interplay of moving forces—which, incidentally, corresponds to an amazing degree with the views of modern physics—is a product of a very special mode of perception. Ordinary waking consciousness sees the world as fixed; it focuses on one thing at a time, isolating it from its surroundings, much like viewing a dark forest with a narrow flashlight beam that illuminates a lone leaf or a solitary stone. Extraordinary consciousness, the other mode of perception that is broad, holistic, and undifferentiated, sees patterns and relationships rather than fixed objects. It is the mode of starlight: dim and silvery, revealing the play of woven branches and the dance of shadows, sensing pathways as spaces in the whole.

The magical and psychic aspects of the Craft are concerned with awakening the starlight vision, as I like to call it, and training it to be a useful tool. Magic is not a supernatural affair; it is, in Dion Fortune's definition, "the art of changing consciousness at will"—of switching the flashlight off and on, of picking out details, of seeing by the stars.

Ordinary consciousness is highly valued in the Craft, but Witches are aware of its limitations. It is, in a sense a grid through which we view the world, a culturally transmitted system of classification. There are infinite ways to look at the world; the "other vision" frees us from the limits of our culture.

"Our fellow men are the black magicians," Don Juan, the Yaqui shaman, tells his student Castaneda in *Tales of Power*. "Think for a moment.

Can you deviate from the path that they've lined up for you? No. Your thoughts and your actions are fixed forever in their terms. I, on the other hand, brought you freedom. Freedom is expensive, but the price is not impossible. So fear your captors, your masters. Don't waste your time and your power fearing me."[3]

In Witchcraft, the "price of freedom," is, first of all, discipline and responsibility. Starlight vision is a natural potential inherent in each of us, but much work is required to develop and train it. Powers and abilities gained through heightened awareness must also be used responsibly, otherwise, like the Ring of Sauron (in Tolkien's *Lord of the Rings*) they will destroy their possessors. Those who would be free must also be willing to stand slightly aside from the mainstream of society, if need be. In modern Western culture, artists, poets, and visionaries, let alone Witches, mystics, and shamans, are often somewhat alienated from their culture, which tends to devalue intangibles in favor of the solid, monetary fruits of success.

But the final price of freedom is the willingness to face that most frightening of all beings, one's own self. Starlight vision, the "other way of knowing," is the mode of perception of the unconscious, rather than the conscious mind. The depths of our own beings are not all sunlit; to see clearly, we must be willing to dive into the dark, inner abyss and acknowledge the creatures we may find there. For, as Jungian analyst M. Esther Harding explains in *Women's Mysteries*, "These subjective factors. . .are potent psychical entities, they belong to the totality of our being, they cannot be destroyed. So long as they are unrecognized outcasts from our conscious life, they will come between us and all the objects we view, and our whole world will be either distorted or illuminated."[4]

Perhaps the most convincing way to present the Craft conception of the self is to examine some of the recent experimental findings of biologists and psychologists. Robert Ornstein, in *The Psychology of Consciousness*, describes experiments with brain-damaged and epileptic subjects demonstrating that the two hemispheres of the brain appear to specialize in precisely the two modes of consciousness we have discussed. "The left hemisphere (connected to the right side of the body) is predominantly involved with analytic, logical thinking, especially in verbal and mathematical functions. Its mode of operation is primarily linear. This hemisphere seems to process information sequentially."[5] Like our flashlight beam, it focuses on one subject at a time, excluding others. It perceives the world as made of separate things, which we may fear or desire, which can be manipulated to suit our purposes. "It seems to have been evolved for the primary purpose of ensuring biological survival."[6]

"The right hemisphere (again, remember, connected to the left side of the body) seems specialized for holistic mentation. Its language ability is quite limited. This hemisphere is primarily responsible for our orientation in space, artistic endeavors, crafts, body image, recognition of faces. It processes information more diffusely than does the left hemisphere, and its responsibilities demand a ready integration of many inputs at once."[7] This is the starlight vision, which sees the universe as a dance of swirling energies, which "does not postulate duration, a future or a past, a cause or an effect, but a patterned, 'timeless' whole."[8]

This mode of awareness is vital to creativity. As Anton Ehrenzweig states in *The Hidden Order of Art,* "The complexity of any work of art, however simple, far outstrips the powers of conscious attention, which with its pin-point focus, can attend to only one thing at a time. Only the extreme undifferentiation of unconscious vision can scan these complexities. It can hold them in a single, unfocused glance and treat figure and ground with equal impartiality."[9]

The following exercise, used to train artists, is helpful in learning to experience the mode of awareness just described.

EXERCISE 1: SHADOW PLAY

Take a blank sheet of paper and a soft pencil or stick of charcoal. Sit down and observe a scene that interests you. Forgetting about objects, names, and things, observe only the play of light and shadow over various forms. Block in the shadows, not with lines but with patches of broad strokes. Do not be distracted by local color; do not worry about reproducing "things." Let the patches of shade create forms. Spend at least ten minutes on this exercise. Remember, the point is not to create a "good" drawing or to prove your artistic talent (or lack of it); the point is to experience another way of seeing, in which separate objects disappear and only pattern remains.

People who are less visually oriented may find themselves more comfortable with the following exercise.

EXERCISE 2: RHYTHM PLAY

Close your eyes. Listen to the sounds around you, forgetting what they represent. Be conscious only of the vast rhythm they create. Even in the city, forget that the whooshes, thumps, clacks, chirrupings, rumbles and bangs are passing cars, workmen's hammers, footsteps, sparrows, trucks, and slamming doors—hear only the intricate, organic pattern in which each is a separate beat.

As we have said, both modes of perception are valued in the Craft, but the holistic vision of the right hemisphere is considered to be more in touch with underlying reality than the linear vision of the left hemisphere. This view is borne out by experiments with biofeedback, which gives people visual information about their involuntary body processes, allowing them to monitor and eventually control such functions as heartbeat or brain waves. Barbara Brown, in *New Mind, New Body,* describes experiments showing that "long before conscious recognition, the body and its subconscious substructure both recognize and make judgments about what goes on in the environment."[10] Subjects were monitored as "naughty" words were flashed on a screen, too briefly to be recognized consciously. Their skin, heart rates, brain waves, and muscles all showed reactions to the "unseen" words. The subconscious can respond correctly to reality even when it is given incorrect information by the conscious mind. In one experiment, subjects were told that they would be given a series of shocks that varied in intensity. Consciously, they perceived that the shocks grew weaker; in reality, the shocks were of the same intensity each time. Skin reactions proved that the subconscious was not fooled—monitors recorded exactly the same skin response to each shock, even when the conscious reaction was different.[11]

In the Faery Tradition of Witchcraft, the unconscious mind is called the Younger Self; the conscious mind is called Talking Self. Because they function through different modes of awareness, communication between the two is difficult. It is as if they speak different languages.

It is Younger Self that directly experiences the world, through the holistic awareness of the right hemisphere. Sensations, emotions, basic drives, image memory, intuition and diffuse perception are functions of Younger Self, which corresponds roughly to Freud's concept of the id, to the personal and collective unconscious described by Jung, and to the "Child" mode of Transactional Analysis. Younger Self's verbal understanding is limited; it communicates through images, emotions, sensations, dreams, visions, and physical symptoms. Classical psychoanalysis developed from attempts to interpret the speech of Younger Self. Witchcraft not only interprets, but teaches us how to speak back to Younger Self.

Talking Self organizes the impressions of Younger Self, gives them names, classifies them into systems. As its name implies, it functions through the verbal, analytic awareness of the left hemisphere and can be compared to the concept of "ego" in both Jungian and Freudian psychology, although it also includes the superego—the set of verbally understood precepts that encourage us to make judgements about right and wrong. In the terms of Transactional Analysis, it would include both "Adult" and "Parent." Talking Self speaks through words, abstract concepts, and numbers.

In the Faery tradition, a third "self" is recognized: the High Self or God Self, which does not easily correspond to any psychological concept. The High Self is the Divine within, the ultimate and original essence, the spirit that exists beyond time, space, and matter. It is our deepest level of wisdom and compassion and is conceived of as both male and female, two motes of consciousness united as one. It is often symbolized as two linked spirals, or as the infinity sign, the 8 on its side. In the Faery tradition, it is called Dian Y Glas, the Blue God. Blue symbolizes spirit; the High Self was said to appear blue when psychicly "seen." The Picts stained themselves blue with woad, according to our traditions, in order to identify with the High Self. "Dian" is related to both Diana and Tana, the Faery name of the Goddess; also to Janicot, the Basque name of the Horned God, and to the given names Jean, Joan, and Jonet, which Margaret Murray documents as being popular in Witch families.[12]

In the esoteric Judaism of the Cabalah, the High Self is named the Neshamah, from the root *Shmh,* "to hear or listen": The Neshamah is She Who Listens, the soul who inspires and guides us. In modern occultism, the High Self often appears as the "Spirit Guide," sometimes in dual form, as in John C. Lilly's account of his LSD experiences in an isolation tank, where he reports meeting two helpful beings: "They say that they are my guardians, that they have been with me before at critical times and that in fact they are with me always, but that I am not usually in a state to perceive them. I am in a state to perceive them when I am close to the death of the body. In this state there is no time. There is an immediate perception of the past, present, and future as if in the present moment."[13]

Lilly is describing the holistic, right-hemisphere awareness linked to Younger Self. The Faery tradition teaches that the High Self is connected to Younger Self, and not directly linked to Talking Self. We do not, fortunately, have to be nearly dead before we can perceive the High Self, once we learn the trick of communication. It is not the conscious mind, with its abstract concepts, that ever actually communicates with the Divine, it is the unconscious mind, the Younger Self that responds only to images, pictures, sensations, tangibles. To communicate with the High Self, the Goddess/God Within, we resort to symbols, to art, poetry, music, myth, and the actions of ritual that translate abstract concepts into the language of the unconscious.

Younger Self—who can be as balky and stubborn as the most cantankerous three-year-old—is not impressed by words. Like a native of Missouri, it wants to be *shown.* To arouse its interest, we must seduce it with pretty pictures and pleasurable sensations—take it out dining and dancing, as it were. Only in this way can the High Self be reached. For this reason, religious truths have not been expressed throughout time as mathematical formulas, but in art, music, dance, drama, poetry, stories, and active rituals. As Robert Graves says, "Religious morals, in a healthy society, are best enforced by drums, moonlight, fasting, dancing, masks, flowers, divine possession."[14]

Witchcraft has no sacred book. Its allegiance is not to "The Word" of the Gospel of John, but to the power of symbolic action that unlocks the starlit awareness of Younger Self, and opens a free flow of communication between all three selves at once. The myths and stories that have come down to us are not dogma to be taken literally, any more than we are meant to take literally the statement that "my love is like a red, red rose." They are poetry, not theology—meant to speak to Younger Self, in Joseph Campbell's words "to touch and exhilarate centers of life beyond the reach of vocabularies of reason and coercion."[15]

Aspects of Witchcraft rituals may sometimes seem silly to very serious-minded people, who fail to realize that ritual is aimed at Younger Self. The sense of humor, of play, is often the key to opening the deepest states of consciousness. Part of the "price of freedom," then, is the willingness to play, to let go of our adult dignity, to look foolish, to laugh at nothing. A child makes-believe that she is a queen; her chair becomes a throne. A Witch makes-believe that her wand has magic power, and it becomes a channel for energy.

Of course, balance is necessary. There is a difference between magic and psychosis—and that difference lies in maintaining the ability to step back, at will, into ordinary consciousness, to return to the awareness that, as my high school health education teacher used to affirm in the height of the psychedelic era, "Reality is that when you jump off a roof, you break your leg." Drugs can open the holistic awareness of Younger Self, but often at the expense of Talking Self's survival judgment: If we "play" at flying in the body, we may smash a femur. But a trained awareness has no quarrel with ordinary reality; it flies further, in the spirit, and gains insights and perceptions that can later be verified by Talking Self.

Humor and play awaken the sense of wonder, the basic attitude that Witchcraft takes to the world. For example, last night my coven held a May Eve ritual, the central action of which involved winding a "Maypole," and weaving into it those things we wish to weave into our lives. Instead of a pole, we used a central cord, and instead of ribbons we had strings of colored yarn, anchored to a central hook on the ceiling of our meeting room. We also had eleven people in the circle. Of course, we knew perfectly well that it is impossible to wind a Maypole with an odd number of people, but we did not want to leave anybody out. So, with a cavalier disregard for ordinary reality, we went right ahead.

The result, to begin with, was chaos and confusion. Everyone was laughing as we dodged in and out, creating a tangled knot of yarn. It was scarcely a scene of mystical power; a ritual magician would have blanched pale and turned in his wand on the spot. But an odd thing began to happen as we continued. The laughter began to build a strange atmosphere, as if ordinary reality was fading away. Nothing existed but the interplay of colored cords and moving bodies. The smiles on faces that flashed in and out of sight began to resemble the secret smiles of archaic Greek statues, hinting at the highest and most humorous of Mysteries. We began to sing; we moved in rhythm and a pattern evolved in the dance—nothing that could ever be mapped or plotted rationally; it was a pattern with an extra element that always and inevitably would defy explanation. The snarl of yarn resolved itself into an intricately woven cord. The song became a chant; the room glowed, and the cord pulsed with power like a live thing, an umbilicus linking us to all that is within and beyond. At last the chant peaked and died; we dropped into trance. When we awoke, all together, at the same moment, we faced each other with wonder.

The creation myth that heads this chapter clearly expresses the attitude of wonder, to the world, which is divine, and to the divine, which is the world.

In the beginning, the Goddess is the All, virgin, meaning complete within Herself. Although She is called *Goddess,* She could just as easily be called *God*—sex has not yet come into being. As yet, there is no separation, no division, nothing but the primal unity. Yet the female nature of the ground of being is stressed—because the process of creation that is about to occur is a *birth* process. The world is born, not made, and not commanded into being.

The Goddess sees her reflection in the curved mirror of space, which may be a magical insight into the form of the universe, the curved space of modern physics. The mirror is an ancient attribute of the Goddess, according to Robert Graves, in her aspect as "the ancient pagan Sea Goddess Marian . . . Miriam, Mariamne (Sea Lamb), Myrrhine, Myrtea, Myrrha, Maria, or Marina, patroness of poets and lovers and proud mother of the Archer of Love. . . . A familiar disguise of this same Marian is the merry-maid, as 'mermaid' was once written. The conventional figure of the mermaid—a beautiful woman with a round mirror, a golden comb and a fish-tail—expresses 'The Love-Goddess rises from the Sea.' Every initiate of the Eleusinian mysteries, which were of Pelasgian [the indigenous, matrifocal people of Greece] origin, went through a love rite with her representative after taking a cauldron bath . . . the mirror did also form part of the sacred furniture of the Mysteries, and probably stood for 'Know thyself.' "[16]

Water is the original mirror; the image conveyed is also that of the moon floating over the dark sea, watching her reflection in the waves. A faint echo can be heard in the opening of Genesis: "The earth was unformed and void, and the spirit of God floated on the face of the water."

There is yet another aspect to the mirror: A mirror image is a reversed image, the same, but opposite, the reverse polarity. The image expresses the paradox: All things are one, yet each thing is separate, individual, unique. Eastern religions tend to focus on the first part of the paradox, holding the view that in reality all things are one and that separation and individuality are illusions. Western religions stress individuality and tend to see the world as composed of fixed and separate things. The Western view tends to encourage individual effort and involvement with the world; the Eastern view encourages withdrawal, contemplation, and compassion. Witchcraft holds to the truth of paradox and sees each view as equally valid. They reflect and complement each other; they do not contradict each other. The world of separate things is the reflection of the One; the One is the reflection of the myriad separate things of the world. We are all "swirls" of the same energy, yet each swirl is unique in its own form and pattern.

The Goddess falls in love with Herself, drawing forth her own emanation, which takes on a life of its own. Love of self for self is the creative force of the universe. Desire is the primal energy, and that energy is erotic: the attraction of lover to beloved, of planet to star, the lust of electron for proton. Love is the glue that holds the world together.

Blind *eros,* however, becomes *amor,*[17] the love that, in Joseph Campbell's terminology, is personal, directed to an individual, rather than the universal, sexless charity of *agape,* or indiscriminate, sexual desire. The Goddess' reflection takes on its own being and is given a name. Love is not only an energizing force, but an individualizing force. It dissolves separation and yet creates individuality. It is, again, the primal paradox.

Miria, "The Wonderful," is of course, Marian-Miriam-Mariamne, who is also Mari, the full moon aspect of the Goddess in the Faery tradition. The sense of wonder, of joy and delight in the natural world, is the essence of Witchcraft. The world is not a flawed creation, not something from which we must escape, not in need of salvation or redemption. However it might appear from day to day, by nature of its deepest being it fills us with wonder.

Divine ecstasy becomes the fountain of creation, and creation is an orgasmic process. Ecstasy is at the heart of Witchcraft—in ritual, we turn paradox inside out and become the Goddess, sharing in the primal, throbbing joy of union. "The fundamental characteristic of shamanism is ecstasy," according to Mircea Eliade, and although he interprets the state somewhat narrowly as "the soul forsaking the body," he admits that "in all probability the ecstatic experience in its many aspects, is co-existent with the human condition, in the sense that it is an integral part of what is called man's gaining consciousness of his specific mode of being in the world. Shamanism is not only a technique of ecstasy; its theology and its philosophy finally depend on the spiritual value that is accorded to ecstasy."[18] Witchcraft is a shamanistic religion, and the spiritual value placed on ecstasy is a high one. It is the source of union, healing, creative inspiration, and communion with the divine—whether it is found in the center of a coven circle, in bed with one's beloved, or in the midst of the forest, in awe and wonder at the beauty of the natural world.

Ecstasy brings about harmony, the "music of the spheres." Music is a symbolic expression of the vibration that is a quality of all beings. Physicists inform us that the atoms and molecules of all things, from an unstable gas to the Rock of Gibralter, are in constant motion. Underlying that motion is an order, a harmony that is inherent in being. Matter sings, by its very nature.

The song is carried forth on waves that become spheres. The waves are the waves of orgasm, light waves, ocean waves, pulsating electrons, waves of sound. The waves form spheres as swirling gases form stars. It is a basic insight of Witchraft that energy, whether physical, psychic, or emotional, moves in waves, in cycles that are themselves spirals. (An easy way to visualize this is to borrow a child's "Slinky" toy—a coiling spiral of very thin metal. When stretched and viewed from the side, the spirals appear very clearly as wave forms.)

The Goddess swells with love and gives birth to a rain of bright spirits, a rain that awakens consciousness in the world as moisture awakens green growth on earth. The rain is the fructifying menstrual blood, the moon's blood that nourishes life, as well as the bursting waters that herald birth, the ecstatic giving forth of life.

The motion, the vibration, becomes so great that Miria is swept away. As She moves further from the point of union, She becomes more polarized, more differentiated, more male. The Goddess has projected Herself; her projected Self becomes the Other, her opposite, who eternally yearns for reunion. Jung would say She has projected her *animus,* her male soul. Differentness awakens desire, which pulls against the centrifugal force of projection. The energy field of the cosmos becomes polarized; it becomes a conductor of forces exerted in opposite directions.

The view of the All as an energy field polarized by two great forces, Female and Male, Goddess and God, which in their ultimate being are aspects of each other, is common to almost all traditions of the Craft. The Dianic tradition, however, while recognizing the Male Principle, accords it much less importance than the Female. Some modern, self-created traditions, especially those stemming from a feminist-separatist political orientation, do not recognize the Male at all. If they work with polarity, they visualize both forces as contained within the female. This is a line of experimentation that has great value for many women, particularly as an antidote to thousands of years of Western culture's exclusive concentration on the Male. However, it has never been the mainstream view of the Craft. I personally feel that, in the long run, a female-only model of the universe would prove to be as constricting and oppressive, to women as well as men, as the patriarchal model has been. One of the tasks of religion is to guide us in relationship to both that which is like ourselves, and that which is unlike ourselves. Sex is the most basic of differences; we cannot become whole by pretending difference does not exist, or by denying either male or female.

It is important, however, to separate the concept of polarity from our culturally conditioned images of male and female. The Male and Female forces represent difference, yet they are not different, in essence: They are the same force flowing in opposite, but not opposed, directions. The Chinese concept of Yin and Yang is somewhat similar, but in Witchcraft the description of the forces is very different. Neither is "active" or "passive," dark or light, dry or moist—instead, each partakes of all those qualities. The Female is seen as the life-giving force, the power of manifestation, of energy flowing into the world to become form. The Male is seen as the death force, in a positive, not a negative sense: the force of limitation that is the necessary balance to unbridled creation, the force of dissolution, of return to formlessness. Each principle contains the other: Life breeds death, feeds on death; death sustains life, makes possible evolution and new creation. They are part of a cycle, each dependent on the other.

Existence is sustained by the on-off pulse, the alternating current of the two forces in perfect balance. Unchecked, the life force is cancer; unbridled, the death force is war and genocide. Together, they hold each other in the harmony that sustains life, in the perfect orbit that can be seen in the changing cycle of the seasons, in the ecological balance of the natural world, and in the progression of human life from birth through fulfillment to decline and death—and then to rebirth.

Death is not an end; it is a stage in the cycle that leads on to rebirth. After death, the human soul is said to rest in "Summerland," the Land of Eternal Youth, where it is refreshed, grows young, and is made ready to be born again. Rebirth is not considered to be condemnation to an endless, dreary round of suffering, as in Eastern religions. Instead, it is seen as the great gift of the Goddess, who is manifest in the physical world. Life and the world are not separate from Godhead; they are immanent divinity.

Witchcraft does not maintain, like the First Truth of Buddhism, that "All life is suffering." On the contrary, life is a thing of wonder. The Buddha is said to have gained this insight after his encounter with old age, disease, and death. In the Craft, old age is a natural and highly valued part of the cycle of life, the time of greatest wisdom and understanding. Disease, of course, causes misery, but it is not something to be inevitably suffered: The practice of the Craft was always connected with the healing arts, with herbalism and midwifery. Nor is death fearful: It is simply the dissolution of the physical form that allows the spirit to prepare for a new life. Suffering certainly exists in life—it is a part of learning. But escape from the Wheel of Birth and Death is not the optimal cure, any more than hara kiri is the best cure for menstrual cramps. When suffering is the result of the social order or human injustice, the Craft encourages active work to relieve it. Where suffering is a natural part of the cycle of birth and decay, it is relieved by understanding and acceptance, by a willing giving-over to both the dark and the light in turn.

The polarity of the Female and Male Principles should not be taken as a general pattern for individual female and human beings. We each contain both principles; we are female and male both. To be whole is to be in touch with both forces—creation and dissolution, growth and limitation. The energy created by the push-pull of forces flows within each of us. It can be tapped individually in rituals or meditations, and it can be attuned to resonate with others. Sex, for instance, is far more than a physical act; it is a polarized flow of power between two people.

The Male Principle is first seen as a nearly androgynous figure: the Child, the flute-playing Blue God of love. His image is connected with that of the personal Blue God, the High Self, which is also androgynous. Gentle youth, beloved son, He is never sacrificed.

The Green aspect is the vegetation God—the corn spirit, the grain that is cut and then replanted; the seed that dies with every harvest and is eternally reborn each spring.

The Horned God, the most "male" in the conventional sense, of the Goddess' projections, is the eternal Hunter, and also the animal who is hunted. He is the beast who is sacrificed that human life may go on, as well as the sacrificer, the one who sheds blood. He is also seen as the sun, eternally hunting the moon across the sky. The waxing and waning of the sun throughout the seasons manifest the cycle of birth and death, creation and dissolution, separation and return.

Goddess and God, Female and Male, Moon and Sun, Birth and Death swing in their orbits—eternal, yet ever changing. Polarity, the force that holds the cosmos together, is love, erotic, transcendent, and individual. Creation did not happen once in a fixed point in time; it goes on eternally, occurring in each moment, revealed in the cycle of the year:

The Wheel of the Year [19]

In love, the Horned God, changing form and changing face, ever seeks the Goddess. In this world, the search and the seeking appear in the Wheel of the Year.

She is the Great Mother who gives birth to Him as the Divine Child Sun at the Winter Solstice. In spring, He is sower and seed who grows with the growing light, green as the new shoots. She is the Initiatrix who teaches Him the mysteries. He is the young bull; She the nymph, seductress. In summer, when light is longest, they meet in union, and the strength of their passion sustains the world. But the God's face darkens as the sun grows weaker, until at last, when the grain is cut for harvest, He too sacrifices Himself to Self that all may be nourished. She is the reaper, the grave of earth to which all must return. Throughout the long nights and darkening days, He sleeps in her womb; in dreams, He is Lord of Death who rules the Land of Youth beyond the gates of night and day. His dark tomb becomes the womb of rebirth, for at Midwinter She again gives birth to Him. The cycle ends and begins again, and the Wheel of the Year turns, on and on.

The rituals of the eight solar holidays, the Sabbats, are derived from the myth of the Wheel of the Year. The Goddess reveals her threefold aspects: as Maiden, She is the virgin patroness of birth and initiation; as Nymph, She is the sexual temptress, lover, siren, seductress; as Crone, She is the dark face of life, which demands death and sacrifice. The God is son, brother, lover, who becomes his own father: the eternal sacrifice eternally reborn into new life.

Sir James Frazer, in *The Golden Bough,* traces many variations of this myth. Most, like the version expounded by Robert Graves in *The White Goddess,* present the God as split into rival Twins embodying his two aspects. The Star Son, Lord of the Waxing Year, vies with his brother the Serpent for the love of the Goddess. On the Summer Solstice, they battle, and the Dark Serpent defeats the Light and supplants Him in the Goddess' favor, only to be Himself defeated at Midwinter, when the Waxing Year is reborn.

This variation is not, in essence, different from the variation we have presented, as long as the Dark and Light Twins are clearly understood to be aspects of the same divinity. But when we see the God as split, we run the risk of suffering a split within ourselves: of identifying totally with the Light and ascribing the Dark to an agent of evil. Star Son and Serpent too easily become Christ-Satan figures. In Witchcraft, the dark, waning aspect of the God is not evil—it is a vital part of the natural cycle.

The essential teaching of the myth is connected with the concept of sacrifice. To Witches, as to other peoples who live close to nature, all things—plants, animals, stones, and stars—are alive, are on some level conscious beings. All things are divine, are manifestations of the Goddess. The death of the grain in the harvest, or the death of a deer in the hunt, was considered a divine sacrifice, freely made out of love. Ritualistic and mythical identification with the sacrificing God honors the life spark, even in death, and prepares us to give way gracefully to new life, when the time comes for each of us to die. Waxing and waning, birth and death, take place within the human psyche and life cycle. Each is to be welcomed in its proper time and season, because life is a process of constant change.

The God chooses to sacrifice in order to remain within the orbit of the Goddess, within the cycle of the natural world, and within the ecstatic, primal union that creates the world. Were He to cling to any point on the wheel and refuse to give way to change, the cycle would stop; He would fall out of orbit and lose all. Harmony would be destroyed; union would be broken. He would not be preserving Himself; He would be denying his true self, his deepest passion, his very nature.

It is vitally important not to confuse this conception of sacrifice with the masochistic self-sacrifice that is so often preached as the ideal by patriarchal religions. In the Craft, the sacrifice of one's nature or individuality is never demanded. Instead, one sacrifices *to* nature. There is no conflict, in Witchraft, between the spiritual and the material; we do not have to give up one to gain the other. The spirit manifests in matter: The Goddess is seen as giving us abundance. But the most abundant summer is followed by winter, as the longest day ends in night. Only when one gives way to the other can life go on.

In Witchcraft, sacrifice is most definitely not the submission to external power held by another person or institution. Nor does it mean giving up one's will or self-respect. Its emotional tone is not self-pity, but pride: it is the sacrifice of Mettus Curtius, who, when told by the augurs that the bottomless crack that had suddenly opened in the Forum was a sign that the Gods demanded the sacrifice of Rome's finest, unhesitatingly leapt into the chasm on horseback, fully armed. He had not a moment's doubt as to his own self-worth; he knew what "Rome's finest" must be, and acted accordingly, out of an inner sense of what was right.

Witchcraft does not demand poverty, chastity, or obedience, but it is not a "looking out for Number One" philosophy, either. It developed in a close-knit clan society, where resources were shared and land held in common. "Charity" was an unknown concept, because sharing was an integral part of society, a basic expectation. "Number One" existed only within the fabric of society and within the web of all life. Witchcraft recognizes that we are all interdependent, and even the most avid member of the "me generation" must ultimately serve the life force, if only as compost.

The sacrifice of the God was represented in human society by the "Sacred King" or priest, who served as consort to the High Priestess, religious leader, and at times, war leader for the clan. Since Frazer compiled *The Golden Bough,* his classic work of folklore and anthropology first published in 1900, writers on the subject of "primitive" religions, especially those oriented toward a Goddess, have generally accepted his thesis that human sacrifice was a vital and regular institution in matrifocal culture. Even well-meaning, sensitive, and thinking men—including Robert Graves who has probably been the greatest force for revival of interest in the Goddess in this century—perpetuate the myths. Joseph Campbell, author of the fine series *The Masks of God,* goes so far as to say that "human sacrifice . . . is everywhere characteristic of the worship of the Goddess."[20]

Craft tradition and archaeological evidence do not support this picture of Goddess worship as bloody and barbaric. The many Paleolithic sites associated with Goddess figures—Laussel, Angles-Sur-Anglin, Cogul, La Magdaleine, Malta, to name just a few—show no evidence of human sacrifice. In the Neolithic, Çatal Hüyük is one of the earliest (circa 6500–5700 BC) and most clearly matriarchal sites excavated. The many shrines decorated with figures of the Mother Goddess and her son-paramour have no provisions for either human or animal sacrifice: no altars, no pits for blood, and no caches of bones. Nor do the Goddess temples of Malta and Sardinia, the passage graves and stone circles of the megalith builders, or the excavated sites of Crete show any evidence that human beings were ever ritually murdered. Where human sacrifice is clearly evident—for example, in the Royal Tombs of the Sumerian city Ur, where entire courts followed the king into death—it is associated with cultures that have already made the shift to patriarchy.

Reconstructing culture from buried bones and artifacts is, of course, difficult; reconstruction from surviving folk customs, which Frazer often attempts, is just as liable to error. If peasants burn corn dollies in the harvest fire, it does not necessarily follow that they once burned living men. To Younger Self, a corn dollie is a perfectly effective symbol of the God's sacrifice; a live victim is not required.

Historical reports of matrifocal cultures most often come from their enemies and conquerors, who are likely to paint a black picture of the religious customs of their foes. If our knowledge of medieval Judaism was limited to historical reports by Catholic Churchmen, we would be bound to conclude that the blood of Christians was needed to bake the ritual Matzohs. Today we recognize this fiction for the libel that it was, but slurs against matrifocal religions have become deeply embedded in religion and mythology and are often hard to identify. For example, the Greek myth of Theseus and the Minotaur was believed to represent Cretan sacrifice of captives to their bull God. But frescoes excavated in the Palace of Minos reveal, instead, the practice of bull-leaping: no doubt a dangerous sport, but one that could hardly be called human sacrifice any more than its modern descendent, bullfighting.

In the Faery Tradition, oral teachings say that in early times the Sacred King or High Priest held office for nine years, after which he underwent a ritual mock death, abdicated, and joined the Council of Elders. Ritual mock death may be the origin of many folk customs involving symbolic sacrifices. In times of great need or disaster, a king might, if his inner being prompted, sacrifice himself. The willingness to give over one's personal existence to serve the people was the true test of kingship, and this requirement lessened the attraction of power for corrupt and selfish individuals. Kingship was not an opportunity to make a killing in the bronze market or collect personal slaves; it was a ritual, mystical identification with the underlying forces of death and life.

Women were never sacrificed in Witchcraft. Women shed their own blood monthly and risk death in service to the life force with every pregnancy and birth. For this reason, their bodies were considered sacred, and held inviolate.

Unfortunately, newspapers, motion pictures, and television today continue to perpetuate the association of Witchcraft and Goddess religion with horror and human sacrifice. Every Manson-like murderer is called a "witch." Outright psychopaths claim to be practicing Witchcraft with degraded rites, and may at times mislead gullible people into believing them. Witchcraft as a religion may not have a universal creed or set liturgy, but on some points there is unanimity. No true Witches today practice human sacrifice, torture, or any form of ritual murder. Anyone who does is not a Witch, but a psychopath.

The world view of Witchcraft is, above all, one that values life. The cosmos is a polarized field of forces that are constantly in the process of swirling into form and dissolving back into pure energy. Polarity, which we call Goddess and God, creates the cycle that underlies the movements of the stars and the changing of the seasons, the harmony of the natural world and the evolution within our human lives. We perceive the interplay of forces in two basic modes, the holistic, intuitive "starlight" mode of the right hemisphere and the unconscious; and the linear, analytic, conscious mode of the left hemisphere. Communication between conscious and unconscious, between Talking Self and Younger Self, and through the latter to the High Self, the spirit, depends on an openness to both modes of awareness. Verbal concepts must be translated into symbols and images; unconscious images must be brought to the light of consciousness. Through open communication, we can become attuned to the cycles of nature, to the primal, ecstatic union that is the force of creation. Attunement requires sacrifice, the willingness to change, to let go of any point on the Wheel and move on. But sacrifice is not suffering, and life in all its aspects, light and dark, growing and decaying, is a great gift. In a world where the endlessly transforming, erotic dance of God and Goddess weaves radiant through all things, we who step to their rhythm are enraptured with the wonder and mystery of being.

Notes

1. Oral teaching of the Faery tradition of Witchcraft.
2. Lee Bartlett, "Interview—Gary Snyder," *California Quarterly,* 1975, Vol. No. 9, pp. 43–50.
3. Carlos Castaneda, *Tales of Power* (New York: Simon & Schuster, 1974), pp. 28–29.
4. M. Esther Harding, *Woman's Mysteries, Ancient & Modern* (New York: Pantheon, 1955), p. 6.
5. Robert E. Ornstein, *The Psychology of Consciousness* (San Francisco: W. H. Freeman, 1972), pp. 51–52.
6. Ornstein, p. 17.
7. Ornstein, pp. 51–52.
8. Ornstein, p. 79.
9. Anton Ehrenzweig, *The Hidden Order of Art* (London: Paladin, 1967), p. 35.
10. Barbara Brown, *New Mind, New Body* (New York: Harper & Row, 1974), p. 75.
11. Brown, p. 75.
12. Margaret A. Murray, *The Witch-Cult in Western Europe* (Oxford: Oxford University Press, 1971), p. 255.
13. John C. Lilly, *The Center of the Cyclone* (New York: Julian Press, 1972), p. 27.
14. Robert Graves, *Food for Centaurs* (New York: Doubleday, 1960), p. 6.
15. Joseph Campbell, *The Masks of God: Creative Mythology* (New York: Viking Press, 1968), p. 4.
16. Robert Graves, *The White Goddess* (New York: Farrar, Straus & Giroux, 1948), p. 395.
17. Campbell, 1968, pp. 176–177.
18. Micrea Eliade, *Rites & Symbols of Initiation,* translated by William R. Trask (New York: Harper & Row, 1958), p. 101.
19. Oral teaching of the Faery tradition.
20. Joseph Campbell, *The Masks of God: Oriental Mythology,* (New York: Penguin Books, 1976), p. 160.

3   *The Coven*

Between the Worlds
New Moon

*"We met tonight in the rented storefront. For a long time, we just talked—
about our fears and doubts about magic and ourselves: that it isn't real, that
it is real, that it will stop, that it's an ego-trip, that we're crazy, that what
we really want is power, that we'll lose our sense of humor and become
pompous about it, that we won't be able to take it seriously, that it won't work,
that it* will *work. . . .*

*At one point, we all took hands, and started breathing together. Suddenly
we realized that a circle had been cast. We passed around the oil, for anointing,
and kissed. Someone began a low humming, and Pat started tapping out a
rhythm on the drum. And we were all chanting, interweaving voices and
melodies, as if different words were coming through each of us:*

> Isis . . . Astarte . . . Ishtar . . .
> Dawn and darkness . . . dawn and darkness . . .
> Moo-oo-oon, Crescent Moo-oo-oon . . .
> Pour out your light and your radiance upon us . . . .
> Shine! Shine! Shine! Shine! Shine!

and through it and behind it all, Beth was wailing on her kazoo, and it sounded like some strange, Arabian oud, or a sobbing jazz saxophone, but we were smiling at the humor of it . . .

At the same moment, we all fell silent. Then we shared fruit, laughed, and talked about humor. We were thinking about a coven name, and someone suggested Compost. It was perfect! Earthy, organic, nurturing—and discouraging to self-inflation.

We are now the Compost coven!

The ritual worked. Whatever magic brings, it will not take away our ability to laugh at ourselves. And those fears grow less and less all the time."

From my Book of Shadows

The coven is a Witch's support group, consciousness-raising group, psychic study center, clergy-training program, College of Mysteries, surrogate clan, and religious congregation all rolled into one. In a strong coven, the bond is, by tradition, "closer than family": a sharing of spirits, emotions, imaginations. "Perfect love and perfect trust" is the goal.

The coven structure makes the organization of Witchcraft very different from that of most other religions. The Craft is not based on large, amorphous masses who are only superficially acquainted; nor is it based on individual gurus with their devotees and disciples. There is no hierarchical authority, no Dalai Lama, no Pope. The structure of Witchcraft is cellular, based on small circles whose members share a deep commitment to each other and the Craft.

Witchcraft tends to attract people who, by nature, do not like to join groups. The coven structure makes it possible for rabid individualists to experience a deep sense of community without losing their independence of spirit. The secret is its small size. A coven (usually pronounced so as to rhyme with oven), by tradition, never contains more than thirteen members. In such a small group, each person's presence or absence affects the rest. The group is colored by every individual's likes, dislikes, beliefs, and tastes.

At the same time, the coven becomes an entity in itself, with a personality of its own. It generates a *raith* form,* an energy swirl that exists over and beyond its membership. There is a quality of synergy about a strong coven. It is more than the sum of its parts; it is an energy pool on which its members can draw.

To become a member of a coven, a Witch must be initiated, must undergo a ritual of commitment, in which the inner teachings and secrets of the group are revealed. Initiation follows a long training period, during which trust and group security are slowly built. When properly timed, the ritual also becomes a rite of passage, that marks a new stage in personal

---

*See page 133 for a full discussion and explanation of the *raith.*

growth. Witchcraft grows slowly; it can never be a mass-market religion, peddled on streetcorners or between flights at the airport. Witches do not proselytize. Prospective members are expected to seek out covens and demonstrate a deep level of interest. The strength of the Craft is felt to be in quality, not quantity.

Originally, coveners were the teachers and priestesses/priests of a large pagan population of noninitiates. They were the councils of elders within each clan, the wise women and wise men who delved beneath the surface of their rites and sought the deeper meanings. At the large solar festivals, the Sabbats, they led the rituals, organized the gatherings, and expounded the meanings of the ceremonies. Each coven had its own territory, which by tradition extended for a league. Neighboring covens might join for the great Sabbats, in order to share knowledge, herbs, spells, and, of course, gossip. Federations of covens were sometimes linked together under a Witch "Queen," or Grandmaster. On full moons, covens met alone for Esbats, when they studied the inner teachings and practiced magic.

During the Burning Times, the great festivals were stamped out or Christianized. Persecution was most strongly directed against coven members, because they were seen as the true perpetuators of the religion. The strictest secrecy became necessary. Any member of a coven could betray the rest to torture and death, so "perfect love and perfect trust" were more than empty words. Covens were isolated from one another, and traditions became fragmented, teachings forgotten.

Today, there is a growing effort throughout the Craft to reestablish communication between covens and share knowledge. But many individual Witches still cannot afford to "come out of the broom closet." Public recognition may mean the loss of their jobs and livelihoods. Known Witches are easy targets for violent crackpots: A Southern California couple were firebombed out of their home after appearing on a television talk show. Other Witches face harrassment by the authorities for traditional practices such as divination, or become scapegoats for local crimes. Unfortunately, prejudice is still widespread. Sensitive people never identify anyone as a Witch without first asking permission privately. In this book, my own friends and coveners have generally been referred to by coven names in order to protect their privacy.

Every coven is autonomous. Each functions as its own authority in matters of ritual, thealogy, and training. Groups of covens who follow the same rites may consider themselves part of the same tradition. To ensure legal protection for their members, many covens band together and incorporate as a church, but the rights of separate covens are always jealously guarded.

Covens usually develop a specific orientation and focus. There are covens that concentrate on healing or teaching; others may lean toward psychic work, trance states, social action, or creativity and inspiration. Some simply seem to throw good parties; after all, "all acts of love and pleasure" are rituals of the Goddess. Covens may include both men and women or be limited to women only. (There are very few all-male covens, for reasons to be discussed in Chapter Six.)

A coven is a group of peers, but it is not a "leaderless group." Authority and power, however, are based on a very different principle from that which holds sway in the world at large. Power, in a coven, is never power *over* another. It is the power that comes from within.

In Witchcraft, power is another word for energy, the subtle current of forces that shape reality. A powerful person is one who draws energy into the group. The ability to channel power depends on personal integrity, courage, and wholeness. It cannot be assumed, inherited, appointed, or taken for granted, and it does not confer the right to control another. Power-from-within develops from the ability to control ourselves, to face our own fears and limitations, to keep commitments, and to be honest. The sources of inner power are unlimited. One person's power does not diminish another's; instead, as each covener comes into her own power, the power of the group grows stronger.

Ideally, a coven serves as the training ground in which each member develops her or his personal power. The support and security of the group reinforces each member's belief in herself. Psychic training opens new awarenesses and abilities, and feedback from the group becomes the ever-present mirror in which we "see ourselves as others see us." The goal of a coven is not to do away with leaders, but to train every Witch to be a leader, a Priestess, or a Priest.

The issue of leadership has plagued the feminist movement and the New Left. Exemplars of power-from-within are sadly lacking on the American political scene. Power-over-others is correctly seen to be oppressive, but too often the "collective ideal" is misused, to tear down the strong instead of to build strength in the weak. Powerful women are attacked instead of supported: "Am I a traitor? They ought to shoot me. Made me into a leader. We're not supposed to have leaders. I will be executed in some underground paper, my character assassinated subterraneously."[1]

The concept of power-from-within encourages healthy pride, not self-effacing anonymity; joy in one's strength, not shame and guilt. In Witchcraft, authority means responsibility. The coven leader must have the inner power and sensitivity to channel the group's energy, to start and stop each phase of the ritual, adjusting the timing to the mood of the circle. A ritual, like a theater production, needs a director.

In practice, leadership is passed from one covener to another in a fully developed group. The wand representing the authority of the leader may be passed to each covener in turn. Different sections of the ritual may be led by different people.

For example, our last Fall Equinox Ritual was inspired by Alan, who is an apprentice but not yet an initiate of Compost Coven. Alan is very much involved with the men's liberation movement and wanted a ritual centered around changing the sex-role conditioning we have each received. Eight of us, from Compost, from Honeysuckle, my women's coven, and from Alan's men's group, planned the ritual together. Here is my account:

Fall Equinox, 1978

A hot night. Seventeen of us met at Guidot's, nine women and eight men. After some socializing, we went upstairs to the ritual room.

Alan, aided by Guidot and Paul, cast the circle, using beautiful invocations, which I think he improvised on the spot. Three or four of us had explained the ritual to the rest, so they were ready. I led the invocation to the Goddess, using the Kore Chant. I began speaking it, and as I switched into the sung chant, it was as if something came in from behind and lifted me out of myself. My voice physically changed, became a low, deep throbbing, with power pouring through into the circle, and then, as everyone picked up the chant, pouring through all of us—the dark moaning wail of summer's passing, sad but beautiful. . . .

Change is . . . touch is . . .
Touch us . . . change us . . .

Alan, Paul, and Guidot invoked the God, Alan calling Him as the Gentle Brother, the Rape Fighter. He wrote a powerful invocation (included in Chapter Six).

We began a banishing dance, widdershins around the circle. As we moved, one person would throw out a phrase—the group took it up and repeated it, chanted it rhythmically, building it, shrieking it, then letting it die away until its power to control us faded with it. Alan began it:

"You must be successful!"

"You must be successful!" "You must be successful!" "Must be! Must be! Must be!" "Must!"

"Nice girls don't *do* that!" "Nice girls don't *do* that!" "Big boys don't cry!" "You're not a real woman!" "Sissy! Sissy! Sissy!"

Sixteen howling echoes took up every cry, frenzied, mocking voices that became, in the dim light, the pursuing Furies of our own minds, taunting, laughing, screaming—then vanishing, like wisps of smoke. By the end we were stamping, shouting—seventeen stark-naked adults, jumping up and down, yelling "No! No! No! No! No!"

Younger Self was awake in its full, primal glory, all right.

Val has come into her own, her power as the Crone. She performed the Mystery (which is secret), aided, I think, by Alan and Paul. I never saw.

Laurel, Brook, and I led the trance, a soft, whispered, three-voiced induction:

> Your fingers are dissolving into. . . .
> Dream deep, and sleep the magic sleep. . . .
> Dissolving into water, and your toes are. . . .

Valerie awakened us. We formed into two groups, for the male and female Mysteries. The men took a long time—I think they got involved in a historical discussion of the rites of Dionysus. When they finished, we one by one moved back into the circle, sitting man and woman alternately. We went around the circle, each saying how we become strong.

"I become strong through facing my fears."
"I become strong through my friends."
"I become strong through making mistakes."
"I become strong through taking a stand."
"I become strong through dreaming."

Then we chanted, raising power to actualize the visions we had seen in trance, of our true, free selves. The chant went on and on, it was so physically pleasurable, feeling the flow of power, the low resonance of the deep male voices, the high, bell-like notes of the women—it swirled around us like a great, warm wave.

After, Alan and I blessed the wine and cakes. As the cup went around the circle, we each said what we were thankful for. The cup went around many times. Then we relaxed, ate, laughed, talked as usual. Alan ended the ritual and opened the circle.

Afterward, I was amazed at how smoothly it all went, with everyone taking different parts. It feels good to be able to step back and let other people take the center, to see them developing their power.

At the present time, both Compost and the women's coven, called Honeysuckle, are covens of elders. Each initiate is capable of leading rituals, directing the energy, and training newcomers. The process of development in each group, however, was very different.

Compost was typical of many of the new, self-initiatory covens that are springing up today without benefit of formal Craft training. I had been taught by Witches many years previously, when I was a college student, but never actually initiated. Most of my knowedge came from dream figures and trance experiences. I had been unable to find a coven I felt was right for me, and for many years I had worked alone. Finally, I decided to see if I could start my own coven, whether or not I was "authorized" to do so. I began teaching a class in Witchcraft through the Bay Area Center for Alternative Education.

Within a few weeks, a group of interested individuals began meeting weekly. Our rituals were collective and spontaneous, like the one described at the opening of this chapter. We resisted set forms and set words.

After a few months had passed, a strong core group developed, and we performed a formal initiation. Our rituals had also taken on a regular pattern, and we decided to set the structure of the rites so that we would have a collective framework, within which we could all be spontaneous and open. Before, the leader—usually me—had decided what was going to happen at any given moment, and everyone else had followed along.

We met many Witches from other covens, and I began studying with a teacher from the Faery Tradition. I began to come into a sense of my own power. As a group, we also realized that the energies we were raising were *real,* not merely symbolic. The group felt a need for an acknowledged leader; at the same time, I felt the need to have my newfound inner power recognized. The coven confirmed me as High Priestess.

Like most people whose sense of inner strength is developing quickly, I occasionally went to extremes. From being a collectivist nonleader, I became a rather heavy-handed High Priestess at times. There are days when my records of rituals read quite differently from either of the two presented in this chapter: "I cast the circle ... I invoked the Goddess ... I led the chant ... I directed the Cone of Power ..." Fortunately, my coveners were both tolerant enough to let me make mistakes and honest enough to tell me when they didn't like what I was doing. We began sharing responsibilities: One covener would bring the salt and water and purify the circle, another would bring the incense and charge the space. The men invoked the Horned God, and we took turns invoking the Goddess and directing the cone of power. I became more relaxed in the role of leader.

As other coveners developed their own strengths, we decided to "pass the wand." Diane, a tremendously warm individual, who radiates a sense of caring, was our unanimous choice. She had always liked our simple, spontaneous rituals best, and under her leadership we let go of a lot of structure and experimented. "I don't feel like formally casting the circle tonight," she might say, "let's just tap the four walls, and chant. Why don't we chant each other's names?" And so we would chant—sometimes for hours, in the process developing one of the simplest and most beautiful rituals we use today.

Diane left for the summer, and we passed the wand to Amber, the youngest member of our coven. Diane warmed the circle with a steady glow, Amber lit it up with skyrockets, fireworks, and colored flames. Talented, charming, lovable, and unsteady, she is a fine musician with an operatic singing voice and a flair for drama. She inspired us to the creation of more theatrical rituals, like many of those presented in Chapter Twelve. But Amber had difficulty functioning at the high level of responsibility that coven leadership demands. She was going through a tense period in her personal life, and, while she usually carried through her commitments, doing so caused her a lot of anxiety and stress. In retrospect, we did her a disservice by not allowing her a longer period of training.

Honeysuckle underwent a different process of formation. It began as a class in the Great Goddess, at a time when I had been High Priestess of Compost for many months, and was already an initiate of the Faery Tradition. I was coming from a much stronger position as a leader, and it took a much longer time before anyone questioned my authority. I was determined not to rush the training of this group, and it was almost a year before I so much as mentioned the word *initiation*. When each woman in turn felt ready to take on more responsibility, was able to question my authority, and was willing to move out from the role of student, she was initiated. A new ritual was created for each member, and each rite crystallized a period of growth.

Finding a coven to join can be difficult. Witches are not listed in the Yellow Pages and rarely place classified ads. Often, however, they do give classes through Open Universities or metaphysical bookstores. Some universities are beginning to offer courses in Witchcraft in their religious studies departments. Occult shops sometimes also furnish leads. The best route, of course, is through personal contacts. Witches feel that when a person is internally ready to join the Craft she will be drawn to the right people.

Unfortunately, a lot of people claim to be Witches who are merely unsavory characters. When you meet someone who calls herself a Witch, listen carefully to your underlying feelings and intuitions. The rituals of many covens are secret, but you should be told or shown enough about them to form a fairly clear picture of what goes on. A true coven will never ask you to do something you feel is wrong for you. Any form of force, coercion, or high-pressure sales tactics are contrary to the spirit of Witchcraft. Real Witches will let you take the initiative in seeking them out.

Witchcraft is not for sale. There are no fees for initiation, and it is considered a breach of ethics to charge money for coven training. Of course, Witches who teach public classes or work as psychic counselors are allowed to charge a fair fee for their time and labor. They will not, however, sell you "blessed" candles for large sums of money or ask you to hand over your life savings in order to remove a curse: Those are favorite dodges of the con artists who prey on the gullible public. A coven may charge dues to cover candles, incense, and other expenses: but the High Priestess will *not* be driving a Mercedes bought by the contributions of her faithful followers.

In a strong coven, members will feel close to each other and turn naturally to each other in times of stress. They generally spend time together socially outside of group meetings and enjoy each other's company. But they also have varied and interesting outside friends and lives and do not spend all of their time together. A coven should not be a retreat from the world, but a supportive structure that helps each member function in the world more fully.

At the present time, there are far more people who want to join covens than there are groups capable of taking in newcomers. If you cannot find a congenial coven, you can either practice the Craft alone or start your own coven.

Working alone is not ideal. Opening up the starlight vision is much more difficult without the support of a group. Those who travel the uncharted pathways of the mind alone run more risk of being caught in subjectivity. Also, working with other people is much more fun.

But, as one Witch who has practiced the Craft by herself for many years says, "Working alone has its good points as well as bad. Your training is rather erratic—but then it is in a lot of covens, anyway. The advantage is that you learn to depend on yourself and learn your limitations. When you do join a coven, you know what you want and what works best for you."

Solitary meditation and visualization practice is part of every Witch's training. Most of the exercises in this book can be done alone, and even the rituals can be adapted. Solitary worship is far preferable to joining the wrong group.

You do not have to be an hereditary or even an initiated Witch in order to start your own coven. Naturally, training helps. But the school of trial and error is also a very fine one.

When a group of interested but inexperienced people come together, the first task is to establish a feeling of security. Openness and trust develop slowly, through both verbal and nonverbal sharing. People need time to socialize, as well as work magic. I often start groups with a pot luck dinner, so that everyone can share a very tangible form of energy: food. Consciousness-raising techniques can also be very effective. We may go around the circle, letting each person tell why she or he came to the group and what she or he hopes to get out of it. Everyone is allowed to speak for a limited period of time without interruptions, so that quieter people are encouraged to express themselves and more voluble individuals do not dominate the conversation. Questions and comments come after everyone has had a turn to speak.

Nonverbal sharing is also important in creating group trust. The following exercises teach the sensing and sharing of energy, which is the basis of Craft rituals. They can be done singly or flow into a smooth sequence. I have written down what I say when leading a group through the exercise. In guiding a group, the actual words spoken are less important than the rhythm of your voice and the timing of pauses. The only way to learn this is by practice. Read through the exercises, become familiar with them, and then improvise in your own natural speech patterns.

EXERCISE 3: SENSING GROUP ENERGY

"The energy we talk about in Witchcraft is real, a subtle force that we can all learn to perceive. Right now, as we are sitting in the circle, be aware of the energy level in the group. Do you feel alert? Aware? Excited? Calm or anxious? Tense, or relaxed? (Pause.)

"Energy travels up and down your spine. Now sit up, as erect as you can without straining. Good. Notice how the energy level has changed. Do you feel more alert? More aware? Good. (Pause.)

"Your breath moves energy in and out of your body. It wakens your body's centers of power. So take a deep breath. Breathe deep . . . breathe all the way down. Breathe from your diaphragm . . . from your belly . . . from your womb. Your stomach should push in and out as you breathe . . . loosen your pants if you need to. Fill your belly with breath. Feel yourself relaxing, recharging. Now notice how the energy of the group has changed. (Pause.)

"Now let's reach out and take hands, linking ourselves together around the circle. Continue to breathe deeply. Feel the energy move around the circle. It may seem like a subtle tingling, or a low heat, or even a sensation of cold. We may all perceive it differently. Some of us may see it—dancing like sparks in the center of the circle. (Long pause.)

(To end here:) "Now take a deep breath, and suck in the power, as if you were sucking through a straw. Feel it travel down your spine, and flow into the earth. Relax."

(Or go on to the next exercise.)

EXERCISE 4: GROUP BREATH

(To begin here, say:) "Let's take hands around the circle and sit (or stand) up straight.

"And now, closing your eyes, let's breathe together—breathing the deep breath of the belly, of the womb. Inhale. . .(slowly), exhale. . .inhale. . .exhale . . . inhale . . . exhale . . . feel yourself relax, as you breathe. Feel yourself become strong . . . with each breath . . . become refreshed . . . with each breath . . . feel your worries floating away . . . with each breath . . . become revitalized . . . as we breathe together . . . inhale . . . exhale . . . inhale . . . exhale . . .

"And feel our breath as it meets in the center of the circle . . . as we breathe as one . . . breathing one breath . . . inhale . . . exhale . . . breathing one circle . . . breathing one, living organism . . . with each breath . . . becoming one circle . . . with each breath . . . becoming one . . ." (long pause).

(End as in Exercise 3, or go on.)

EXERCISE 5: THE TREE OF LIFE

(This is one of the most important meditations, which is practiced individually, as well as in the group. In solitary practice, begin by sitting or standing erect, and breathing deeply and rhythmically.)

"And as we breathe, remember to sit erect, and as your spine straightens, feel the energy rising . . . (pause).

"Now imagine that your spine is the trunk of a tree. . .and from its base roots extend deep into the earth . . . into the center of the earth Herself . . . (pause).

"And you can draw up power from the earth, with each breath . . . feel the energy rising . . . like sap rising through a tree trunk . . .

"And feel the power rise up your spine . . . feel yourself becoming more alive . . . with each breath . . .

"And from the crown of your head, you have branches, that sweep up and back down to touch the earth . . . and feel the power burst from the crown of your head . . . and feel it sweep through the branches until it touches the earth again . . . making a circle . . . making a circuit . . . returning to its source . . .

(In a group:) "And breathing deeply, feel how all our branches intertwine . . . and the power weaves through them . . . and dances among them, like the wind . . . feel it moving . . ." (long pause).

(End as in Exercise 3, or go on.)

EXERCISE 6: POWER CHANT

(This should always begin with a Group Breath—Exercise 4.)

"Now let your breath become sound . . . any sound that you like . . . a moan . . . a sigh . . . a giggle . . . a low hum . . . a howl . . . a melody . . . chant the wordless sounds of the vowels . . . ."

(Wait. In a new group, there may be silence for a moment. Slowly, someone will begin to sigh, or hum very quietly. Others will gradually join in. The chant may develop into a strong hum, or a swelling wave of open-throated notes. People may begin to chortle, bark, or howl like animals, if they feel so inclined. The chant may peak suddenly, and drop to silence, or it may rise and fall in several tides of power. Let it direct itself.

When everyone is silent, allow a quiet time of relaxation. Before the group has time to get restless, earth the power as in Exercise 7.)

EXERCISE 7: EARTHING POWER

(Also called *grounding,* earthing power is one of the basic techniques of magic. Power must be earthed every time it is raised. Otherwise, the force we feel as vitalizing energy degenerates into nervous tension and irritability. In the earlier exercises, we grounded the energy by sucking it in and letting it flow through us into the earth. That technique is often useful when working alone.)

"Now sink to the ground and relax. Place your palms flat on the ground, or lie flat. Let the power sink through you into the earth." (Even if you are meeting in a penthouse fifteen floors above the earth, visualize the energy flowing down to the actual ground.) "Relax, and let the force flow through you . . . let it flow deep into the earth . . . where it will be cleansed and renewed. Relax and let yourself drift peacefully."

These five exercises contain the essence of a Craft ritual. The circle is cast by taking hands; power is raised, shared, and earthed. Sharing of wine and food generally follows—magic is hungry work! As the wine cup is passed around, toasts are made and people express thanks to the Goddess for good things that have come to them. This part of the meeting is relaxed and informal, a good time for sharing impressions and discussing what has gone on. People may move out of the circle at this time, but the meeting *must* be formally ended before anyone goes home. Meetings that dribble off at the end leave people without a sense of closure and completion. If magic has been worked, the energy absorbed then tends to turn into anxiety and irritation, instead of peace and vitality. A meeting can be ended quite simply by having everyone take hands and say together:

> The circle is open, but unbroken,
> May the peace of the Goddess go in our hearts;
> Merry meet, and merry part.
> And merry meet again. Blessed be.

A kiss is then passed around the circle (clockwise).

Sharing poems, songs, stories, pictures, and creative work in the circle also helps build a feeling of closeness. In Honeysuckle, when we are taking in a group of new members we devote an evening to sharing our life stories in the circle. We also jog together regularly and have gone backpacking as a group. Compost occasionally makes "excursions"—for example, to the Chinese Moon Festival parade. We devoted one meeting to watching *The Wizard of Oz* on television and to skipping down the street singing "Follow the Yellow Brick Road."

As the group grows more unified, certain interpersonal conflicts will inevitably arise. The very cohesiveness of the group itself will make some members feel left out. Each person is part of the whole, but also an individual, partly separated from the rest. Some people tend to see the group as a solid entity that completely enfolds everyone else, while they alone are partly left out. Sexual attraction often arises between coveners, and, while the first bright flush of love will draw power into the group, a quarreling couple will cause disruption. If the two break up, and no longer feel they can work in the group together, a real problem arises. A coven leader who is strong and charismatic often becomes the focus of other member's projections. She may be seen as the all-giving earth mother, the eternally-desirable-yet-unattainable woman, or the all-wise prophetess. It is always tempting for her to believe these flattering images and psychically feed on the energy charge they contain; but if she does she stunts her own growth as a real human being. Sooner or later, she will fumble and the image will be shattered; the results can be explosive.

A certain amount of group time and energy spent on resolving interpersonal conflicts is necessary and desirable, part of the growth process that goes on in a healthy coven. But it is all too easy for a group to degenerate into a sort of amateur encounter session or shouting match. A coven cannot function as a therapy group. Problems between members can often be solved more effectively by using magic than by endless discussion. For example, instead of verbally reassuring an insecure covener, place her in the center of the circle and chant her name. If two members cannot work together, but neither wants to leave, the group may need to cast lots, leaving the decision up to the Goddess. And if a High Priestess seems in danger of being seduced by her own public relations campaign, the less star-struck members of the group should gently tell her so. Objective, constructive criticism is one of the great benefits of the coven structure.

A coven becomes a safe space in which members feel free to release their inhibitions: laugh, dance, act silly, burst into song, chant spontaneous poetry, make bad puns, and let Younger Self come out and play. Only then can the higher states of awareness be reached. Many techniques have been developed to drop the "censor" of Talking Self and to let the inner voice speak freely.

Nudity is one such technique. When we take off our clothes, we drop our social masks, our carefully groomed self-images. We become open. The mystical meaning of the naked human body is "truth." Different people need different levels of private space; while some romp happily on nude beaches, others cannot feel comfortable naked until trust has been built over a long period of time. In our covens, public rituals are always clothed. If guests invited to private "sky-clad" ceremonies feel uncomfortable disrobing, they are welcome to wear whatever they like. Vulnerability cannot be forced on anyone, except destructively.

Here is one of the exercises we use to begin opening the inner voice and releasing the blocks to expression:

EXERCISE 8: WORD ASSOCIATION TRANCE

(Everyone should lie down and position themselves comfortably. Turn off the lights. Begin with a Group Breath—Exercise 4. When everyone is relaxed, proceed:)

"Now we're going to go around the circle, clockwise. I'll start by saying a word, and the next person will say the first word that pops into her mind. Then the person after that will respond to her word, and so on, around the circle. Don't think about the word, just relax, breathe deep, and let it come."

(Start. The sequence might go like this:)

"Green/Pea/Soup/Hot/Cold/Ice/Snow/White/Black/Bird/Fly/Sky/Starry/ Night/Dark."

(After a few rounds:)

"Now we're each going to repeat the last person's word before we add our own."

(The sequence might go like this:)

"Dark Cave/Cave Bury/Bury Deep/Deep Sea/Sea Wave/Wave Flag/Flag Star/Star Light/Light Ray/Ray Sun."

(After a few rounds:)

"Now we're each going to repeat the last two words before adding our own."

(Now the sequence might run like this:)

"Ray Sun Shine/Sun Shine Day/Shine Day Forever/Day Forever Night/ Forever Night Sky/Night Sky Star/Sky Star Light."

(This is an actual invocation we use, which was created by a group during this exercise. As the trance continues, words become entities in themselves. The combinations form constantly shifting scenes, which flash vividly before the inner eye. Gradually, the cycle may die away, and people simply describe what they see:)

"I see a dark sky, dotted with a million stars—one of them shoots across the sky . . ."

"I see a blazing comet, with a golden tail trailing behind . . ."

"I see a trailing peacock's tail with iridescent eyes . . ."

"I see an eye looking at me . . ."

"I see a face, the dark face of a beautiful woman . . ."

(Descriptions may be elaborate or simple. Some may obtain striking visions, others hear sounds or voices, or feel new sensations. A few people may drift off to sleep. After a time, the group will fall silent, each member floating in her own vision. Allow time for everyone to fully experience her inner world, then say:)

"Now breathe deeply and say farewell to your visions. In a moment, we're going to open our eyes and awaken, fully and completely, feeling refreshed and renewed. When I count to three, we will open our eyes and wake up. Now take a deep breath . . . inhale. . . exhale . . . one . . . two . . . three. . . . Open your eyes, and awaken, refreshed and renewed."

It is extremely important to bring everyone fully back into ordinary consciousness. Turn on the lights and change the atmosphere completely. Share food and drink (but not alcohol); move around and talk. Otherwise, participants may remain slightly entranced, a condition that becomes draining and depressing.

This is especially good for opening up the creative imagination and could be used in art or writing classes as well as in covens.

Ritual is partly a matter of performance, of theater. Some people delight in this aspect of Witchcraft; others become shy and frozen in front of a group. The quieter coveners, however, may channel power in other ways. Brook, for example, rarely wants to cast the circle or invoke the Goddess, but when she chants, her voice, ordinarily pleasant but unremarkable, becomes an eerie, more-than-human channel for power.

Magical training varies greatly from coven to coven, but its purpose is always the same: to open up the starlight consciousness, the other-way-of-knowing that belongs to the right hemisphere and allows us to make contact with the Divine within. The beginner must develop four basic abilities: relaxation, concentration, visualization, and projection.

Relaxation is important because any form of tension blocks energy. Muscular tension is felt as mental and emotional stress, and emotional stresses cause physical and muscular tension and *dis*-ease. Power trying to move through a tense body is like an electric current trying to force its way through a line of resistors. Most of the juice is lost along the way. Physical relaxation also seems to change brain wave patterns and activate centers that aren't ordinarily used.

EXERCISE 9: RELAXATION

(This can be done in a group, alone, or with a partner. Begin by lying down on your back. Do not cross your limbs. Loosen any tight clothing.)

"In order to know how relaxation feels, we must first experience tension. We are going to tense all the muscles of the body, one by one, and keep them tense until we relax our entire bodies with one breath. Don't clench the muscles so they cramp, just tense them lightly.

"Start with your toes. Tense the toes in your right foot . . . and now your left foot. Tense your right foot . . . and your left foot. Your right ankle . . . and your left ankle. . . .

(Continue throughout the whole body, part by part. From time to time, remind the group to tense any muscles that they have let slack.)

"Now tense your scalp. Your whole body is tense. . .feel the tension in every part. Tense any muscles that have gone slack. Now take a deep breath . . . inhale . . . (pause) . . . exhale . . . and relax!"

"Relax completely. You are completely and totally relaxed." (In a sing-song tone:) "Your fingers are relaxed, and your toes are relaxed. Your hands are relaxed, and your feet are relaxed. Your wrists are relaxed, and your ankles are relaxed."

(And so on, throughout the entire body. Periodically pause and say:)

"You are completely and totally relaxed. Completely and totally relaxed. Your body is light, it feels like water, like it is melting into the earth."

"Allow yourself to drift and float peacefully in your state of relaxation. If any worries or anxieties disturb your peace, imagine they drain from your body like water and melt into the earth. Feel yourself being healed and renewed."

(Remain in deep relaxation for ten to fifteen minutes. It is good to practice this exercise daily, until you can relax completely simply by lying down and letting go, without needing to go through the entire process. People who have difficulty sleeping will find this extremely helpful. However, do not allow yourself to drift off into sleep. You are training your mind to remain in a relaxed but alert state. Later, you will use this state for trance work, which will be much more difficult if you are not in the habit of staying awake. If you practice this at night before sleeping, sit up, open your eyes and consciously end the exercise before dozing.

Many of the other exercises can be most effectively practiced in a state of deep relaxation. Experiment to find what works best for you.)

Visualization is the ability to see, hear, feel, touch, and taste with the inner senses. Our physical eyes do not *see*, they merely transmit nerve impulses touched off by light stimuli to the brain. It is the brain that *sees*, and it can see inner images as clearly as those in the outer world. In dreams, all five senses are vivid. With practice, most people can develop the ability to use the inner senses vividly while awake.

Some people naturally see images, others may hear or feel impressions. A few people find it difficult or impossible to visualize, but most find the facility will improve with exercise.

Visualization is important because it is through internal images and sensations that we communicate with Younger Self and the High Self. When the inner senses are fully awake, we may see visions of extraordinary beauty, smell the blossoms of the Isle of Apples, taste ambrosia, and hear the songs of the Gods.

EXERCISE 10: GROUNDING AND CENTERING

Before beginning visualization practice, we should ground and center ourselves. This is again one of the basic techniques of magical work. *Grounding* means to establish an energy connection with the earth. The Tree of Life exercise is one method of grounding. Another is to visualize a cord or pole extending from the base of your spine into the center of the earth. Center yourself by aligning your body along its center of gravity. Breathe from your center—from your diaphragm and abdomen. Feel energy flow up from the earth and fill you.

Grounding is important because it allows you to draw on the earth's vitality, rather than depleting your own. When channeling energy, it serves as a psychic lightning rod—forces run through you into the earth, rather than "burning out" your mind and body.

EXERCISE 11: SIMPLE VISUALIZATIONS:

This exercise is for those of you who have difficulty visualizing. Ground and center. Close your eyes, and imagine that you are looking at a white wall or a blank screen. Practice visualizing simple geometric forms: a line, a dot, a circle, a triangle, an ellipse, and so on.

When you are able to see the forms clearly, visualize the screen in color: red, yellow, blue, orange, green, violet, and black in turn. It may help to look at a colored object with your eyes open, first—then close your eyes and mentally see the color.

Finally, practice visualizing the geometric forms in various colors. Change the colors and forms until you can mentally picture them at will.

EXERCISE 12: THE APPLE

Visualize an apple. Hold it in your hands; turn it around; feel it. Feel the shape, the size, the weight, the texture. Notice the color, the reflection of light on its skin. Bring it up to your nose and smell it. Bite into it, taste it; hear the crunch as your teeth sink in. Eat the apple; feel it slide down your throat. See it grow smaller. When you have eaten it down to the core, let it disappear.

Repeat with other foods. Ice cream cones are also excellent subjects.

EXERCISE 13: THE PENTACLE

Visualize a line of flickering blue flame, like a gas flame from a Bunsen burner. Now mentally draw a pentacle, a five-pointed star with one point up, in the invoking direction: starting at the top and moving down to the left. (See illustration on opposite page.) Watch it form out of the blue flame. Hold the image in your mind for a few moments.

Now retrace it in the banishing direction, starting at the lower left-hand corner and moving up. As you do so, watch it disappear.

Practice until it comes to you easily. This visualization is part of casting a circle.

EXERCISE 14: THE KNOT

Visualize yourself tying a knot—any knot you can tie easily in reality. Try not to see a mental picture of yourself from outside; instead, put yourself in the picture. See your hands moving, and feel the string. Feel every movement you would make, then draw the knot closed, and feel the string pull taut.

This visualization is used to bind spells.

More complex visualizations are given in later chapters.

Concentration is the ability to focus on an image, thought, or task, to narrow one's field of awareness and shut out distractions. Like a muscle, it grows stronger with exercise.

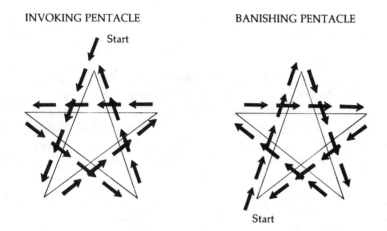

INVOKING PENTACLE   BANISHING PENTACLE

Start

Start

Many people today practice forms of Eastern meditation—yoga, Zen, Transcendental Meditation—which are excellent for developing concentration. The more you practice the visualizations, the easier it is to concentrate on the images. The following three exercises will help improve your inner focus:

EXERCISE 15: CANDLE GAZING

In a quiet, darkened room, light a candle. Ground and center, and gaze quietly at the candle. Breathe deeply, and let yourself feel warmed by the light of the candle. Let its peaceful radiance fill you completely. As thoughts surface in your mind, experience them as if they came from outside. Do not let the flame split into a double image: keep your eyes focused. Remain for at least five or ten minutes, then relax.

EXERCISE 16: THE DIAMOND

Again, light a candle in a dim quiet room. Ground and center. Gaze at the candle, and visualize a diamond in the center of your forehead, between and just above your eyebrows. The diamond reflects the light of the candle, and the candle reflects the light of the diamond. Feel the reverberation of energy. Hold for at least five or ten minutes, then relax.

EXERCISE 17: MIRROR, MIRROR

Ground and center. In a mirror, gaze into your own eyes. Focus your attention on the space between them. Repeat your own name to yourself, over and over. Again, as thoughts surface, experience them as if they were outside you. After five or ten minutes, relax.

Projection is the ability to send out energy. It comes quite naturally to most people, once they are aware of its "feel." Projection is also used in another sense to mean the ability to travel "out-of-body": That form of projection will be discussed in Chapter Nine. In the Tree of Life exercise and during the Group Breath and Power Chant, we have already experienced what it feels like to send out energy. Here are two other exercises:

EXERCISE 18: THE ROCK

Ground and center. Imagine that you are standing on the seashore, looking out over the waves. In your strongest hand, you hold a heavy rock. Pick it up, inhale, and as you exhale, let it fly! Watch it splash into the sea just below the horizon.

Now look up again. Realize that you can see a horizon twice as far away. Mentally stretch to see it. In your hand, you hold a rock twice as large as the first. Again, take a deep breath, and, as you exhale, throw with all your might. Watch it splash into the far waves.

Once again, look up and realize that you can see a horizon twice as far away again. In your hand, you hold a rock twice as heavy. Take one more deep breath, and as you exhale, throw hard! Watch it splash.

Practice this exercise until you can feel the release of power that goes with the rock.

EXERCISE 19: THE HAMMER

Ground and center. Visualize a heavy hammer in your hand. A stubborn nail is sticking out of a board in front of you. With all your strength, drive the nail into the board. Repeat, doing it three times in all.

Covens have many different ways of taking on new members. Some hold open classes or study groups. We prefer to have initiates take on individual apprentices. Each newcomer gets individualized instruction, tailored to her particular needs. And each coven member has a chance to be an authority, and is forced to conceptualize her own knowledge of the

Craft in order to teach it. Apprentices and their teachers develop a strong bond, so each newcomer feels she has a special relationship to one group member. Apprentices also develop a bond with each other as a group. They attend rituals together, so that nobody has to be the "only new kid on the block."

When I train an apprentice, I think of myself as being somewhat like a dance teacher. I suggest a regular discipline, including many of the exercises in this chapter, the "basic barre-work" of magic. Also, I try to identify areas of weakness and imbalance, and prescribe corrective exercises. For example, for one student whose mind continually wanders I might suggest concentration practice. For Paul, on the other hand, who studied for years with a sect of Buddhists and can, in his own words, "bore holes through walls," I suggested daily jogging. During rituals, apprentices have a chance to combine skills learned in solitary practice into an intricate dance of power with the coven and each other.

As a basic, daily discipline, I recommend three things. The first is regular physical exercise. The importance of this cannot be overstressed. Unfortunately, it is one of the hardest things to get people to do. The Craft tends to attract mental and spiritual types rather than brawny athletes. But magic and psychic work requires tremendous vitality—literally, the energy of the *raith,* of Younger Self. That vitality is replenished and renewed by physical activity—much as the motion of an automobile's wheels turns the generator, which recharges the batteries. Too much mental and spiritual work that is not balanced by physical exercise drains our etheric batteries. Yoga is sometimes good, but it is usually taught as a spiritual discipline that opens the psychic centers, rather than increasing physical vitality. For our purposes, jogging, swimming, bicycling, tennis, or roller-skating are better—something active and enjoyable that gets us out into the elements. Witches who are physically disabled, of course, may be limited to sedentary exercises such as isometrics. If they can spend some time each day outdoors, on the grass or under a tree where they can soak up elemental energies, they will reap many of the same benefits as the marathon runners.

The second thing I recommend for students is daily relaxation practice and a daily meditation, visualization, or concentration exercise. These often change as the student develops. Some people practice several at once, but one is enough. Too many are cumbersome. At one point in my own training, I woke up in the morning and did a trance exercise at my typewriter for up to an hour, then twenty minutes of yoga, including meditations on the four elements and the Circle Visualization in Chapter Four. Later in the day I practiced deep relaxation and a lying-down trance. At night, I did a candle-gazing, a water purification, and a variety of personal spells. Unfortunately, I had very little time left for actually *living*. After a few weeks, I decided that moderation was the essence of wisdom, in magic, as in other things.

The third practice I suggest is the keeping of a magical diary, called a Book of Shadows. Traditionally, this was the "recipe book" of rituals, spells, chants and incantations, hand-copied by each Witch from her teacher. Today, although I blush to admit it, such information is generally xeroxed for coven distribution. The Book of Shadows is more of a personal journal. It may include descriptions of rituals, records of dreams, reactions to exercises, poems, stories, and trance journeys. Solitary Witches can use their Book of Shadows to develop some of the objectivity that generally comes from working in a coven. Trances and meditations can be written out in the journal. Tristine Rainer, in *The New Diary,* even describes techniques for using journal writing to remember past lives.[2]

Womb, support group, magical training college, and community of friends—the coven is the heart of the Craft. Within the circle, each Witch is trained to develop her inner power, her integrity of mind, body and spirit. Like families, covens sometimes have their squabbles. But whenever the circle is cast, whenever they raise the cone and call on the Gods together, they recognize in each other the Goddess, the God, the life spirit of all. And so, when every initiate is challenged at the gate to the circle, she speaks the only password: "Perfect love and perfect trust."

Notes

1. Kate Millett, *Flying* (New York: Ballantine Books, 1974), p. 14.
2. Tristine Rainer, *The New Diary* (Los Angeles: Tarcher, 1978), pp. 259–261.

4 Creating Sacred Space

Between the Worlds

THE CASTING OF THE CIRCLE

The room is lit only by flickering candles at each of the cardinal points. The coveners stand in a circle, their hands linked. With her **athame,** *her consecrated knife, unsheathed, the High Priestess* steps to the altar and salutes sky and earth. She turns and walks to the Eastern corner, followed by two priestesses, one bearing the chalice of salt water, the other the smoldering incense. They face the East. The High Priestess raises her knife and calls out:*

> Hail, Guardians of the Watchtowers of the East,
> Powers of Air!
> We invoke you and call you,
> Golden Eagle of the Dawn,
> Star-seeker,
> Whirlwind,
> Rising Sun,
> Come!
> By the air that is Her breath,

---

*For literary convenience, I have designated the High Priestess as casting the circle. But any qualified covener, female or male, may take her role.

Send forth your light,
Be here now!¹

As she speaks, she traces the invoking pentagram in the air with her knife. She sees it, glowing with a pale blue flame, and through it feels a great onrush of wind, sweeping across a high plain lit by the first rays of dawn. She breathes deeply, drawing in the power, then earths it through her knife, which she points to the ground.

As she sprinkles water three times, the second Priestess cries out, "With salt and water, I purify the East!" The third Priestess draws the invoking pentagram with incense, saying,

"With fire and air, I charge the East!"

The High Priestess, knife held outward, traces the boundaries of the circle. She sees it take shape in her mind's eye as they continue to each of the four directions, repeating the invocation, the purification, and the charging:

Hail, Guardians of the Watchtowers of the South,
Powers of Fire!
We invoke you and call you,
Red Lion of the noon heat,
Flaming One!
Summer's warmth,
Spark of life,
Come!
By the fire that is Her spirit,
Send forth your flame,
Be here now!

Hail, Guardians of the Watchtowers of the West,
Powers of Water!
We invoke you and call you,
Serpent of the watery abyss,
Rainmaker,
Gray-robed Twilight,
Evening Star!
By the waters of Her living womb,
Send forth your flow,
Be here now!

Hail, Guardians of the Watchtowers of the North,
Powers of Earth,
Cornerstone of all Power.
We invoke you and call you,
Lady of the Outer Darkness,
Black Bull of Midnight,
North Star,

Center of the whirling sky.
Stone,
Mountain,
Fertile Field,
Come!
By the earth that is her body,
Send forth your strength,
Be here now!

The High Priestess traces the last link of the circle, ending in the East.
Again she salutes sky and earth, turns and touches the tip of her athame to
the central cauldron, and says,

The circle is cast.
We are between the worlds,
Beyond the bounds of time,
Where night and day,
Birth and death,
Joy and sorrow,
Meet as one.

The third Priestess takes a taper to the South point candle and with it
lights candles in the central cauldron and on the altar, saying,

The fire is lit,
The ritual is begun.

They return to the circle. The second Priestess smiles at the covener on
her left, and kisses her or him, saying,

"In perfect love and perfect trust."
The kiss is passed around the circle.

"The unfolding of God . . . involves the creation of new space,
in which women are free to become who we are. . . . Its center is
on the boundary of patriarchal institutions . . . its center is the
lives of women who begin to liberate themselves toward wholeness."[2]
"Entry into the new space . . . also involves entry into new time.
. . . The center of the new time is on the boundary of patriarchal
time. . . . It *is* whenever we are living out of our
own sense of reality, refusing to be possessed, conquered, and
alienated by the linear, measured-out, quantitative time of the
patriarchal system."[3]

Mary Daly

In Witchcraft, we define a new space and a new time whenever we
cast a circle to begin a ritual. The circle exists on the boundaries of ordinary
space and time; it is "between the worlds" of the seen and unseen, of
flashlight and starlight consciousness, a space in which alternate realities

meet, in which the past and future are open to us. Time is no longer measured out; it becomes elastic, fluid, a swirling pool in which we dive and swim. The restrictions and distinctions of our socially defined roles no longer apply; only the rule of nature holds sway, the rule of Isis who says "What I have made law can be dissolved by no man."⁴ Within the circle, the powers within us, the Goddess and the Old Gods, are revealed.

Casting the circle is an enacted meditation. Each gesture we make, each tool we use, each power we invoke, resonates through layers of meaning to awaken an aspect of ourselves. The outer forms are a cloak for inner visualizations, so that the circle becomes a living mandala, in which we are centered.

When we cast a circle, we create an energy form, a boundary that limits and contains the movements of subtle forces. In Witchcraft, the function of the circle is not so much to keep *out* negative energies as to keep *in* power so that it can rise to a peak. You cannot boil water without putting it in a pot, and you can't raise power effectively unless it is also contained. Leaving the circle during the ritual is discouraged because it tends to dissipate the energy, although cats and very small children seem to pass across without disturbing the force field. Adults usually cut a "gate" in pantomine with an *athame,* should they need to leave the circle before the ritual is ended.

The casting of the circle is the formal beginning of the ritual, the complex "cue" that tells us to switch our awareness into a deeper mode. In ritual, we "suspend disbelief" just as we do when watching a play: We allow the critical and analytical functions of Talking Self to relax so that Younger Self may respond fully and emotionally to what happens. Younger Self, as we have seen, responds best to actions, symbols, tangibles —so this change in consciousness is acted out, using a rich array of tools and symbols.

In the permanent stone circles of the Megalithic era, where rituals were enacted for hundreds of years, great reservoirs of power were built up. Because the stones defined the sacred space, there was no need to draw out the circle as we do. The form of circle casting most Witches use today probably originated during the Burning Times, when meetings were held secretly, indoors, and it became necessary to create a temple in a simple hut. Witches may have taken over some forms from Cabalists. It is said that Witches often harbored Jews from Christian persecution and that they exchanged knowledge. (I must admit that, while Witches in general like to believe this is true, Jews don't seem to have heard of it—or, if they have, aren't advertising the fact.)

Before any ritual there is always a period of purification, during which participants can clear away worries, concerns, and anxieties that may hamper their concentration. Some covens simply aspurge (sprinkle) each member with salt water while casting the circle. At very large rituals, this is the only practical method. But for small groups and important workings, we use a more intense meditative exercise called the Salt-Water Purification.

Salt and water are both cleansing elements. Water, of course, washes clean. Salt preserves from decay and is a natural disinfectant. The ocean, the womb of life, is salt water, and so are tears, which help us purify the heart of sorrow.

EXERCISE 20: SALT-WATER PURIFICATION

(This is one of the basic individual meditations that should be practiced regularly. During periods of high anxiety or depression or when undertaking heavy responsibilities, it is helpful to practice this daily.)

Fill a cup with water. (Use your ritual chalice, if you have one. With your *athame* (or other implement), add three mounds of salt, and stir counterclockwise.

Sit with the cup in your lap. Let your fears, worries, doubts, hatreds, and disappointments surface in your mind. See them as a black stream, which flows out of you as you breathe and is dissolved by the salt water in the cup. Allow yourself time to feel deeply cleansed.

Now hold up the cup. Breathe deeply, and feel yourself drawing up power from the earth (as in the Tree of Life exercise.) Let the power flow into the salt water, until you can visualize it glowing with white light.

Sip the water. As you feel it on your tongue, know that you have taken in the power of cleansing, of healing. Fear and unhappiness have become transformed into the power of change.

Empty the leftover water into a running stream. (Alas, in these decadent times the nearest stream is usually running out of the kitchen faucet and down the drain.)

EXERCISE 21: GROUP SALT-WATER PURIFICATION

Coveners assemble in a circle, with incense and point candles lit. The High Priestess goes to the altar, grounds and centers herself. She takes the cup of water in her right hand, saying "Blessed be, thou creature of water." She takes the dish of salt in her left hand, and says, "Blessed be, thou creature of earth." She holds them both up to the sky with arms outstretched, and lets power flow into them, saying,

> Salt and water,
> Inner and outer,
> Soul and body,
> Be cleansed!
> Cast out all that is harmful!

> Take in all that is good and healing!
> By the power of the Mother of all life,
> And her lover the Horned God,
> So mote* it be!"

She sets them down on the altar, and takes her *Athame* in her strongest hand, saying, "Blessed be, thou creature of art." She spills three mounds of salt into the water and stirs it counterclockwise, saying,

> May this *athame* be purified,
> And may these tools and this altar be purified,

as she shakes a few drops over the altar, then salutes sky and earth:

> "In the names of Life and Death, so mote* it be!"

She then holds the cup to her heart and charges the water with power. When she can feel it glowing, she returns to the circle. The cup is sent around, and each person performs her or his private purification. Others may sing softly as the cup goes around. In a large group, three or four cups of water are charged at the same time; otherwise the cup may take hours to go around the circle.

When the cup returns to the High Priestess, she sends a kiss around the circle. Then she begins the casting of the circle. If the meeting space is felt to need special cleansing, the following Banishing can be performed.

EXERCISE 22: BANISHING

After the purification, the High Priestess takes the sword or *athame* and goes to the center of the circle. She points the blade to earth and sky, and says, forcefully,

> Spirits of evil,
> Unfriendly beings,
> Unwanted guests,
> Begone!
> Leave us, leave this place, leave this circle,
> That the Gods may enter.
> Go, or be cast into the outer darkness!
> Go, or be drowned in the watery abyss!
> Go, or be burned in the flames!
> Go, or be torn by the whirlwind!
> By the power of the Mother and the Horned One,

---

*"So mote it be" means "So must it be" and is traditional for ending a spell or magical working in the Craft.

All the coven together shouts:

> We banish you! We banish you! We banish you!
> Begone!

All scream, shout, clap hands, ring bells, and make noise to frighten away negative forces.

Bath water can be "charged,"* and a few salt crystals added, and coveners can take a ritual bath before entering the circle. This is more fully described in Chapter Ten, on Initiation. Due to the limitations of time and hot water, it is best done at home.

The concept of the quartered circle is basic to Witchcraft, as it is to many cultures and religions. The four directions and the fifth, the center, each correspond and resonate to a quality of the self, to an element, a time of day and year, to tools of the Craft, symbolic animals, and forms of personal power. Constant visualization of these connections create deep internal links, so that physical actions trigger inner states. The action of casting the circle then awakens all parts of the self, and puts us in touch with mind, energy, emotions, body and spirit, so that we are constantly made whole.

The "Guardians of the Watchtowers" are energy forms, the *raiths* or spirits of the four elements. They bring the elemental energy of earth, air, fire and water, into the circle, to augment our human power. The vortex of power created when we invoke the four directions guards the circle from intrusions, and draws in the higher powers of the Goddess and God.

Each movement in a ritual has meaning. When we move "sunwise" or clockwise, "deosil," we follow the direction the sun appears to move in the sky, and draw in power. Deosil is the direction of increase, of fortune, favor and blessing. When we move "widdershins" or counterclockwise, we are going against the sun, and this direction is used for decrease and banishings.

The tools, the physical objects we use in Witchcraft, are the tangible representatives of unseen forces. The mind works magic, and no elaborately forged knife or elegant wand can do any more than augment the power of a trained mind. The tools are simply aids in communicating with Younger Self, who responds much better to tangibles than to abstracts.

There are two basic schools of thought about tools in the Craft: the Ceremonial Magic school and what I call the kitchen magic school. Ceremonialists are purists, who feel that magical tools should never be handled by others or used for any but ritual purposes. Objects can become

---

*To magically "charge" an object means to imbue it with energy.

reservoirs of psychic power, which may be dissipated by, for example, slicing fruit with your *athame*. Kitchen magic Witches, on the other hand, feel that the Goddess is manifest in ordinary tasks as well as magic circles. When you slice fruit with your *athame,* you consecrate the fruit, and a kitchen chore becomes a sacred task. Whichever school of thought you follow, it is a breach of manners to handle another Witch's tools without asking permission.

Tools may be bought, hand-made yourself, given as gifts, or found, sometimes in unusual circumstances. Mother Moth of Compost found her *athame* lying on the white line in the middle of the freeway when she was driving home late one night. A set of tools are sometimes given to a new initiate by the coven. When buying magical tools, never haggle over the price.

Correspondences may differ in varying traditions, and interpretations of symbolism may not always agree. The following are the correspondences used in the Faery Tradition (complete tables are given in the tables beginning on page 201):

The East

The East corresponds to the element Air, to the mind, dawn, spring, to pale, airy colors, white and violet, to the eagle and high-flying birds, and the power to *know.* Its tools are the *athame* and the sword, which are used interchangeably. The *athame* is traditionally a double-bladed, black-handled knife, but people use anything from kitchen knives to Swiss Army knives complete with corkscrew, so indispensable for opening ritual wine. Many Witches do not own a sword; they are dramatic at large, open rituals but awkward in close quarters.

EXERCISE 23: AIR MEDITATION

Face East. Ground and center. Breathe deep, and be conscious of the air as it flows in and out of your lungs. Feel it as the breath of the Goddess, and take in the life force, the inspiration, of the universe. Let your own breath merge with the winds, the clouds, the great currents that sweep over land and ocean with the turning of the earth. Say, "Hail, Arida, Bright Lady of the Air!"

EXERCISE 24: *ATHAME* OR SWORD MEDITATION

Ground and center. Hold your *athame* or sword in your strongest hand. Breathe deeply and take in the power of Air, the power of the mind. The power of this tool is that of discrimination, of drawing lines, setting limits, making choices, and carrying them out. Remember choices you have made and carried through in spite of difficulties. Feel the power of your mind to influence others and the strength of your responsibility not to misuse that power. You have the force to act ethically, in accord with what you believe is right. Let the power of your intelligence, your knowledge, your moral courage, flow into your tool.

The South

The South corresponds to the element Fire, to energy or spirit, to noon, summer, fiery reds and oranges, to the solar lion and the quality of *will.* Its tool is the wand, which may be a slender branch of hazel, a stout oak staff, or a magically shaped piece of driftwood. The wand is used to channel energy, to direct a cone of power, and to invoke God or Goddess.

EXERCISE 25: FIRE MEDITATION

Face South. Ground and center. Be conscious of the electric spark within each nerve as pulses jump from synapse to synapse. Be aware of the combustion within each cell, as food burns to release energy. Let your own fire become one with candle flame, bonfire, hearth fire, lightning, starlight, and sunlight, one with the bright spirit of the Goddess. Say, "Hail, Tana, Goddess of Fire!"

EXERCISE 26: WAND MEDITATION

Ground and center. Hold your wand in your strongest hand. Breathe deeply, and feel the power of Fire, of energy. Be aware of yourself as a channel of energy. You can change spirit into matter, idea to reality, concept into form. Feel your own power to create, to do, to be an agent of change. Be in touch with your *will*—your power to do what you must, to set a goal and work toward it. Let your will flow into your wand.

The West

The West corresponds to the element Water, to emotions, to twilight, autumn, to blues, grays, deep purples, and sea greens, to sea serpents, dolphins, fish, to the power to *dare.* From the West comes the courage to face our deepest feelings. Its tool is the cup or chalice, which holds the salt water or wine.

EXERCISE 27: WATER MEDITATION

Face West. Ground and center. Feel the blood flowing through the rivers of your veins, the liquid tides within each cell of your body. You are fluid, one drop congealed out of the primal ocean which is the womb of the Great Mother. Find the calm pools of tranquility within you, the rivers of feeling, the tides of power. Sink deep into the well of the inner mind, below consciousness. Say, "Hail, Tiamat, Serpent of the Watery Abyss!"

EXERCISE 28: CUP MEDITATION

Gound and center. Hold your cup cradled in both hands. Breathe deep, and feel the power of Water, of feeling and emotion. Be in touch with the flow of your own emotions: love, anger, sorrow, joy. The cup is the symbol of nurturing, the overflowing breast of the Goddess that nourishes all life. Be aware of how you are nurtured, of how you nurture others. The power to feel is the power to be human, to be real, to be whole. Let the strength of your emotions flood the cup.

The North

The North is considered the most powerful direction. Because the sun never reaches the north, it is the direction of Mystery, of the unseen. The North Star is the center, around which the skies revolve. Altars face North in the Craft. North corresponds to Earth, to the body, to midnight, winter, brown, black and the green of vegetation. From the North comes the power to keep silent, to listen as well as speak, to keep secrets, to know what not to say. The Goddess as Dark Maiden, the new moon that is not yet visible, and the God as Sacred Bull, are the totems of the North, and its tool is the pentacle, the prime symbol of the Craft. A five-pointed star with one point up, set within the circle of the full moon, the pentacle can be engraved on a plate, glazed on a ceramic platter, or molded out of "baker's clay"—bread dough and salt. It is used for grounding energy or as a platter for serving the sacred cakes.

EXERCISE 29: EARTH MEDITATION

Face North. Ground and center. Feel your bones, your skeleton, the solidity of your body. Be aware of your flesh, of all that can be touched and felt. Feel the pull of gravity, your own weight, your attraction to the earth that is the body of the Goddess. You are a natural feature, a moving mountain. Merge with all that comes from the earth: grass, trees, grains, fruits, flowers, beasts, metals and precious stones. Return to dust, to compost, to mud. Say, "Hail, Belili, Mother of Mountains!"

EXERCISE 30: THE PENTACLE MEDITATION—THE FIVE STAGES OF LIFE

Ground and center. Hold your pentacle in both hands. Breathe deep, and feel the power of earth, of the body. The pentacle is your own body, four limbs and head. It is the five senses, both inner and outer. Be in touch with your own power to see, to hear, to smell, to taste, to touch. The pentacle is the four elements plus the fifth—essence. And it is the five stages of life, each an aspect of the Goddess:

1. *Birth:* the beginning, the time of coming into being

2. *Initiation:* adolescence, the time of individuation

3. *Love:* the time of union with another, of full adulthood, sexuality, responsibility

4. *Repose:* the time of advancing age, of reflection, integration, wisdom

5. *Death:* the time of ending, of letting go, of moving on toward rebirth

Look at your pentacle, or draw one on a sheet of paper. Label the five stations, going clockwise around the points, and experience each stage in turn, as it occurs in a life span and within the span of each new activity or relationship. Trace the interlocking lines and reflect on their meanings. Love is linked to Birth and Death. Death is linked to Love and Initiation.

In the Goidelic* tree alphabet, each of the five stages was symbolized by a tree, whose name began with one of the five vowels:[5]

A: Birth—*ailm*, silver fir

O: Initiation—*onn*, gorse or furze

U: Love—*ura*, heather

E: Repose—*eadha*, the aspen

I: Death—*idho*, the yew

Chant the sounds of the vowels and feel the power of each stage in turn. Touch your pentacle to your body, and let the life force of your own flesh flow into it.

EXERCISE 31: THE IRON PENTAGRAM

(A pentagram is a drawn or written pentacle. This is a meditative tool of the Faery Tradition and an important training exercise.)

Ground and center. In your Book of Shadows, draw a pentacle with interlocking lines and label the points, in order, clockwise: "Sex," "Self," "Passion," "Pride," and "Power."

Sex is the manifestation of the driving life force energy of the universe. It is

---

*Goidelic refers to the Gaelic Celts (Irish, Scots, Manx) as opposed to the Brythonic Celts (Welsh, Cornish and Bretons).

polarity, the attraction of God and Goddess, the on-off pulse that sustains the universe, the orgasmic, ecstatic harmony that sings within each being.

Self is identity, individuality. Each of us is a unique manifestation of the Goddess, and that individuality is highly valued in the Craft. Self-love is the foundation of all love. "Celebrate yourself, and you will see that Self is everywhere."

Passion is the force of emotion that gives color and depth and vitality to life. Joy, sorrow, ecstasy, anger, fear, pain, love—the Goddess manifests in all human emotions. We cannot feel any of them in their full intensity unless we are willing to face them all.

Pride encourages us to create, to do, to share, to grow, and to enjoy the rightful fruits of our achievements. True pride is not based on comparisons or competition, it is an absolute sense of one's inner worth. Pride carries with it the responsibility of acting in accordance with one's self-respect and respect for Self in others.

Power is energy, inner power, not power over others. When the five points are in balance, the life force flows freely, filling us with vitality. Power is integrity, creativity, courage: the mark of a person who is whole.

Meditate on each of the points in turn, and then explore the links and connections: "Sex—Passion," "Self—Pride," "Passion—Power," and so on. Lie down with your arms and legs outstretched so that you form a star. Let your head and each of your limbs be a point on the pentacle. When you are "on the points," they will all be in balance. If some points feel weak, work on developing those qualities. Absorb the strength of the Iron Pentagram.

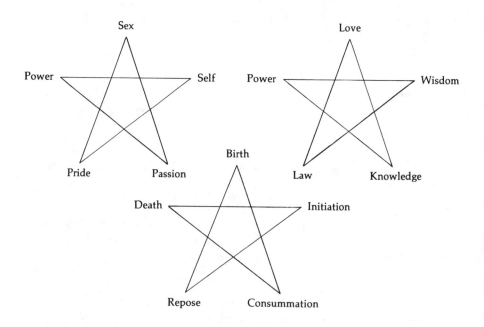

EXERCISE 32: THE PENTAGRAM OF PEARL

The Pentagram of Pearl is a meditative tool, like the Iron Pentagram. Its points are Love, Wisdom, Knowledge, Law, and Power.

Begin as for the Iron Pentagram.

Love is the moving energy of life. It is both blindly erotic and deeply personal, a passionate, prideful, powerful caring for oneself and others. It is the law of the Goddess and the essence of magic.

Wisdom and *Knowledge* can best be understood together. Knowledge is learning, the power of the mind to understand and describe the universe. Wisdom is knowing how to apply knowledge—and how not to apply it. Knowledge is knowing what to say; wisdom is knowing whether or not to say it. Knowledge gives answers; wisdom asks questions. Knowledge can be taught; wisdom grows out of experience, out of making mistakes.

Law is natural law, not human law. When we break natural laws, we suffer the consequences as a natural result of our actions, not as a punishment. If you break the law of gravity, you will fall. Magic functions within natural law, not outside of it. But natural law may be broader and more complex than we realize.

Power, again, is the power that comes from within, when love, knowledge, wisdom and law are united. Power, rooted in love and tempered by knowledge, law, and wisdom, brings growth and healing.

Again, meditate on the points and the links between them. Lie in the pentacle position, feel the points as part of yourself, and become aware of your own imbalances. Absorb the beauty of the Pentagram of Pearl.

Center

The center of the circle is the point of transformation. It corresponds to pure essence, to timelessness, to transparent light, to the power to *go,* to move, change, transform. Its magical tool is the cauldron, which may be the traditional three-legged cast iron pot, or a clay or metal bowl. The cauldron holds fire: a candle, incense, smoldering herbs, or a bonfire. It may also be a cooking pot, in which fire transforms the food we will eat.

EXERCISE 33: TRANSFORMATION MEDITATION

Ground and center. Whisper softly, over and over, "She changes everything She touches, and everything She touches, changes." Feel the constant processes of change within yourself, in your body, your ideas and emotions, your work and relationships. Within every unmoving stone, atoms are in constant flux. Feel the changes all around you, changes you have made, are about to make. Even ending the meditation is part of the process of change that is life. Say, "Hail, Kore, whose name cannot be spoken, the Ever-Changing One!"

EXERCISE 34: CAULDRON MEDITATION

Ground and center. Hold the cauldron in both hands. Breathe deep, and feel the power of transformation. You hold the Cauldron of Ceridwen, where the dead come to life. You hold the cauldron in which was brewed the broth that imparts all knowledge and understanding. The cauldron is the womb of the Goddess, the gestation ground of all birth. Think of the transformations you undergo every day. In a moment, you die and are reborn a thousand times. Feel your power to end and begin anew, your ability to gestate, to create, to give birth to new things, and let that power flow into your cauldron.

Meditations on the elements are part of the training of every Witch. After experiencing the energy of each magical element separately, the apprentice is taught to combine them, in preparation for learning to cast a circle.

EXERCISE 35: THE CIRCLE VISUALIZATION EXERCISE

(You may lie down, sit comfortably, or get up and enact this exercise. Face each direction either physically or mentally.)

Ground and center. Face East. Visualize your *athame* in your strongest hand, and draw an Invoking Pentacle (as in Exercise 13). See it burning with a pale, blue flame. Say, "Hail, Guardians of the Watchtowers of the East, Powers of Air."

Walk through the pentacle, and see a great wind sweeping across a vast plain of waving grass. Breathe deeply, and feel the air on your face, in your lungs, through your hair. The sun is rising, and in its rays a golden eagle shines as it flies toward you. When you are filled with the power of air, say, "Hail and farewell, Shining Ones." Walk back through the pentacle.

Turn and face the South. Again, draw the Invoking Pentacle. Say, "Hail, Guardians of the Watchtowers of the South, Powers of Fire."

Walk through the pentacle. You are on a blazing veldt under the hot sun. It is high noon. Feel the sun's fire on your skin and absorb its power. In the distance, red-gold lions sun themselves. When you feel attuned to fire, say, "Hail and farewell, Radiant Ones." Walk back through the pentacle.

Turn and face the West, and again draw the pentacle. Say, "Hail, Guardians of the Watchtowers of the West, Powers of Water."

Walk through the pentacle. You are on a cliff above a pounding sea. Feel the spray and the force of the waves. It is twilight, and the blue-green waves are edged with violet as the sun disappears. Dolphins and sea serpents dive and play in the foam. When you feel attuned to the power of water, say, "Hail and farewell, Flowing Ones" and walk through the pentacle.

Turn and face North. Draw the pentacle, and say, "Hail, Guardians of the Watchtowers of the North, Powers of Earth.

Walk through the pentacle. You are in the midst of a lush, fertile landscape, on the slopes of a mountain. Around you are green, growing herbs nourished by fresh springs, and tall silent trees fed by the minerals and nutrients in the earth. In the distance, grain is waving in the fertile fields. Wild goats cling to the craggy heights above you, while below, herds of wild cattle thunder across the plain. It is midnight; the moon is hidden but the stars are bright. The Great Bear and Little Bear circle the North Star, the still center point of the whirling wheel of the sky. Say, "Hail and farewell, Silent Ones."

Visualize all four pentacles around you in a circle of blue flame. Above your head is an eight-rayed star. Breathe deep, and draw in power from the star. Let it fill you; feel it flood every cell of your body with light, a cone of light that extends deep into the earth around you. Thank the star, and let the light return to its source. Open the circle by visualizing the pentacles flying off into space.

Additional tools used in most covens include a cord, a necklace, a censer, and a Book of Shadows, which has been discussed in Chapter Three. The cord is the symbol of binding, of belonging to a particular coven. In some traditions, the color of the cord reflects the degree of advancement in the Craft of its bearer. The censer is used to hold the incense, and is identified with either the East or the South, Air or Fire. The necklace is the circle of rebirth, the sign of the Goddess. It can be of any design that is personally pleasing.

Of course, candles, herbs, oils, and incenses are also used in Witchcraft. Unfortunately, I don't have space to go into a detailed discussion of their uses and correspondences, especially as that information is given in the Appendix, and is available from other sources.[6] In general, a Witch depends less on traditional associations of herbs, odors, and colors than on her own intuition. If the "proper" materials aren't available, we improvise.

The tools are usually kept on an altar, which may be anything from a hand-carved antique chest to a box covered with a cloth. When used for regular meditation and magical practice, the altar becomes charged with energy, a vortex of power. Generally, a Witch's altar faces north, and the tools are placed in their corresponding directions. Images of the Goddess and God—statues, shells, seeds, flowers, or a mirror—take a central position.

EXERCISE 36: CONSECRATING A TOOL

(Tools can be charged—imbued with psychic energy—and consecrated within a group ritual, during an initiation, or individually. I will describe the rite for an *athame:* for other tools, simply make the necessary adjustments.)

Set up the altar as you want it, and light the candles and incense. Perform the Salt-Water Purification, and cast a circle by doing the Circle Visualization. Ask the Goddess to be with you.

Hold your *athame* in your strongest hand, saying "Blessed be, thou creature of art." Do the *Athame* or Sword Meditation.

Touch it to the symbols of each of the four elements in turn: incense for Air, the wand for Fire, the cup for Water, and the pentacle for Earth. Meditate on the power of each element, and visualize that power flowing into the *athame.* Say "May you be charged with the power of (Air, Fire, etc.) and serve me well in the (East, South, etc.), between the worlds, in all the worlds. So mote it be."

Pass your *athame* through the candle flame, and touch it to the central cauldron. Visualize white light filling and charging it. Say "May you be charged from the center of all, above and below, throughout and about, within and without, to serve me well between the worlds, in all the worlds. So mote it be."

Draw or inscribe your own personal symbols on the blade or hilt. Trace over them with your own saliva, sweat, menstrual blood, or other secretions, to create the link with your tool. Breathe on it, and imagine your own personal power flowing into it.

Touch it to your heart, and your lips. Raise it to sky, and point it to earth. Wrap your cord around it (or imagine it, if you don't have a cord) and visualize a shield of light binding the power. Say "Cord go round, power be bound, light revealed, now be sealed."

Earth the power, thank the Goddess, and open the circle by thanking each of the directions and visualizing the pentacles dissolving.

In casting a circle, the outer forms used are less important than the strength of the inner visualization. When the High Priestess calls the Guardians of the East, for example, she feels the wind and sees the sun rising with her inner sight. She is also visualizing the flaming pentacles and the circle of light surrounding the coven. In a strong coven, one person may perform the outward actions, but all will be internally visualizing the circle and attuning themselves to the elements.

The outer forms can be very simple. Alone, it may be enough to simply visualize a ring of white light around the room, or turn to each direction in turn and tap the wall. A group may join hands and picture the circle, or one member may walk around the others. The circle may be marked out ahead of time with chalk, stones, string, flowers, leaves, or shells, or drawn invisibly with the *athame* as it is cast.

This chapter opens with a description of a formal circle casting. At first, trying to remember the words and actions, visualize the elements, and feel the power will be far more difficult than trying to pat your head and rub your stomach at the same time. But with practice your concentration will improve until the entire sequence flows easily and naturally. You may wish to create your own invocations, instead of using the ones given. Here are other examples:

A CIRCLE FOR HEALING DURING STRUGGLE
BY *Alan Acacia*

hail guardians of the watchtower of the east, powers of air:

blow the staleness away, fill our lungs.
help us bring freshness
into our lives.
let there be clear skies, clear minds
for us to see our way.
let our words create a safe space.
blessed be.

hail guardians of the watchtower of the south, powers of fire:

come into our hearts, warm us.
help us emerge from hibernation, isolation,
to greet each other.
let passion glow on our birthright
as we fight injustice.
let our emotions out
from all their hiding places.
blessed be.

hail guardians of the watchtower of the west, powers of water:

rain on us, quench our thirst.
help us remember
the ocean womb from which we come.
now let all of us be connected.
let our moods be flowing back & forth
until all is one.
let the drought of separation be over.
blessed be.

hail guardians of the watchtower of the north, powers of earth:

strengthen our resolve, keep us centered.
help us be here, now.

let our bodies be strong
for loving each other.
let the dizziness of the workday pass,
& all of us find ourselves together
on one planet.
because of our struggles & magic
may a greater circle be cast
of love & social harmony.
blessed be.

VALERIE'S RHYMING INVOCATIONS TO THE FOUR QUARTERS

East:
Quicksilver messenger
Master of the crossroads
Springtime step lightly
Into my mind
Golden one whisper
Airy ferryman
Sail from the East on the wings of the wind.

South:
Desert flower, flaming will
Crackle with energy under my skin
Red lion roaring
Pulses racing
Roaming the South
I am open: come in.

West:
Pearl-gray warrior
Ghostly quest
Prince of Twilight
Sailing West
Intuition, sundown lady
Ancient serpent of the Sea
Pearly Queen of twilight waters
Silverfoot come silently.

North:
Mother of mountains, mother of trees,
Mother of midnight, mother of earth.
Root and leaf and flower and thorn,
Come to us, come to us, out of the North.

INVOCATIONS FROM THE SUMMER SOLSTICE RITUAL (STARHAWK)

[With these, begin in the North]
Earth my bone, my body,
Mountain my breast
Green grass and leafy tree
My trailing hair,
Rich dark dust, oozing mud
Seed sending white root deep,
Carpet of molding leaves,
Be our bed!
By the earth that is Her body,
Powers of the North send forth your strength.

Air, my breath, breeze of morning,
Stallion of the dawn star,
Whirlwind, bearing all that soars in flight,
Bee and bird,
Sweet fragrance,
Wailing storm's voice,
Carry us!
By the air that is Her breath,
Powers of the East send forth your light.

Fire my heart, burn bright!
My spirit is a flame,
My eye misses nothing.
A blaze leaps from nerve to nerve
Spark of the solar fire!
An answering heat rises, unbearable delight!
The flames sing, consume us!
By the fire that is Her spirit,
Powers of the South, send forth your flame.

Water my womb, my blood,
Wash over us, cool us.
Waves sweep ashore on white wings,
The rush, hiss, the rumble of stones
As the tide recedes,
That rhythm, my pulse,
Flood, gushing fountain,
We pour ourselves out,
Sweep us away!
By the waters of Her living womb,
Powers of the West, send forth your flow.

The energy field created by a circle can also be used for protection. This can be done very simply:

EXERCISE 37: PROTECTIVE CIRCLE

Visualize a circle or bubble of white light around yourself, with the energy running clockwise. Tell yourself it is an impenetrable barrier no harmful forces can cross. If you have time, perform the Circle Visualization or quickly call each of the four elements in turn.

EXERCISE 38: PERMANENT PROTECTIVE CIRCLE

(A permanent circle of protection can be established around your home or place of work. The following ritual can be done alone, or in a group with each person carrying one of the objects.)

Ground and center. Go around the house widdershins with a bell, a broom, and charged salt water. Ring the bell to scare away negative energies. Sweep away unwanted forces with the broom—or use a wand to wave them out. Sprinkle each entrance—each window, door, mirror, and major water outlets, with salt water. Also sprinkle the corners of every room. If necessary, perform a Banishing as in Exercise 22. Do the Salt-Water Purification.

Now go around the house clockwise, with salt water, *athame,* and incense. Draw an invoking pentacle at each entrance with the *athame,* and then with salt water. Concentrate on forming a seal of protection that cannot be broken. Finally, with the incense, charge each entrance and corner, inviting good forces to enter. Say,

> Salt and sea,
> Of ill stay free,
> Fire and air,
> Draw all that is fair.
> Around and around,
> The circle is bound.

Formally cast a circle in the room you will use for rituals. Chant and raise power to fill the house with protection. Then thank the Goddess, earth the power, and open the circle.

You can reinforce a protective circle by visualizing it. Do so before magical work or sleep.

The circle is cast; the ritual is begun. We have created the sacred space, a space fit for the Gods to enter. We have cleansed ourselves and centered ourselves; our mental bonds have dropped away. Free from fear, we can open to the starlight. In perfect love, and perfect trust, we are prepared to invoke the Goddess.

Notes

1. This set of invocations is written and paraphrased by me from traditional Faery invocations.
2. Mary Daly, *Beyond God the Father* (Boston: Beacon Press, 1973), p. 40.
3. Daly, p. 41.
4. Helen Diner, *Mothers and Amazons* (New York: Anchor Press, 1973), p. 169.
5. Robert Graves, *The White Goddess* (New York: Farrar, Straus & Giroux, 1948), Chaps. 10–11.
6. As a good general reference on traditional materials, and an excellent source book for Dianic Witchcraft, see Z. Budapest, *The Feminist Book of Lights and Shadows* (Venice, Calif.: Luna Publications, 1976)—available through The Feminist Wicca, 442 Lincoln Blvd., Venice, CA 90291.

5 The Goddess

Between the Worlds:

THE CHARGE OF THE GODDESS[1]

Listen to the words of the Great Mother, who of old was called Artemis, Astarte, Dione, Melusine, Aphrodite, Ceridwen, Diana, Arionrhod, Brigid, and by many other names:

"Whenever you have need of anything, once in the month, and better it be when the moon is full, you shall assemble in some secret place and adore the spirit of Me who is Queen of all the Wise. You shall be free from slavery, and as a sign that you be free you shall be naked in your rites. Sing, feast, dance, make music and love, all in My presence, for Mine is the ecstasy of the spirit and Mine also is joy on earth. For My law is love unto all beings. Mine is the secret that opens upon the door of youth, and Mine is the cup of wine of life that is the Cauldron of Ceridwen that is the holy grail of immortality. I give the knowledge of the spirit eternal and beyond death I give peace and freedom and reunion with those that have gone before. Nor do I demand aught of sacrifice, for behold, I am the mother of all things and My love is poured out upon the earth."

Hear the words of the Star Goddess, the dust of whose feet are the hosts of heaven, whose body encircles the universe:

"I who am the beauty of the green earth and the white moon among the stars and the mysteries of the waters, I call upon your soul to arise and come unto me. For I am the soul of nature that gives life to the universe. From Me all things proceed and unto Me they must return. Let My worship be in the heart that rejoices, for behold—all acts of love and pleasure are My rituals. Let there be beauty and strength, power and compassion, honor and humility, mirth and reverence within you. And you who seek to know Me, know that your seeking and yearning will avail you not, unless you know the Mystery: for if that which you seek, you find not within yourself, you will never find it without. For behold, I have been with you from the beginning, and I am that which is attained at the end of desire."

The symbolism of the Goddess has taken on an electrifying power for modern women. The rediscovery of the ancient matrifocal civilizations has given us a deep sense of pride in woman's ability to create and sustain culture. It has exposed the falsehoods of patriarchal history, and given us models of female strength and authority The Goddess—ancient and primeval; the first of deities; patronness of the Stone Age hunt and of the first sowers of seeds; under whose guidance the herds were tamed, the healing herbs first discovered; in whose image the first works of art were created; for whom the standing stones were raised; who was the inspiration of song and poetry—is recognized once again in today's world. She is the bridge, on which we can cross the chasms within ourselves, which were created by our social conditioning, and reconnect with our lost potentials. She is the ship, on which we sail the waters of the deep self, exploring the uncharted seas within. She is the door, through which we pass into the future. She is the cauldron, in which we who have been wrenched apart simmer until we again become whole. She is the vaginal passage, through which we are reborn.

A historical and/or cross-cultural overview of the Goddess and her symbols would itself require several volumes, and I will not attempt it in the limited space of this book, especially as much good material is already available.[2] Instead, I will limit myself to discussing the Goddess as seen through Witchcraft, and focus on her function and meaning for women and men today.

People often ask me if I *believe* in the Goddess. I reply "Do you believe in rocks?" It is extremely difficult for most Westerners to grasp the concept of a manifest deity. The phrase "believe *in*" itself implies that we cannot *know* the Goddess, that She is somehow intangible, incomprehensible. But we do not *believe* in rocks—we may see them, touch them, dig them out of our gardens, or stop small children from throwing them at each other. We know them; we connect with them. In the Craft, we do not *believe* in the Goddess—we connect with Her; through the moon, the stars, the ocean, the earth, through trees, animals, through other human beings, through ourselves. She is here. She is within us all. She is the full circle: earth, air, fire, water, and essence—body, mind, spirit, emotions, change.

The Goddess is first of all earth, the dark, nurturing mother who brings forth all life. She is the power of fertility and generation; the womb, and also the receptive tomb, the power of death. All proceeds from Her; all returns to Her. As earth, She is also plant life; trees, the herbs and grains that sustain life. She is the body, and the body is sacred. Womb, breast, belly, mouth, vagina, penis, bone, and blood—no part of the body is unclean, no aspect of the life processes is stained by any concept of sin. Birth, death, and decay are equally sacred parts of the cycle. Whether we are eating, sleeping, making love, or eliminating body wastes, we are manifesting the Goddess.

The Earth Goddess is also air and sky, the celestial Queen of Heaven, the Star Goddess, ruler of things felt but not seen: of knowledge, mind, and intuition. She is the Muse, who awakens all creations of the human spirit. She is the cosmic lover, the morning and evening star, Venus, who appears at the times of love-making. Beautiful and glittering, She can never be grasped or penetrated; the mind is drawn ever further in the drive to know the unknowable, to speak the inexpressible. She is the inspiration that comes with an indrawn breath.

The celestial Goddess is seen as the moon, who is linked to women's monthly cycles of bleeding and fertility. Woman is the earthly moon; the moon is the celestial egg, drifting in the sky womb, whose menstrual blood is the fertilizing rain and the cool dew; who rules the tides of the oceans, the first womb of life on earth. So the moon is also Mistress of Waters: the waves of the sea, streams, springs, the rivers that are the arteries of Mother Earth; of lakes, deep wells, and hidden pools, and of feelings and emotions, which wash over us like waves.

The Moon Goddess has three aspects: As She waxes, She is the Maiden; full, She is the Mother; as She wanes, She is the Crone. Part of the training of every initiate involves periods of meditation on the Goddess in her many aspects. I don't have space to include all of these, but I will share with you the meditations on the three aspects of the moon:

EXERCISE 39: WAXING MOON MEDITATION

Ground and center. Visualize a silver crescent moon, curving to the right. She is the power of beginning, of growth and generation. She is wild and untamed, like ideas and plans before they are tempered by reality. She is the blank page, the unplowed field. Feel your own hidden possibilities and latent potentials; your power to begin and grow. See her as a silver-haired girl running freely through the forest under the slim moon. She is Virgin, eternally unpenetrated, belonging to no one but herself. Call her name "Nimuë!" and feel her power within you.

EXERCISE 40: FULL MOON MEDITATION

Ground and center, and visualize a round full moon. She is the Mother, the power of fruition. She nourishes what the New Moon has begun. See her open arms, her full breasts, her womb burgeoning with life. Feel your own power to nurture, to give, to make manifest what is possible. She is the sexual woman; her pleasure in union is the moving force that sustains all life. Feel the power in your own pleasure, in orgasm. Her color is the red of blood, which is life. Call her name "Mari!" and feel your own ability to love.

EXERCISE 41: WANING MOON MEDITATION

Ground and center. Visualize a waning crescent, curving to the left, surrounded by a black sky. She is the Old Woman, the Crone who has passed menopause, the power of ending, of death. All things must end to fulfill their beginnings. The grain that was planted must be cut down. The blank page must be destroyed, for the work to be written. Life feeds on death—death leads on to life, and in that knowledge lies wisdom. The Crone is the Wise Woman, infinitely old. Feel your own age, the wisdom of evolution stored in every cell of your body. Know your own power to end, to lose as well as gain, to destroy what is stagnant and decayed. See the Crone cloaked in black under the waning moon; call her name "Anu!" and feel her power in your own death.

The triad of the moon becomes the pentad, the five fold star of birth, initiation, love, repose, and death. The Goddess is manifest in the entire life cycle. Women are valued and respected in old age, as well as youth.

Birth and childhood, of course, are common to all cultures. But our society has not, until recently, conceptualized the stage of initiation, of personal exploration and self-discovery, as necessary for women. Girls were expected to pass directly from childhood to marriage and motherhood—from control by their fathers to control by their husbands. An initiation demands courage and self-reliance, traits that girls were not encouraged to develop. Today, the stage of initiation may involve establishing a career, exploring relationships, or developing one's creativity. Women who have missed this stage in their youth often find it necessary to go back to it later in life. The later stages of life can only fully be experienced after the initiation is completed and an individualized self has been formed.

The stage of love is also called *consummation,* and it is the stage of full creativity. Relationships deepen and take on a sense of commitment. A woman may choose to mother children or to nurture a career, a project, or a cause. An artist or writer reaches her mature style.

Creations, whether they are children, poems, or organizations, take on a life of their own. As they become independent, and their demands diminish, the stage of repose is reached. With age comes a new initiation, this one reflective, less physically active but deepened by the insights of experience. Old age, in Witchcraft, is seen very positively, as the time when activity has evolved into wisdom. It brings about the final initiation, which is death.

These five stages are embodied in our lives, but they can also be seen within every new enterprise or creative project. Each book, each painting, each new job is born first as an idea. It undergoes an initiatory period of exploration, which is frightening at times, because we are forced to learn new things. As we grow comfortable with a new skill or concept, the project can be consummated. It exists independently; as we rest from it, other people read the book, view the painting, eat the food, or apply the knowledge we have taught. Finally, it is over; it dies, and we go on to something new.

The pentacle, all five-lobed leaves, and five-petaled flowers are sacred to the Goddess as pentad. The apple is especially her emblem, because, when it is sliced crosswise, the embedded seeds form a pentacle.

The nature of the Goddess is never single. Wherever She appears, she embodies both poles of duality—life in death, death in life. She has a thousand names, a thousand aspects. She is the milk cow, the weaving spider, the honeybee with its piercing sting. She is the bird of the spirit and the sow that eats its own young. The snake that sheds its skin and is renewed; the cat that sees in the dark; the dog that sings to the moon— all are Her. She is the light and the darkness, the patroness of love and death, who makes manifest *all* possibilities. She brings both comfort and pain.

It is easy to respond to the concept of Goddess as Muse or Mother, to inspiration, nurturing, and healing power. It is more difficult to understand the Goddess as Destroyer. Judeo-Christian dualism has conditioned us to think of destruction as synonymous with evil. (Although, Goddess knows, the Jehovah of the Old Testament was far from all sweetness and light.) Most of us live removed from nature, cut off from the experiences that constantly remind more "primitive" people that every act of creation is an act of aggression. To plant a garden, you must dig out the weeds, crush the snails, thin the seedlings as they reach toward the light. To write a book, you must destroy draft after draft of your own work, cutting apart paragraphs and striking out words and sentences. Creation postulates change; and any change destroys what went before.

The Creatrix-Destroyer is manifest in fire, which destroys all it feeds on in order to create warmth and light. Fire is the nurturing hearth, the creative fire of the forge, the joyous bonfire of celebration. But the Goddess is also the raging fire of anger.

The power of anger is difficult to face. We identify anger with violence, and women have been conditioned to feel that our anger is wrong and unacceptable. Yet anger is a manifestation of the life force. It is a survival emotion, a warning signal that something in our environment is threatening. Danger triggers a physical, psychic, and emotional response that mobilizes our energy to change the situation. Being human, we respond to verbal and emotional attacks as threats, which arouse anger. But when we cannot admit our own anger, instead of recognizing the threat in the environment, we experience ourselves as wrong. Instead of flowing outward to change the environment, our energy becomes locked into internal efforts at repression and control.

The Goddess liberates the energy of our anger. It is seen as sacred, and its power is purified. Like a forest fire in undisturbed wilderness, it sweeps away the underbrush so that the seedlings of our creativity can receive the nourishing sunlight. We control our *actions;* we do not attempt to control our *feelings.* Anger becomes a connecting force that spurs honest confrontations and communications with others.

I have spoken of the Goddess as psychological symbol and also as manifest reality. She is both. She exists, *and* we create Her. The symbols and attributes associated with the Goddess speak to Younger Self and, through it, to the High Self. They engage us emotionally. We know the Goddess is not the moon—but we still thrill to its light glinting through branches. We know the Goddess is not a woman, but we respond with love as if She were, and so connect emotionally with all the abstract qualities behind the symbol.

Many shapes and symbols represent the Goddess. Eyes, which schematically are also breasts, symbolize her nurturing powers and the gift of inner sight. The crescent represents the moon: a waxing and waning crescent, back to back, becomes the labrys or double ax, the weapon of Goddess cultures. Triangles, ovals, and lozenges, the shapes of the female genitals, are her symbols, as well. As part of an initiate's training, she is taught to visualize symbols, to meditate on them and play with them in her imagination until they reveal their meaning directly. Any symbol or aspect of the Goddess can be a basis for meditation, but as I have space for only one example, I will choose the double spiral:

EXERCISE 42: THE DOUBLE SPIRAL

Ground and center. Visualize a double spiral. When you see it clearly, let it grow until you stand within it, and follow it inward, moving counterclockwise. It becomes a maze of high, clipped hedges, then a labyrinth of stone walls; its winding turns are the passageway to a hidden secret. As you move through the spiral, the world dissolves, form dissolves, until you are in the hidden heart where birth and death are one. The center of the spiral shines; it is the North Star, and the arms of the spiral are the Milky Way, a myriad of stars slowly revolving around the still center point. You are in Spiral Castle, at the back of the North Wind. Explore it in your imagination. See who you meet, what you learn. You are in the womb of the Goddess, floating free. Now feel yourself pushed and squeezed, moving out through the spiral, which is now the vaginal passage of rebirth. Move clockwise through the double spiral of your DNA. Now it becomes a whirlwind—fly with it. Let is become the twining tendril of a plant—a crystal—a shell—an orbiting electron. Time is a spiral—the cycles endlessly repeating, yet always moving. Know the spiral as the underlying form of all energy. As you emerge, let it return to its small, abstract, symbolic form. Thank it, and let it disappear.

The Charge of the Goddess, at the opening of this chapter, reflects the Craft understanding of the Goddess. It begins with a long list of Goddess names, drawn from many cultures. These are not seen as separate beings but, rather, different aspects of the same Being that is all beings. The names used may change with the seasons or preferences of the speaker: for example, the Goddess might be named Kore in the sping, after the Maiden aspect of the Greek Goddess. A Witch of Jewish heritage might call on the ancient Hebrew Goddess as Ashimah or Asherah; an Afro-American Witch might prefer Iemaja, the West African Goddess of the sea and love.[3] In most traditions of the Craft, the inner name of the Goddess is recognized to embody great power, and so is kept secret, revealed only to initiates. The outer names most commonly used are Diana, for the Goddess of the moon, and Aradia, her daughter, whom legends say was sent to earth to liberate people by teaching them the arts of magic.[4]

"Need of anything" refers to both spiritual and material needs. In Witchcraft, there is no separation. The Goddess is manifest in the food we eat, the people we love, the work we do, the homes in which we live. It is not considered ignoble to ask for needed goods and comforts. "Work for yourself, and you will see that Self is everywhere," is a saying of the Faery Tradition. It is through the material world that we open ourselves to the Goddess. But Witchcraft also recognizes that when material needs are satisfied deeper needs and longings may remain. These can only be satisfied by connection with the nurturing, life-giving forces within, which we call *Goddess.*

The coven meets at the full moon, in honor of the Goddess at the height of her glory. The tides of subtle power are considered to be strongest when the moon is full. The Goddess is identified with the fructifying lunar energy that illumines the secret dark; the feminine, tidal, pulsating power that waxes and wanes in harmony with woman's menstrual flow. The sun is identified with her male, polar self, the God, whose festivals are celebrated at eight points of power in the solar cycle.

The Goddess is the liberator, and it has been said that "Her service is perfect freedom."[5] She is the liberator because She is manifest in our deepest drives and emotions, which always and inevitably threaten the systems designed to contain them. She is love and anger, which refuse to fit comfortably into the social order. To be "free from slavery" once meant that, within the ritual circle, all were equal, whether they were peasant, serf, or noble in the outside world. Slavery, today, can be mental and emotional as well as physical: the slavery of fixed perceptions, of conditioned ideas, of blind beliefs, of fear. Witchcraft demands intellectual freedom and the courage to confront our own assumptions. It is not a belief system; it is a constantly self-renewed attitude of joy and wonder to the world.

The naked body represents truth, the truth that goes deeper than social custom. Witches worship naked for several reasons: as a way of establishing closeness and dropping social masks, because power is most easily raised that way, and because the human body is itself sacred. Nakedness is a sign that a Witch's loyalty is to the truth before any ideology or any comforting illusions.

Rituals are joyful and pleasurable. Witches sing, feast, dance, laugh, joke, and have fun in the course of rituals. Witchcraft is serious—but not pompous or solemn. As in Hasidic Judaism or Bhakti Yoga, joy and ecstasy are seen as the pathways to the Divine. The "ecstasy of the spirit" is not separate from "joy on earth." One leads to the other—and neither can truly be realized without the other. Earthly joys, unconnected with the deep, feeling power of the Goddess, become mechanical, meaningless—mere sensations that soon lose their appeal. But spiritual ecstasies that attempt to escape the senses and the body become equally arid and rootless, draining vitality instead of nourishing it.

The law of the Goddess is love: passionate sexual love, the warm affection of friends, the fierce protective love of mother for child, the deep comradeship of the coven. There is nothing amorphous or superficial about love in Goddess religion; it is always specific, directed toward real individuals, not vague concepts of humanity. Love includes animals, plants, the earth itself—"all beings," not just human beings. It includes ourselves and all our fallible human qualities.

Ceridwen is one of the forms of the Celtic Goddess, and her cauldron is the womb-cauldron of rebirth and inspiration. In early Celtic myth, the cauldron of the Goddess restored slain warriors to life. It was stolen away to the Underworld, and the heroes who warred for its return were the originals of King Arthur and his Knights, who quested for its later incarnation, the Holy Grail. The Celtic afterworld is called the Land of Youth, and the secret that opens its door is found in the cauldron: The secret of immortality lies in seeing death as an integral part of the cycle of life. Nothing is ever lost from the universe: Rebirth can be seen in life itself, where every ending brings a new beginning. Most Witches do believe in some form of reincarnation. This is not so much a doctrine as a gut feeling growing out of a world view that sees all events as continuing processes. Death is seen as a point on an ever-turning wheel, not as a final end. We are continually renewed and reborn whenever we drink fully and fearlessly from "the cup of wine of life."

The love of the Goddess is unconditional. She does not ask for sacrifice—whether human or animal—nor does She want us to sacrifice our normal human needs and desires. Witchcraft is a religion of self-celebration, not self-abnegation. Sacrifice is *inherent* in life, in constant change that brings constant losses. Offerings: a poem, a painting, a pinch of grain, may express our thankfulness for her gifts, but only when they are made freely, not from a sense of obligation.

In the Star Goddess passage, we see the imagery of the celestial encircler, the moon, the waters, the green earth from which all proceeds and to which all must return. She is the "soul of nature," which vivifies all things.

Any act based on love and pleasure is a ritual of the Goddess. Her worship can take any form and occur anywhere; it requires no liturgy, no cathedrals, no confessions. Its essence is the recognition, in the midst of pleasure, of its deepest source. Pleasure, then, is not superficial but becomes a profound expression of the life force; a connecting power linking us to others, not the mere sensation of satisfying our own isolated needs.

Witchcraft recognizes that any virtue becomes a vice unless it is balanced by its own opposite. Beauty, when unsustained by strength, is vapid, lifeless. Power is insufferable when untempered by compassion. Honor, unless balanced by humility, becomes arrogance; and mirth, when not deepened by reverence, becomes mere superficiality.

Finally we learn the Mystery—that unless we find the Goddess within ourselves we will never find Her without. She is both internal and external; as solid as a rock, as changeable as our own internal image of Her. She is manifest within each of us—so where else should we look?

The Goddess is "the end of desire," its goal and its completion. In Witchcraft, desire is itself seen as a manifestation of the Goddess. We do not seek to conquer or escape from our desires—we seek to fulfill them. Desire is the glue of the universe; it binds the electron to the nucleus, the planet to the sun—and so creates form, creates the world. To follow desire to its end is to unite with that which is desired, to become one with it, with the Goddess. We are already one with the Goddess—She has been with us from the beginning. So fulfillment becomes, not a matter of self-indulgence, but of self-*awareness*.

For women, the Goddess is the symbol of the inmost self, and the beneficent, nurturing, liberating power within woman. The cosmos is modeled on the female body, which is sacred. All phases of life are sacred: Age is a blessing, not a curse. The Goddess does not limit women to the body; She awakens the mind and spirit and emotions. Through Her, we can know the power of our anger and aggression, as well as the power of our love.

For a man, the Goddess, as well as being the universal life force, is his own, hidden, female self. She embodies all the qualities society teaches him *not* to recognize in himself. His first experience of Her may therefore seem somewhat stereotyped; She will be the cosmic lover, the gentle nurturer, the eternally desired Other, the Muse, all that he is not. As he becomes more whole and becomes aware of his own "female" qualities, She seems to change, to show him a new face, always holding up the mirror that shows what to him is still ungraspable. He may chase Her forever, and She will elude him, but through the attempt he will grow, until he too learns to find Her within.

To invoke the Goddess is to awaken the Goddess within, to become, for a time, that aspect we invoke. An invocation channels power through a visualized image of Divinity. In some covens, one Priestess is chosen to represent the manifest Goddess to the rest. In our covens, She is invoked into each member of the circle.

An invocation can be a set piece of poetry or music, sung or spoken by an individual or the group. In our covens, we usually chant as a group, sometimes wordlessly and spontaneously, sometimes using a set phrase that is repeated over and over again. A multivoiced chant will sometimes involve one Priestess repeating a simple "bass" line—"All That Is Wild and Free," for example—while another chants a repeating cycle—"Green Bud Leaf   Bud Leaf Bright," and so on (see below)—and a third chanting a long poetic piece, while the entire coven softly chants the vowel sounds. It is impossible to reproduce the effect on the printed page, unfortunately, but the bare words follow. When you use the invocations given here, please play with them, experiment with melodies and plain-song incantings, rearrange them, combine them, interweave them, change them, and take inspiration from them to make your own:

REPEATING CHANTS (TO THE GODDESS)

MOON Mother Bright Light Of All   Earth Sky   We CALL You.

LUNA Momma Shiny Shine COME.

HAIL Old Moon Secret WISE One HAIL Old Moon Secret WISE One.

She SHINES For All   She FLOWS Through All.

All That Is WILD And Free   All That Is WILD And Free.

REPEATING CYCLE: "GREEN BUD LEAF"

(This developed out of a Word Association Trance, as in Exercise 8. Words should be stressed evenly, with no breaks between groups, which are separated for ease of memorization. The entire cycle repeats over and over.)

Green Bud Leaf/Bud Leaf Bright/Leaf Bright Flower/
Bright Flower Grow/Flower Grow Fruit/Grow Fruit Ripe/
Fruit Ripe Seed/Ripe Seed Die/Seed Die Earth/
Die Earth Dark/Earth Dark Waken/Dark Waken Green/
Waken Green Bud . . .

SUMERIAN CHANT:

(Half-sung on two or three notes—repeat entire chant)
NAMmu NAMmu O NamMU AE EE AE EE O NamMU
NINmah NINmah O NinMAH AE EE AE EE O NinMAH
MAmi MAmi O MaMI AE EE AE EE O MaMI
MAma MAma O MaMA AE EE AE EE O MaMA
MAH MAH O MAH MAH AE EE AE EE O MAH MAH . . .

INVOCATION TO THE DEWY ONE

All-dewy Sky-sailing Pregnant Moon
Who shines for all,
Who flows through all.
Light of the world which is yourself.
Maiden, Mother, Crone,
The Weaver   The Green One
Isis Astarte Ishtar
Aradia Diana Cybele
Kore Ceridwen Levanah
Luna Mari Anna
Rhiannon Selena Demeter Mah

See with our eyes, Hear with our ears,
Touch with our hands, Breathe with our nostrils,
Kiss with our lips, Open our hearts,
Come into us!
Touch us, Change us, Make us whole.

HONOR TO THE GODDESS, LADY OF MANY NAMES,
TO DEMETER, THE IMMEASURABLE ONE, & TO THE MAIDEN
BY KAREN LYND CUSHEN

'Take, Eat, This is My Body   'Take, Drink, This is My Blood
Which shall Rise in You   The emptied Cup shall be
& Be Made Whole'   Refilled'

Goddess of the Harvest,
the fruit of Whose joy in the return of Your Daughter,
sustains us even as You make bleak the earth
at Her leaving

The earth is rent
& Persephone
the Maiden Whose name may not be spoken
is swallowed by the land of the dead

She will come again,
in Whose footfalls spring the flowers & the grain
carrying up with Her
dark memories of whence She came

Demeter
Near in our grief
because yearly we see Your own sorrow
ravage the face of earth
& Your Daughter
Close at the hour of our death
because yearly death claims Her
We know hope because we remember
again & again
Persephone healing Herself
& You with Her, rising

Demeter, Mother
We who have lain on Your knees
& slept in Your arms, give You honor,
Anoint us & place us at night

in the red heart of Your fire;
we shall not flinch
& let none in terror
snatch us from that hearth.
Anneal us at unspeakable heat
& give us a slow cooling
that pliant we may return
evergreen with the spring

We Your holy grain
honor You not in slaughter
but as we plow, plant our feet, scatter Your seed
in Your Daughter's returning footsteps
& reap

We the threshing floor
Ground of Your Being
where you stand smiling with sheaves & poppies in Your hand
watching the winnowing

In the heat of the morning we wake
our parched throats thirsty for the cup of Eleusis
cooling draught of the reaper
Our limbs longing to sway again in the wind
in Your ancient dances

Out of our dreams, our myths, our nursery tales
those ghettoes in which survive Your memory
we behold the Ear of Corn
we know the song You sung,
Song of the Sacred Body
Yours & Our Own
& honor You, Lady of Many Names,
Maiden & Immeasurable One.

KORE CHANT: SPRING AND FALL EQUINOX

Her name cannot be spoken,
Her face was not forgotten,
Her power is to open,
Her promise can never be broken.

(*Spring*)
All sleeping seeds She wakens,
The rainbow is Her token,

Now winter's power is taken,
In love, all chains are broken.

(*Fall*)
All seeds She deeply buries,
She weaves the thread of seasons.
Her secret, darkness carries,
She loves beyond all reason.

She charges everything She touches, and
Everything She touches, changes. [Repeat—chant.]
Change is, touch is; Touch is, change is.
Change us! Touch us! Touch us! Change us!

Everything lost is found again,
In a new form, In a new way.
Everything hurt is healed again,
In a new life, In a new day.
[Repeat any and all verses.]

INVOCATION TO THE GODDESS AS MOTHER
BY SUSAN STERN

Mama!
From my heart,
From my blood, Mama
I call you . . .

My heart of your heat
Limb of your Northwind
Water of your Water
Cunt of your Hillside
Cock of your Springtime
Eyes of Your Stars,
    Mama
Eyes of your sun,
    Mama
Of your Sol, Mama
My soul of your Sol
    Mama
Come Mama!
Come into our circle
Our womb
Be with us now, Mama
Be with us now!

MOONMOTHER

BY LAUREL

moonmother
i am your child of innocence
your natural born
no laws but yours can tame me
no love but your own

everlasting
everchanging
thousand formed
your eyes are ducks on the wing
your foot is dancing foam
i am your dancer
you are the dance
song without limit
drummer and tune
a whole orchestra
of your love
i could walk
your golden path
straight to the sun
two-step my way
to your heart

o send me away
let me swing on your star
inconstant ripple
stream lake pond
ocean
whirlpool
crashing great one
earthsucker
the one and only true love
    you leave treasure everywhere
sand dollars
smooth stone
your edible green hair

this is our life mama
yours and mine
all the flickering powers
all the shimmering lights
currents alternate
and direct
i might hold the cork

but you are the flow
the circuit
the breaker
the spare dry cell
insanity at midnight
prayers at dawn
ecstasy in the noon heat
mirage that points
to the real splendor
gold and saffron
ruby and red
sunrise
moonset
the single song of all
that is
was
and ever shall be

Blessed be.

INVOCATION TO THE QUEEN OF SUMMER

Queen of Summer
Queen Bee
Sweet-smelling
Flowering One
Honey Nectar
Overflowing fountain
Full-blown rose
Intoxicating dancer
Whispering wind
Singer
Spell-binder
Blossom and thorn
Rhiannon
Arianrhod
Aphrodite
Ishtar
Cybele
Come into us
Carry us off!

Notes

1. The Charge of the Goddess is traditional to almost all branches of Witchcraft. It appears in many varying forms; in this version, I have modernized the language. No one knows

when or by whom it was first composed, or even whether it is authentically ancient, but it is loved and preserved by Witches because it so perfectly expresses our concept of the Goddess.

2. One of the best recent historical sources on the Goddess is: Merlin Stone, *When God Was A Woman* (New York Dial Press, 1976)

3. Many books are available that explore Goddess religion historically and cross-culturally. The classic work is still Robert Graves, *The White Goddess* (New York: Farrar, Straus & Giroux, 1966).

4. Charles Leland, *Aradia, Gospel of the Witches* (New York: Weiser, 1974).

5. "It was said of the lotus-crowned Goddess in the Corinthian Mysteries, long before the phrase was applied to the ideally benign Father-God, 'Her service is perfect freedom' " (Graves, p. 485).

6 The God

Between the Worlds

The High Priest steps into the center of the circle and picks up the drum. Beating a strong, pounding rhythm, he begins the chant:

> Seed sower, grain reborn,
> Horned One come!

Other voices join his. Hands clap out the rhythm on bare thighs; feet stamp the floor. There is one great shout:

> "Io! Evohe!"

Silence. A soft tenor begins to sing:

> Bright sun, Dark death,
> Lord of winds, Lord of the dance,
> Sun child, Winter-born king,
> Hanged One,
> Untamed! Untamed!
> Stag and stallion, Goat and bull,
> Sailor of the last sea, Guardian of the gate,
> Lord of the two lands,
> Ever-dying, Ever-living, Radiance!
> Dionysus, Osiris, Pan, Dumuzi, Arthur,

Robin, Janicot, Hou!
Move us! Touch us! Shake us!
Bring us through!

All is quiet. The High Priest sets down the drum, and says simply, "He is here." The coven echoes, "He is here!" "Blessed be."

I grow old, I grow old,
I shall wear the bottoms of my trousers rolled.

Shall I part my hair behind? Do I dare to eat a peach?
I shall wear white flannel trousers, and walk upon the beach.
I have heard the mermaids singing, each to each.

I do not think that they will sing to me.

T. S. Eliot[1]

"It is very much in style today to urge men to feel. However, this urging is partially reminiscent of taunting a crippled man to run."

Herb Goldberg[2]

The image of the Horned God in Witchcraft is radically different from any other image of masculinity in our culture. He is difficult to understand, because He does not fit into any of the expected stereotypes, neither those of the "macho" male nor the reverse-images of those who deliberately seek effeminacy.[3] He is gentle, tender, and comforting, but He is also the Hunter. He is the Dying God—but his death is always in the service of the life force. He is untamed sexuality—but sexuality as a deep, holy, connecting power. He is the power of feeling, and the image of what men could be if they were liberated from the constraints of patriarchal culture.

The image of the Horned God was deliberately perverted by the medieval Church into the image of the Christian Devil. Witches do not believe in or worship the Devil—they consider it a concept peculiar to Christianity. The God of the Witches is sexual—but sexuality is seen as sacred, not as obscene or blasphemous. Our God wears horns—but they are the waxing and waning crescents of the Goddess Moon, and the symbol of animal vitality. In some aspects, He is black, not because He is dreadful or fearful, but because darkness and the night are times of power, and part of the cycles of time.[4]

There have always been traditions of the Craft in which the God is given little recognition.[5] In the Craft, separate Women's Mysteries and separate Men's Mysteries may be performed.[6] But in most Witch traditions the God is seen as the other-half of the Goddess, and many of the rites and holidays are devoted to Him as well as to Her.

In the medieval Witch cult, the God may have obtained prominence over the Goddess for a time. Most Witch confessions speak of "the devil," as the Christian priests transcribed the Witches' words for their non-Christian God. Fewer mention the Goddess, who is usually called "The Queen of Elphame." However, the interrogators of Witches were looking for evidence of Devil worship, not Goddess worship. They recorded evidence that supported their accusations of Satanism and ignored or twisted other evidence. Tortured suspects who reached the end of their endurance were often given already prepared statements to sign, which expressed what the Christian Priests wished to believe, rather than the truth.

A common practice in the medieval Craft was for the High Priest and Priestess to enact the parts of God and Goddess, who were believed to be physically incarnate in the rites. One old account cited by Margaret Murray expresses the importance of this custom to illiterate peasants, for whom seeing was believing: The High Priest mocked those "who offered to trust in God who left them miserable in the world, and neither he nor his son Jesus Christ ever appeared to them when they called on him, as he had, who would not cheat them."[7] For most Witches, "that earthly Sabbath was to her the true Paradise, where there was more pleasure than she could express, and she believed also that the joy which she took in it was but the prelude to a much greater glory, for her god so held her heart that no other desire could enter in."[8]

In the women's movement, Dianic/separatist Witchcraft[9] has become the fashion, and some women may have difficulty understanding why a feminist would bother with the Horned God at all. Yet there are few if any women whose lives are not bound up with men, if not sexually and emotionally, then economically. The Horned God represents powerful, positive male qualities that derive from deeper sources than the sterotypes and the violence and emotional crippling of men in our society. If man had been created in the Horned God's image, he would be free to be wild without being cruel, angry without being violent, sexual without being coercive, spiritual without being unsexed, and able to truly love. The mermaids, who are the Goddess, would sing to him.

The Goddess is the Encircler, the Ground of Being; the God is That-Which-Is-Brought-Forth, her mirror image, her other pole. She is the earth; He is the grain. She is the all-encompassing sky; He is the sun, her fireball. She is the Wheel; He is the Traveler. His is the sacrifice of life to death that life may go on. She is Mother and Destroyer; He is all that is born and is destroyed.

For men, the God is the image of inner power and of a potency that is more than merely sexual. He is the undivided Self, in which mind is not split from body, nor spirit from flesh. United, both can function at the peak of creative and emotional power.

In our culture, men are taught that masculinity demands a lack of feeling. They are conditioned to function in a military mode; to cut off their emotions and ignore the messages of their bodies; to deny physical discomfort, pain, and fear, in order to fight and conquer most efficiently. This holds true whether the field of conquest is the battlefield, the bedroom, or the business office.

It has become something of a cliché to say that men have been trained to be aggressive and dominant and women have been taught to be passive and submissive, that men are allowed to be angry and women are not. In patriarchal culture, both women and men learn to function within a hierarchy, in which those at the top dominate those below. One aspect of that dominance is the privilege of expressing anger. The general chews out the sergeant; the private cannot. The boss is free to blow his stack, but not his assistant. The boss's wife yells at her maid, not vice versa. Because women have usually been at the bottom of hierarchies, from the business world to the traditional family, they have borne the brunt of a great deal of male anger, and been the ultimate victims of violence. Anger can be seen as a response to an attack; very few men are in positions where they can afford to directly confront their attackers.

Men's anger, then, becomes twisted and perverted. It is threatening to recognize the true source of his rage, because he would then be forced to recognize the helplessness, powerlessness, and humiliation of his position. Instead, he may turn his anger on safer targets—women, children, or still less powerful men. Or his anger may turn to self-destruction: disease, depression, alcoholism, or any of a smorgasbord of readily available addictions.

Patriarchy literally means "rule of the fathers," but in a patriarchy, very few men are allowed to enact the role of "father" outside the limited family sphere. The structure of hierarchical institutions is pyramidal: One man at the top controls many below. Men compete for money and power over others; the majority, who do not reach the top of the chain of command, are forced to remain immature, enacting the roles of either dutiful or rebel sons. The good sons eternally seek to please the father by obedience; the bad sons seek to overthrow him and take his place. Either way, they are cut off from their own true desires and feelings.

And so our religions reflect a cosmos in which Father God exhorts his "children" to obey the rules and do what they are told, lest they align themselves with the Great Rebel. Our psychology is one of war between sons and fathers who eternally vie for exclusive possession of the mother, who, like all women under patriarchy, is the ultimate prize for success. And progressive politics are reduced to alignments of rebel sons, who overthrow the father only to institute their own hierarchies.

The Horned God, however, is born of a Virgin mother. He is a model of male power that is free from father-son rivalry or oedipal conflicts. He has no father; He is his own father. As He grows and passes through his changes on the Wheel, He remains in relationship to the prime nurturing force. His power is drawn directly from the Goddess: He participates in Her.

The God embodies the power of feeling. His animal horns represent the truth of undisguised emotion, which seeks to please no masters. He is untamed. But untamed feelings are very different from enacted violence. The God is the life force, the life cycle. He remains within the orbit of the Goddess; his power is always directed toward the service of life.

The God of the Witches is the God of love. This love includes sexuality, which is also wild and untamed as well as gentle and tender. His sexuality is fully *felt,* in a context in which sexual desire is sacred, not only because it is the means by which life is procreated but also because it is the means by which our own lives are most deeply and ecstatically realized. In Witchcraft, sex is a sacrament, an outward sign of an inward grace. That grace is the deep connection and recognition of the wholeness of another person. In its essence, it is not limited to the physical act—it is an exchange of energy, of subtle nourishment, between people. Through connection with another, we connect with all.

In the Craft, the male body, like the female body, is held sacred, not to be violated. It is a violation of the male body to use is as a weapon, just as it is a violation of the female body to use it as an object or a proving ground for male virility. To feign desire when it is absent violates the body's truth, as does repression of desire, which can be fully felt even when it cannot be satisfied. But to *feel* desire and longing is to admit need, which is threatening to many men in our culture.

Under patriarchy, men, while encouraged to expect a great deal of nurturing care from women, are taught not to admit their need for nurturing, their need to be passive at times, to be weak, to lean on another. The God, in Witchcraft, embodies longing and desire for union with the prime, nurturing force. Instead of seeking unlimited mothering from actual, living women, men in Witchcraft are encouraged to identify with the God and, through Him, to attain union with the Goddess, whose mother-love knows no bounds. The Goddess is both an external and internal force: When her image is taken into a man's mind and heart, She becomes part of him. He can connect with his own nurturing qualities, with the inner Muse who is a source of unfading inspiration.

The God is Eros, but He is also Logos, the power of the mind. In Witchcraft, there is no opposition between the two. The bodily desire for union and the emotional desire for connection are transmuted into the intellectual desire for knowledge, which is also a form of union. Knowledge can be both analytic and synthetic; can take things apart and look at differences, or form a pattern from unintegrated parts and see the whole.

For women raised in our culture, the God begins as a symbol of all those qualities that have been identified as male and that we have not been encouraged to own. The symbol of the God, like that of the Goddess, is both internal and external. Through meditation and ritual, a woman who invokes the God creates his image within herself and connects with those qualities she lacks. As her understanding moves beyond culturally imposed limitations, her image of the God changes, deepens. He is the Creation, which is not simply a replica of oneself, but something different, of a different order. True creation implies separation, as the very act of birth is a relinquishment, a letting go. Through the God, the woman knows this power in herself. His love and desire stretch across the abyss of separation, taut as a harpstring, humming one note which becomes the single song, the uni-verse, of all. That vibration is energy, the true source of power-from-within. And so the God, like the Goddess, empowers woman.

For both women and men, the God is also the Dying God. As such, He represents the giving over that sustains life: Death in the service of the life force. Life is characterized by many losses, and, unless the pain of each one is fully felt and worked through, it remains buried in the psyche, where, like a festering sore that never fully heals, it exudes emotional poison.[10] The Dying God embodies the concept of loss. In rituals, as we enact his death over and over again, we release the emotions surrounding our own losses, lance the wounds, and win through to the healing promised by his rebirth. This psychological purging was the true purpose of dramatic tragedy, which originated, in Greece, out of the rites of the dying God Dionysus.

In Witchcraft, death is always followed by rebirth, loss by restitution. After the dark of the moon, the new crescent appears. Spring follows winter; day follows night. Not all Witches believe in literal reincarnation; many, like Robin Morgan, view it as "a *metaphor* for that mystically cellular transition in which the dancers DNA and RNA immortally twine themselves."[11] But in a world view that sees everything as cyclical, death itself cannot be a final ending, but rather some unknown transformation to some new form of being. In enacting and reenacting the death of the God, we prepare ourselves to face that transformation, to live out the last stage of life. The God becomes the Comforter and Consoler of Hearts, who teaches us to understand death through his example. He embodies the warmth, tenderness, and compassion that are the true complement of male aggression.

The Dying God puts on horns and becomes the Hunter, who metes out death as well as suffering it. Few of us today directly participate in life processes; we no longer raise or hunt our own meat, but get it plastic-wrapped at the supermarket. It is difficult for us to understand the concept of the Divine Hunter. But in a culture of hunters the hunt meant *life,* and the hunter was the life giver of the tribe. The tribe identified with its food animals; hunting involved tremendous skill and knowledge of the habits and psychology of the prey. Animals were never killed needlessly, and no parts of the kill were wasted. Life was never taken without recognition and reverence for the spirit of the prey.

Today, the only thing most of us hunt for regularly is parking places. But the Hunter has another aspect: that of searching, of seeking. He embodies all quests, whether physical, spiritual, artistic, scientific, or social. His image is poemagogic: It both symbolizes and sparks the creative process, which is itself a Quest. The God seeks for the Goddess, as King Arthur seeks for the Grail, as each of us seeks for that which we have lost and for all that has never yet been found.

Like the Goddess, the God unifies all opposites. As in the invocation that opens this chapter, He is both the bright sun, the light-giving, energizing force, and the darkness of night and death. The two aspects, as I have said before, are complementary, not contradictory. They cannot be identified as "good" and "evil": both are part of the cycle, the necessary balance of life.

As Lord of Winds, the God is identified with the elements and the natural world. As Lord of the Dance, He symbolizes the spiral dance of life, the whirling energies that bind existence in eternal motion. He embodies movement and change.

The Sun Child is born at the Winter Solstice, when, after the triumph of darkness throughout the year's longest night, the sun rises again. In Witchcraft, the celebrations of the Goddess are lunar; those of the God follow the mythological pattern of the Wheel of the Year.

At the Winter Solstice, he is born as the embodiment of innocence and joy, of a childlike delight in all things. His is the triumph of the returning light. At Brigid or Candlemas (February 2)[12] his growth is celebrated, as the days grow visibly longer. At the Spring Equinox, He is the green, flourishing youth who dances with the Goddess in her Maiden aspect. On Beltane (May 1), their marriage is celebrated with maypoles and bonfires, and on the Summer Solstice it is consummated, in a union so complete it becomes a death. He is named Summer-Crowned King instead of Winter-Born, and the crown is of roses: the bloom of culmination coupled with the stab of the thorn. He is mourned at Lughnasad (August 1), and at the Fall Equinox He sleeps in the womb of the Goddess, sailing over the sunless sea that is her womb. At Samhain, (Halloween, October 31), He arrives at the Land of Youth, the Shining Land in which the souls of the dead grow young again, as they wait to be reborn. He opens the gates that they may return and visit their loved ones, and rules in the Dreamworld as He too grows young, until at the Winter Solstice He is again reborn.[13]

This is the myth: the poetic statement of a process that is seasonal, celestial, and psychological. Enacting the myth in ritual, we enact our own transformations, the constant birth, growth, culmination, and passing of our ideas, plans, work, relationships. Each loss, each change, even a happy one, turns life upside down. We each become the Hanged One: the herb hung up to dry, the carcass hung to cure, the Hanged Man of the Tarot, whose meaning is the sacrifice that allows one to move on to a new level of being.

The association of love and death is a strong one in the mythology of many cultures. In Witchcraft, love is never associated with actual physical violence, and nothing could be more antithetical to the spirit of the Craft than the current rash of violent pornography. The God does not perpetrate acts of sadomasochism on the Goddess nor preach to Her the "power of sexual surrender." It is He that surrenders, to the power of his own feeling. Nowhere but in love do we live so completely in the all-consuming present; and at no time but when we are in love are we so searingly conscious of our own mortality. For even if love lasts—and both popular songs and personal experience assure us it does not—or metamorphosizes into a sweeter and deeper, if less fiery form, sooner or later one lover will die and the other will be left alone. The Craft does not try to resolve that dilemma, but to intensify it, because only through that bittersweet realization, through the embrace of Pan whose hairy thighs rub us raw even as they bring us ecstasy, can we learn to be fully alive.

And so the God is the proud stag who haunts the heart of the deepest forest, that of the Self. He is the stallion, swift as thought, whose crescent hooves leave lunar marks even as they strike sparks of solar fire. He is the goat-Pan, lust and fear, the animal emotions that are also the fostering powers of human life; and He is the moon-bull, with its crescent horns, its strength, and its hooves that thunder over the earth. These are only a few of his animal aspects.

Yet He is untamed. He is all that within us that will never be domesticated, that refuses to be compromised, diluted, made safe, molded, or tampered with. He is free.

As God of the waning year, He sails the Last Sea for the Dreamland, the Otherworld, the internal space in which creativity is generated. The mythic Shining Isle is our own internal source of inspiration. He is the Self voyaging the dark waters of the unconscious mind. The gates He guards are the threshold that divides the unconscious from the conscious, the gates of night and day through which we pass to go beyond the illusion of duality, the gates of form through which we pass in and out of life.

While He is ever-dying, He is also ever-reborn, ever-living. In the moment of his transformation, He becomes immortal, as love is immortal although its objects may fade. He glows with the radiance that sparks life.

The God, like the Goddess, has many names. He appears, linked with Her, throughout time, from the Paleolithic caves to the bulls of ancient Crete to the medieval tales of Robin Hood and his merry men.[14] Any of his names or aspects can be used as a focus for meditation.

Although there are many men in modern Witchcraft, in general they are less immediately attracted to the Craft than women. No matter how simplistically or superstitiously the Craft is understood, it offers women a model of female strength and creative power; in that, it has remarkably little competition from other religions. But for men, it demands a giving up of traditional forms of power and traditional concepts of religion. What it offers men is more subtle and not always easy to comprehend.

Men are not subservient or relegated to second-class spiritual citizenship in Witchcraft.[15] But neither are they automatically elevated to a higher status than women, as they are in other religions. Men in the Craft must interact with strong, empowered women who do not pretend to be anything less than what they are. Many men find the prospect disconcerting.

The Craft also demands a new relationship to the female body. No longer can it be seen as an object or vilified as something dirty. A woman's body, its odors, secretions, and menstrual blood, are sacred, are worthy of reverence and celebration. Women's bodies belong to themselves alone; no spiritual authority will back a man's attempt to possess or control her.

The body is not to be celebrated in isolation. Men in the Craft must come to terms with woman's power: the power of a whole woman, a completed woman, whose mind and spirit and emotions are fully awakened. A man must also know and accept the power of his own, inner, female self; to generate a source of nurturing and inspiration within, rather than demanding it exclusively from without.

Witchcraft also means losing the "Great Man" model of spirituality. Jesus, Buddha, Krishna, Moses, and the whole horde of preachers, prophets, gurus, and group leaders who claim to teach in their names, or the names of secular descendents, lose their halos. In Witchcraft, there are no comforting, all-knowing father figures who promise answers for everything at the price of one's personal autonomy. The Craft calls on each of us to be our own authority, and that can be an uncomfortable position.

In fact, there is no more God the Father. In the Craft, the cosmos is no longer modeled on external male control. The hierarchy is dissolved; the heavenly chain of command is broken; the divinely revealed texts are seen as poetry, not truth. Instead, a man must connect with the Goddess, who is immanent in the world, in nature, in woman, in his own feelings—in all that childhood religions taught him needed to be overcome, transcended, conquered, in order to be loved by God.

But the very aspects of Witchcraft that seem threatening also hold out to men a new and vibrant spiritual possibility: that of wholeness, connection, and freedom. Men of courage find relationships with strong, powerful women exhilarating. They welcome the chance to know the Female within, to grow beyond their culturally imposed limitations and become whole.

Attempts to live out the model of God-father isolate men in emotionally frozen life situations. Many men welcome release from the eternal son-father conflict of patriarchy. They delight in a model of male power that is nonhierarchical, that is neither slave nor master. While individuals may not escape external authority in their own lives, they see it for what it is: an arbitrary set of rules to a complex game. They may play or withdraw, but their identities and self-esteem no longer depend on their place in the power pyramid.

In the Craft, the split between mind and body, flesh and spirit, is healed. Men are free to be spiritual without being unsexed, because God and Goddess embody the deeply moving force of passionately felt sexuality. They can connect with their own true feelings, their needs, their weaknesses as well as strengths. Rituals are active, physical, energetic, and cathartic. Ecstasy and wild, untamed energy are given a spiritual value, not relegated to the football field or the corner bar.

It is uncomfortable to be one's own authority, but it is the only condition under which true personal power can develop. Men and women are no longer content to be tame dogs or whipping boys: to place life-and-death decisions in the hands of a "fearless leader," a Pope, or a Jim Jones. Personal authority demands integrity and responsibility, but without it we cannot be free.

Within covens, men can experience group support and the affection of other men, as well as women. They can interact in situations that are not competitive or antagonistic. Men in covens can become friends with other men.

Finally, Witchcraft is fun. It offers men a chance to play, to act silly, to let the inner child come out. There are no fronts to uphold, no masculine dignity that must remain unbreached. Out of foolishness and play, creativity is born.

The God is within and without. Like the Goddess, He is invoked in many ways: singing, chanting, drumming, dancing, a whispered poem, a wild shout. However we call Him, He awakens within us:

REPEATING CHANTS (TO THE GOD)

SEED Sower GRAIN Reborn HORNED ONE COME!

BRIGHT Sun DARK Death Lord Of the Winds COME

HAR HAR HOU HOU
DANCE Ici DANCE La!
JOUE Ici JOUE La!
HAR HAR HOU HOU!
DANCE Here DANCE There!
PLAY Here PLAY There![16]

The SUN Child The Winter-Born KING
[or] The SUN Child The Summer-Crowned KING

IO! EVOHE IO! EVOHE!
(Pronounced Yoh! Ay-VOH-hay!)

Evohe is one of the names of the God, derived from an ancient name of Dionysus, and cited as a Witches' cry in accounts of the Burning Times.[17]

REPEATING CYCLE

Sun Shine Day/Shine Day Forever/Day Forever Night/
Forever Night Sky/Night Sky Star/Sky Star Light/
Star Light Sun/Light Sun Shine/

EQUINOX INVOCATION OF THE MALE ASPECT
BY Alan Acacia

horned god, tamed by love, fierce with passion
join us now

gentle one, sharer, one without possessions
be here now

lover to men as well as women, little child, old man
join us now

strong in struggle, proud of earth from which you
    spring, and to which you fall
be here now

loyal son, caring father, loving brother, rape fighter
join us now

rebel, seed sower, sissy, one who gives support to us,
we need your energy, we call for your presence
be here now

INVOCATION TO THE GOD OF SUMMER

Lord of the colors of day
Untamed Awakener of Hearts
Comforter of sorrows
The namer
Clear-sighted dancer
Morning's son
Vine-ripened Seed
Many-jeweled one
Hunter   Wild beast
Guide
Come to us!
You are dry Drink of us!
We are the dew-filled flowers
That open To your golden shaft

INVOCATION TO THE GODDESS & GOD
BY VALERIE

Kouros seedsower, Kore underground
Leaflight, bloodroot, grain reborn
Turning the Wheel we keep you in mind,
Lovelight, spermshine, flower & thorn.

Spinning the web we call you forth,
Turning the Wheel with ageless love.

Earth Her body, Air Her breath,
Fire Her spirit, Water Her flow,
Transformed in the halls of Death,
Life on life we come and go.

Spinning the Web we call you forth,
Turning the Wheel with ageless love.

Kouros Horned One, Kore above,
Starlight, heart's joy, ancient mirth,
Spinning the Web we call you forth,
Turning the Wheel with ageless love.

INVOCATION TO THE GROUND OF BEING

Nameless One	of many names
Eternal	and ever-changing One
Who is found nowhere	but appears everywhere
Beyond	and within all.
Timeless	circle of the seasons,
Unknowable mystery	known by all.
Lord of the dance,	Mother of all life,
Be radiant within us,	Engulf us with your love,

See with our eyes, Hear with our ears, Breathe with
our nostrils, Touch with our hands, Kiss with our lips,
Open our hearts!
That we may live free at last
Joyful in the single song
Of all that is, was, or ever shall be!

SONG TO PAN
BY MARK SIMOS

Should the raven catch your hair
And seat a king of scarlet
Upon the heart's steep stair
Then, oh, the sights will you see there—
A breaking of the crystal
Under a dark green glare.

A dark green glare, from eyes on fire,
From pools of deepest amber—
Circle your castle round with briar,
Still Pan will find your chamber.

Fill it to the brim, don't say when,
Drink your fill and drink again,
Hear the ocean roaring.
Fill it to the brim, don't say when,
It's Pan that keeps on pouring.

Walnut hands, the eyes of a bear—
He who seeks his sorrows out
May find the lion's share.
With self-same breath He tempts and warns—
The fire that keeps the chill at bay
Is the very flame that burns.

The flame that burns, the song that slays,
When you hear what it is saying—
Let Panic chase us through the maze,
But Pan is only playing.

Fill it to the brim, don't say when,
Drink your fill and drink again,
Hear the ocean roaring.
Fill it to the brim, don't say when,
It's Pan that keeps on pouring.

Dark watcher with tangled brows
Puts his finger to his lips,
Let's hear no more of vows,
Of promises we'll never keep,
Nor of the secret dream
That slips away as we rise from sleep.

As we rise from sleep,
As we rub our eyes,
To set the salt tears falling,
You can cover your ears to drown his cries—
Yet Pan just keeps on calling.

Notes

1. T. S. Eliot, *The Waste Land, and Other Poems* (New York: Harcourt Brace Jovanovich, (1958), p. 8.
2. Herb Goldberg, *The Hazards of Being Male* (New York: New American Library, 1977), p. 58.
3. In San Francisco, certain groups of male transvestites and transsexuals see deliberately adopted effeminacy as a conscious, political identification with the Female life principle. The Horned God, however, while partaking of the Female, is in essence the image of the Male, not a denial of masculinity in favor of the feminine.
4. As many black leaders and thinkers have pointed out, the constant identification of "black" with "evil" is rooted in racism and perpetuated by Judeo-Christian religious imagery. The Craft has always valued the dark as well as the light: Both Goddess and God have aspects in which they are imaged as black, and these are aspects of power and wonder, not horror.
5. All traditions of the Craft recognize the Goddess, and all, except for some lesbian-feminist traditions that originated in the past few years, recognize the God to some extent. But there are broad variations in how much attention and ritual time is given to the God. In some covens, He is never invoked; in others, He may be called in only on the Summer and Winter Solstice, or only on the other solar holidays. Other traditions, however, give Him "equal time"; He may rule the winter months while the Goddess rules the summer, or he may simply be invoked at every ritual. In our tradition, He is invoked at every ritual where men are present, and often, but not always, in women-only rituals.
6. At the present time, there are many all-women covens devoted to the practice of

Women's Mysteries. There are very few all-male covens; the ones I know of are gay, and are more devoted to the Goddess than the Horned God. Male "mysteries" abound in American society—but the concept of such groups in a spiritual context that honors the Female Principle is open for exploration.

7. Margaret Murray, *The Witch Cult in Western Europe* (Oxford, England: Oxford University Press, 1971), p. 30.

8. Murray, p. 15.

9. Not all Dianic traditions are separatist: In Morgan McFarland's tradition, for example, covens include men, but the Horned God is considered subordinate to the Goddess and is invoked only on the Summer and Winter Solstices.

10. My understanding of the concept of loss derives from personal discussions with my mother, over the course of the research and writing of her book. See Dr. Bertha Simos, *A Time to Grieve: Loss as a Universal Human Experience* (New York: Family Service Association, 1979).

11. Robin Morgan, *Going Too Far* (New York: Random House, 1977), p. 306.

12. Holidays begin on the eve of the date given (except for Halloween, for which I have given the commonly known date).

13. There are many variations of this myth known throughout the Craft—in some, the God becomes warring twins; in other traditions, aspects of his transformation may be celebrated on other dates. Whatever the superficial differences, the underlying poetic truth remains the same.

14. A more complete explanation of the identification of Robin Hood with the Horned God of the Witches is given by Margaret Murray in *The God of the Witches* (London: Oxford University Press, 1970), pp. 41–42.

15. Some covens, of course, do not admit men; I am speaking of the Craft as a whole—apart from the separatist traditions.

16. Murray, *The God of the Witches*, p. 40.

17. In Burning Time accounts, it often appears as "A boy"—an obvious mishearing of *Evohe* (see Murray, *The God of the Witches*, p. 141). The true meaning of the name is connected with the esoteric meanings of the vowels. Chant it—and see what happens.

7 *Magical Symbols*

Between the Worlds

WORDPLAY

i/mage mag/ic magician imagination mage mag/net imagic imagnetic imagenetic imagenesis

Imagic—the image is the heart of magic which is made by imagination—what we see in the mind's eye makes magic—makes us magic—the mage—who casts the net—the *magenet*—magic magnet—net of subtle power dipping into the lifestream—glowing in the dark—a web that surrounds the earth Her body—magnetic field—*imagnetic*—how we are attracted to magic—it draws us in—we are fish caught in a magic net—*imagenetic*—because our genes remember, our cells remember, the source, the origin, the beginning—*imagenesis*—creation out of image—creation of the image—from the image all is born—all is magic—*imagnosis*—this, through what we imagine, we know.

Smooth stone with a hole in the center/ candles of blue, green, gold/ musk/ silver/ a round mirror/ myrrh/ seven-pointed star/ silk cord/ eight-spoked wheel/ the number of increase/ the red cord/ silk/ gold/ lead/ the planetary symbols/ drums/ the shapes of letters/ the shapes of eyes/ the shape of a heart/ the shape of a sound/ the shape of magic.

"Do you know the old language?
I do not know the old language.
Do you know the language of the old belief?"

Robert Duncan[1]

"Do you believe in an invisible reality behind appearances?"

Dion Fortune[2]

"No ideas, but in things."

William Carlos Williams

"White magic is poetry, black magic is anything that actually works."

Victor Anderson (High Priest of the Faery tradition)

"Black is beautiful."

Aphorism of the Black Power Movement

"It's our limitations that keep us sane."

Dr. Bertha Simos
(Starhawk's mother)

Magic is the craft of Witchcraft, and few things are at once so appealing, so frightening, and so misunderstood. To work magic is to weave the unseen forces into form; to soar beyond sight; to explore the uncharted dream realm of the hidden reality; to infuse life with color, motion, and strange scents that intoxicate; to leap beyond imagination into that space between the worlds where fantasy becomes real; to be at once animal and god. Magic is the craft of shaping, the craft of the wise, exhilarating, dangerous—the ultimate adventure.

The power of magic should not be underestimated. It works, often in ways that are unexpected and difficult to control. But neither should the power of magic be overestimated. It does not work simply, or effortlessly; it does not confer omnipotence. "The art of changing consciousness at will" is a demanding one, requiring a long and disciplined apprenticeship. Merely waving a wand, lighting a candle, or crooning a rhymed incantation do nothing in and of themselves. But when the force of a trained awareness is behind them, they are far more than empty gestures.

Learning to work magic is a process of neurological repatterning, of changing the way we use our brains. So, for that matter, is learning to play the piano—both processes involve the development of new pathways for neurons to follow, both require practice and take time, and both, when mastered, can be emotional and spiritual channels for great beauty. Magic requires first the development and then the integration of right-hemisphere, spatial, intuitive, holistic, patterning awareness. It opens the gates between the unconscious and the conscious mind, between the starlight and flashlight vision. In so doing, it deeply influences an individual's growth, creativity, and personality.

The language of the old belief, the language of magic, is expressed in symbols and images. Images bridge the gap between the verbal and non-verbal modes of awareness; they allow the two sides of the brain to communicate, arousing the emotions as well as the intellect. Poetry, itself a form of magic, is imagic speech. Spells and charms worked by Witches are truly concrete poetry.

A spell is a symbolic act done in an altered state of consciousness, in order to cause a desired change. To cast a spell is to project energy through a symbol. But the symbols are too often mistaken for the spell. "Burn a green candle to attract money," we are told. The candle itself, however, does nothing—it is merely a lens, an object of focus, a mnemonic device, the "thing" that embodies our idea. Props may be useful, but it is the mind that works magic.

Particular objects, shapes, colors, scents, and images do work better than others to embody particular ideas. Correspondences between colors, planets, metals, numbers, plants, and minerals make up a great body of magical lore. I have included some sets of correspondences beginning on page 201. But the most powerful spells are often improvised, out of materials that feel right or that simply happen to come to hand.

Spells are an important aspect of magical training. They require the combined faculties of relaxation, visualization, concentration, and projection (see the exercises in Chapter Three), and so they provide practice in coordinating these skills and developing them further.

Spell casting also forces us to come to terms with the material world. Many people who are attracted to the spiritual path of Witchcraft find themselves uneasy with the idea of using magic for practical ends or toward material goals. Somehow it seems wrong to work for oneself, to want things and to get things. But this attitude is a holdover of the Judeo-Christian world view that sees spirit and matter as separate and that identifies matter with evil and corruption. In Witchcraft, the flesh, the material world, are not sundered from the Goddess, they are the manifestation of the divine. Union with the Goddess comes through embracing the material world. In Witchcraft, we do not fight self-interest; we follow it, but with an awareness that transmutes it into something sacred.

"Work for yourself, and soon you will see that Self is everywhere," is a saying of the Faery Tradition. The paradox is that in spell casting we may start with the personal self, but in order to work the magic we are forced to expand and recognize the Self that moves through all beings. Magic involves a deliberate self-identification with other objects and people. To do a healing, we must *become* the healer, the one who is healed, and the energy of healing. To attract love, we must become love.

Spell casting is the lesser, not the greater, magic; but the greater magic builds on the less. Spells are extremely sophisticated psychological tools that have subtle but important effects on a person's inner growth.

A spell may highlight otherwise hidden complexes. A person who has conflicts about success, for example, will find great difficulty in concentrating on a money spell. Practical results may be far less important than psychological insights that arise during the magical working. Discovering our inner blocks and fears is the first step in overcoming them.

Spells also go one step further than most forms of psychotherapy. They allow us not only to listen to and interpret the unconscious but also to speak to it, in the language it understands. Symbols, images, and objects used in spells communicate directly with Younger Self, who is the seat of our emotions and who is barely touched by the intellect. We often understand our feelings and behavior but find ourselves unable to change them. Through spells, we can attain the most important power—the power to change ourselves.

The practice of magic also demands the development of what is called the magical *will.* Will is very much akin to what Victorian schoolmasters called "character": honesty, self-discipline, commitment, and conviction.

Those who would practice magic must be scrupulously honest in their personal lives. In one sense, magic works on the principle that "It is so because I say it is so." A bag of herbs acquires the power to heal because I say it does. For my word to take on such force, I must be deeply and completely convinced that it is identified with truth as I know it. If I habitually lie to my lovers, steal from my boss, pilfer from supermarkets, or simply renege on my promises, I cannot have that conviction.

Unless I have enough personal power to keep commitments in my daily life, I will be unable to wield magical power. To work magic, I need a basic belief in my ability to do things and cause things to happen. That belief is generated and sustained by my daily actions. If I say I will finish a report by Thursday and I do so, I have strengthened my knowledge that I am a person who can do what I say I will do. If I let the report go until a week from next Monday, I have undermined that belief. Of course, life is full of mistakes and miscalculations. But to a person who practices honesty and keeps commitments, "As I will, so mote it be" is not just a pretty phrase; it is a statement of fact.

Spells work in two basic ways. The first, which even the most confirmed skeptics will have no trouble accepting, is through suggestion. Symbols and images implant certain ideas in Younger Self, in the unconscious mind. We are then influenced to actualize those ideas. Obviously, psychological spells and many healing spells work on this principle. It functions in other spells, too. For example, a woman casts a spell to get a job. Afterward, she is filled with new self-confidence, approaches her interviewer with assurance, and creates such a good impression that she is hired.

However, spells can also influence the external world. Perhaps the job hunter "just happens" to walk into the right office at the right time. The cancer patient, without knowing that a healing spell was cast, has a spontaneous remission. This aspect of magic is more difficult to accept. The theoretical model that Witches use to explain the workings of magic is a clear one and coincides in many ways with the "new" physics. But I do not offer it as "proof" that magic works—nor do I wish to convince anyone to drop their doubts. (Skeptics make better magicians.) It is simply an elaborate—but extremely useful—metaphor.

That metaphor is based on the world view that sees things not as fixed objects, but as swirls of energy. The physical world is formed by that energy as stalagtites are formed by dropping water. If we cause a change in the energy patterns, they in turn will cause a change in the physical world—just as, if we change the course of an underground river, new series of stalagtites will be formed in new veins of rock.

When our own energy is concentrated and channeled, it can move the broader energy currents. The images and objects used in spells are the channels, the vessels through which our power is poured and by which it is shaped. When energy is directed into the images we visualize, it gradually manifests physical form and takes shape in the material world.

Directing energy is not a matter of simply emoting. It is fashionable in some occult circles to proclaim piously that "thoughts are things, and therefore we should think only positive thoughts, because the negative things we think will come to pass." It is hard to imagine a philosophy that could more swiftly produce extreme paranoia. Were it true, the death rate would rise phenomenally. Overpopulation would be the least of our worries—and no elected politicians would survive long enough to be inaugurated. If thoughts and emotions alone could cause things to happen, thousands of my contemporaries would have married the Beatles in 1964. And I would not be writing at this desk—I would be sunning myself in Tahiti, where the crowds would undoubtedly be fierce.

Emotion is a strobe light; directed energy is a laser beam. No matter how much hate, envy, and rage we direct at tailgaters, business competitors, exlovers, and close relations, we will not esoterically affect either their physical or mental health—although we may affect our own.

Even concentrated power is a small stream compared with the vast surges of energy that surround us. The most adept Witch cannot be successful in all her spells; the opposing currents are often too strong. As John C. Lilly says, "It is all to easy to preach 'go with the flow.' The main problem is identifying what the flow is, here and now."[3] Witchcraft teaches us first to identify the flow and then to decide whether or not it is going where we want to go. If not, we can try to deflect it, or we may have to change our course.

To twist our metaphor slightly, casting a spell is like sailing a boat. We must take into account the currents—which are our own unconscious motivations, our desires and emotions, our patterns of actions, and the cumulative results of all our past actions. The currents are also the broader social, economic, and political forces that surround us. The winds that fill our sails are the forces of time and climate and season; the tides of the planets, the moon, and the sun. Sometimes all the forces are with us; we simply open our sail and run before the wind. At other times, the wind may run against the current, or both run counter to our direction, and we may be forced to tack back and forth, or furl the sail and wait.

Sensing the energy climate is a matter of intuition and experience. Some Witches make a detailed study of astrology in an effort to plan their magical workings at the optimum times. Personally, I prefer simply to work when I feel the time is right. Of all the planets, the moon's influence on subtle energies is the strongest. Subtle power increases as the moon waxes, so the time of the waxing moon is best for spells involving growth or increase, such as money spells. The power peaks when the moon is full, and that is the best time for workings of culmination and love. During the waning moon, power subsides and turns inward: the waning period is used for banishing, binding, and discovering hidden secrets.

Spells can be adjusted to fit the time. For example, if you are obsessed with the need to do a money spell on the waning moon, focus on banishing poverty. A friend of mine whose business had been limping along for two years did precisely that and realized soon afterward that most of his problems stemmed from his partner's miscalculations and lack of management. At the same time, his partner decided to quit. The waning moon had done its work. By the next full moon, the business had begun to turn around.

Energy pursues the path of least resistance. Material results are more easily achieved through physical actions than through magical workings. It is simpler to lock your door than to protect your house with psychic seals. No magic spell is going to bring results unless channels are open in the material world. A job spell is useless unless you also go out and look for a job. A healing spell is no substitute for medical care.

The visualization we create in a spell should be that of the desired end—not necessarily the means by which it will come about. We picture the accident victim running on the beach—not the bones knitting. We keep our focus on our destination, without attempting to chart every movement we will make on the way. Spells usually work in unexpected ways. In order to assure that the power does not inadvertantly cause harm, we bind the spell. We "set" the form we have created, so that the energy becomes fixed in the pattern we desire.

EXERCISE 43: BINDING A SPELL:

When you have finished casting a spell, visualize yourself tying a knot in a cord wrapped around the symbol or image on which you have focused. Tell yourself you are setting the form of the spell, as a clay pot is set when it is fired. Say,

> By all the power
> Of three times three,
> This spell bound around
> Shall be.
> To cause no harm,
> Nor return on me.
> As I do will,
> So mote it be!

Spells that influence another person depend on a psychic link. Power pours through you toward another—but in order for the connection to be made you must be at least partly identified with that other person. You *become* the other, as well as becoming the energy you send. For this reason, "What you send returns on you, three times over." The energy you project to another affects *you* even more strongly than the other person—because you have generated it, you have become it, and you have become its object. If you send out healing energy, you are healed in turn. If you hex or curse, you yourself are cursed.

Witches, therefore, are extremely reluctant to hex anybody.[4] Some traditions expressly forbid hexing, cursing, or even healing another without their consent. Other Witches feel strongly that "A Witch who cannot hex, cannot heal." By that they mean that to use magic for destruction is not synonymous with using it for evil. Cancer must be destroyed for healing to take place. A person who threatens the safety of others must be stopped. This is most safely done with a binding spell, focused on the image of preventing him or her from doing harm. The returning energy, then, will be basically protective. If you bind a rapist, you may find yourself prevented from committing rape, but if that interferes with your daily activities you have no business practicing Witchcraft anyway. The spell may work itself out in many different ways: The rapist may be caught and convicted, or he could become impotent or even undergo a religious conversion. *How* it works is not your concern, as long as it accomplishes your goal.

Even binding spells should never be undertaken lightly. It is best to discuss them thoroughly in the coven, and and proceed only when everyone is in agreement. *Never* hex someone just because they annoy you, because you dislike them, or they cause you inconvenience, or in order to profit at their expense. Such misuses of magic are demeaning, dangerous, and self-defeating. They will do far more harm to you than to anybody else.

Magic should not be used to gain power over others—it should be seen as part of the discipline of developing "power-from-within." Spells that attempt to control another person should be avoided. This particularly applies to love spells focused on a specific person. More than any other form of spells, these work far more strongly on the person who casts them than they do on the intended object. They inevitably backfire, complicating one's life beyond belief. Of course, if you feel you have grown too emotionally complacent, and need to be thoroughly shaken up ... go ahead. Look on it as a "learning experience."

General spells to attract love create fewer problems, although they tend to be more effective for attracting sex than love per se. Love itself is a discipline, requiring an internal readiness. Unless you yourself are open to love, no spell will bring it into your life. It may, however, bring you a lot of amusement.

People often worry about being attacked magically. Actually, psychic attacks occur extremely rarely and are even more rarely effective. Paranoia is a far more pressing danger than psychic warfare. However, people can be attacked in many subtle ways. Envy and hostility need not be focused in a spell to create an uncomfortable emotional climate. Protective meditations and spells can be helpful in many mundane situations (see Chapter Four). The following meditation is effective whenever negative energy is being directed at you:

EXERCISE 44: PROTECTIVE FILTER

Ground and center. Visualize yourself surrounded by a net of glowing white light. See it as a semiporous energy field. Any force that hits this barrier is transmuted into pure creative energy. Whatever anger or hostility are sent to you, they only feed your own power. Take in that power; absorb it; glow with it. Maintain the filter around yourself as you go through the day.

In the following spells, raise power by breathing or chanting, as in the exercises given previously. You can cast a circle formally or simply by visualizing it. Don't forget to earth the power and open the circle at the end. Names of materials used are given in capital letters, for ease of reference.

Spell casting is the lesser magic, but imagery and symbols are also used in the greater magic of rituals, where they become the keys to self-transformation and the links that connect us to the divine, within and without.

ANGER SPELL

Visualize a circle of light around yourself.

Cup a BLACK STONE in your hands and raise it to your forehead.

Concentrate and project all your anger into the stone.

With all your might, hurl it out of the circle into a lake, stream, river, or the ocean. Say:

> With this stone
> Anger be gone.
> Water bind it,
> No one find it.

Earth the power.

Release the circle.
(To be done alongside flowing water.)

THE INDRINKING SPELL

(For self-acceptance when you've made a mistake or are filled with guilt or regrets.)

Cast a circle.

Sit facing North, and light a BLACK or WHITE CANDLE.

Hold in both hands your CUP, filled with CLEAR WATER. You should have before you an IMAGE OF THE GODDESS and a GREEN PLANT, in earth.

Visualize all the negative things you are feeling about yourself, the mistakes you have made, the things you have done wrong. Talk to yourelf and admit you feel bad. Tell yourself, out loud, exactly what you have done wrong, and why. Let your emotion build energy, and project it all into the cup. Breathe on the water.

Raise power.

Visualize the Goddess as forgiving Mother. Imagine her hands cover yours. Hear Her say,

> I am the Mother of all things,
> My love is poured out upon the earth.
> I drink you in with perfect love,
> Be cleansed. Be healed. Be changed.

Pour out the water onto the plant, and feel your self-hate draining out of you. (It is possible this ritual will kill the plant.)

Fill the CUP with RED WINE or MILK.

Raise more power, and visualize yourself as you would like to be, free of guilt and sorrow, changed so that you will not repeat the same errors. Charge the cup with strength and the power to be the person you want to be.

Again, visualize the Goddess. Her hands cover yours, and She says,

> Mine the cup, and Mine the wine of life.
> Drink deep!

Drink the wine or milk. Feel yourself filled with strength. Know that you have changed, that you are, from that very moment, a new person, not bound by the patterns and errors of the past.

Bind the spell.

Earth the power.

Open the circle.

SPELL FOR LONELINESS

Cast a circle.

Raise energy.

Sit facing North and light a GRAY CANDLE.

In a MORTAR AND PESTLE, grind a SHARK'S TOOTH (or other sharp bone) to powder.

Say,

You
have no bones
and never sleep.
You
swim always
within me.

Allow loneliness to fill you and project it into the powder.

Chant,

Fire take you!
Fire have you!
Fire free you!

Shout, "Now be gone!" and release the feeling into the powder.

Spit three times into the powder and burn it in a BRASS BOWL, with ALOES, NETTLES, and THORNS.

Douse the fire with SALT WATER.

Earth the power.

Bind the spell.

Release the circle.

You will feel light of heart and free of loneliness.

SPELL FOR FALLOW PERIODS

On the first day of the dark of the moon, begin to sprout some seeds of wheat, barley, rye, or alfalfa.

Keep them in the dark three days, and then three days in the light.

On the morning of the seventh day, rise at dawn and bathe in water infused with CLOVER, BASIL, and ROSE PETALS.

Wear white, or go naked.

Cast a circle.

Raise energy.

Sit facing East, and light a WHITE CANDLE.

Say,

As the grain grows,
As the sun grows,
As the moon grows.

Chant,

I grow,
I reap,
I receive.

Visualize each stage concentrating and projecting the image into the SPROUTS.

Eat the sprouts.

Say,

Bud in me,
Blosom in me,
Fruit in me.

Say each line three times, visualizing and concentrating.

Save SEVEN SPROUTS and wrap in BLACK SILK.

Bind the spell.

Earth the power.

Release the circle.

That night, bury the sprouts with a SILVER COIN (a dime is OK).

SAFE SPACE SPELL

(Can be done on a Sunday, Monday, or Friday.)

Cast a circle.

Raise energy.

Sit facing South, and light a GREEN, BLUE, or YELLOW CANDLE.

Hold in both hands a CUP of MILK mixed with SUGAR and SAFFRON.

Visualize, one after another, all the people and places who have made you feel safe and secure. Concentrate and project the feeling into the milk.

Raise the cup to your mouth and breathe the feeling of security into it.

Look at the candle flame and visualize three women, one dressed in black, one in white, one in red. They move toward you and merge into one figure. Imagine She places her hands over yours and lifts the cup to your lips.

Say, "I have been with you from the beginning."

Drink the milk.

Earth the power and feel the safe space within yourself.

Bind the spell.

Release the circle.

SPELL TO KNOW THE CHILD WITHIN

Cast a circle.

Sit facing south, and light a GREEN or BLUE CANDLE.

You should have a child's DOLL or STUFFED ANIMAL. Take it in your hands and sprinkle it with SALT WATER.

Say, "I name you _____." (Use your own childhood name or nickname.)

Hold it in your arms, croon to it, rock it, and talk to it. Tell it everything you would have liked to hear as a child. Let it talk to you, and tell you how it feels and what it wants. Let your voice change. Play.

Raise energy, and visualize that you are pouring it into the doll, who is your own child self. Create an image of of your child self as you would have liked to be, and project it into your doll. Continue until the doll is glowing with white light and love.

Kiss the doll. Wrap it in WHITE CLOTH and lay it to rest on your altar.

Bind the spell.

Earth the power.

Open the circle.

(Repeat as often as you need or want to.)

SPELL TO BE FRIENDS WITH YOUR WOMB

(To be done on the first night of your menstruation. Especially helpful for those women who suffer from cramps, or irregular or excessive bleeding.)

Cast a circle.

Light a RED CANDLE. Face South.

With the third finger of your left hand, rub a few drops of your menstrual blood on the candle.

Raise power. Feel the blood's essence drawn into the flame. Let the light warm you and fill you. Feel your own blood as the essence of the life force.

Draw light from the candle into your womb. Let it fill you and spread slowly through your entire body from your womb center, charging you with energy and warmth.

Bind the spell.

Earth the power.

Open the circle.

Herbal Charms

Herbal charms, as I make them, are small bags filled with herbs and other symbolic objects. They are made of a simple square or circle of cloth of the proper color, tied with thread of the proper color, and then charged with energy. They can be worn on the person or kept in the house to attract what you desire. If you wish, they can be made of silk or velvet and elaborately embroidered with symbols—or they can be simple cotton tied with string. You can create your own herbal charms tailored to your own needs. Here are some suggested combinations:

TO ATTRACT MONEY

Use a square of green cloth, filled with borage, lavender, High Joan the Conqueress Root, and saffron (or any four appropriate herbs), a few crystals of rock salt, and three silver coins. (Dimes, although no longer solid silver, seem to work fine). Tie with gold and silver thread in eight knots.

TO ATTRACT LOVE

Use a circle of rose-colored or red (for more sexually passionate love) cloth. Fill it with acacia flowers, myrtle, rose petals or buds, jasmine flowers, and lavender. Add a red felt heart and a copper coin or ring. Tie it with blue thread or ribbon, in seven knots.

TO HEAL A BROKEN HEART

Use a circle of blue cloth, filled with All-Heal, Balm of Gilead buds, feverfew, myrtle, and rose petals (white). Take a white felt heart cut into two pieces, sew it together with blue thread while charging the charm, and add it to the herbs. Add a copper coin to draw new love. Tie it with white thread.

FOR PROTECTION

Use a circle of blue cloth, filled with nine protective herbs. Add a silver coin, or better, a silver crescent moon (perhaps an earring). Tie it with white or silver thread.

TO GET A JOB

Use a square of green cloth. Fill it with bay laurel, lavender, and High Joan the Conqueress Root. Add four other herb governed by—

- *Mercury*—for a job involving communications
- *The Moon*—for a job involving healing, women's work or health, or psychology
- *Jupiter*—for a job involving leadership and responsibility, or the law
- *Mars*—for a job requiring aggressive, assertive action
- *The Sun*—for a job outdoors, in agriculture or nature, or for an easygoing, enjoyable job
- *Saturn*—for architecture, history, or any job where you will be limiting others' actions or freedom (police work, for example)

Add a silver coin, for wealth, and pictures of any important tools you may use in your work. Tie it with purple thread.

FOR INNER POWER

Use a square of royal purple cloth, filled with bay leaf, Dragon's Blood, elder flowers, High Joan the Conqueress Root, rosemary, vervain, oak leaf, holly leaf or berries, and mistletoe. Tie with blue thread, and embroider or draw on your own personal symbol.

FOR ELOQUENCE

Use a circle of yellow or iridescent cloth. Fill it with fennel, hazel, mandrake, and valerian. Add a silver coin, and tie with orange and violet thread.

TO WIN IN COURT

Use a square of blue cloth, filled with bay laurel, High Joan the Conqueress Root, St. Joan's Wort, and vervain. If you are being persecuted by an enemy, add a pine nut or part of a cone, some tobacco, and some mustard seed. Put in a small picture of an open eye, so that justice will look favorably on you. Tie with purple thread.

Feel free to improvise on these charms, to add symbols of your own or to try other combinations of herbs. What feels best to you will work best.

TO CHARGE AN HERBAL CHARM

Assemble all your materials on your altar.

Cast a circle.

Light a CANDLE of an appropriate color. If you wish, burn INCENSE.

Raise energy.

In MORTAR and PESTLE, grind together all the herbs for your charm. Visualize the image or emotion you desire, and project it into the herbs as you grind them together. Draw or create any other symbols you may wish.

Gather together the herbs and other objects into the cloth. Twist the top around them and tie it once with thread.

Breathe on the charm and charge it with air.

Pass it through the candle flame, and charge it with fire.

Sprinkle a few drops of WATER on it, and charge it with water.

Dip it into SALT, or touch it to your PENTACLE, and charge it with earth.

Hold it in your hands, breathe on it, and charge it fully with all the energy you can raise, concentrating on your visualization.

Drop to the ground, relax, and earth the power.

Bind the spell, tying it as you do so.

Open the circle.

HEALING IMAGE SPELL

Create your poppet (a wax or cloth doll) to represent the person you wish to help already completely healed and whole. Do not represent the problem; rather, create the image of the solution. Concentrate as you make the poppet.

Cast a circle.

Light a BLUE CANDLE.

Sprinkle your POPPET with SALT WATER. Say, "Blessed be, thou creature made by art. By art made, by art changed. Thou art not wax (cloth, wood, etc.) but flesh and blood. I name thee _____ (name the person you wish to heal). Thou art s(he), between the worlds, in all the worlds. Blessed be."

Hold the poppet in your hands. Breathe on it, and charge it with energy. Visualize your friend completely healed, completely well. Charge particular parts of the doll especially strongly to correspond with the parts of your friend that are hurt or diseased.

Visualize your friend completely charged with white light, well, happy, and filled with energy.

Bind the spell.

Earth the power.

Open the circle.

Keep the poppet on your altar until your friend is healed. Then, cast another circle, again take the poppet, sprinkle it with water, and say, "Blessed be, child of light. By art changed, by art unmade. I take from thee thy name _____ (your friend's name) and name thee poppet, creature of wax (or cloth, or whatever). Between the worlds, in all the worlds, so mote it be. The link is broken. Blessed be."

Open the circle. If the poppet contains physical links, burn it in an open fire. If not, dispose of it any way you wish, or give it to your friend as a keepsake.

TO BIND AN ENEMY

Cast a circle.

Light a BLACK CANDLE. Burn INCENSE of Saturn.

Sprinkle your poppet with SALT WATER. Say, "Blessed be, thou creature made by art. By art made, by Art changed. Thou art not wax (cloth, etc.) but flesh and blood. I name thee _____ (the person you are binding). Thou art (s)he, between the worlds, in all the worlds, So mote it be.

Hold the poppet in your hands. Visualize a silver net falling over it, and binding the person it represents.

Take RED RIBBON and wrap it around the poppet, tying it firmly, and binding all parts of the body that could conceivably harm others. Charge the binding with power.

Say,

> By air and earth,
> By water and fire,
> So be you bound,
> As I desire.
> By three and nine,
> Your power I bind.
> By moon and sun,
> My will be done.
> Sky and sea
> Keep harm from me.
> Cord go round,
> Power be bound,
> Light revealed,
> Now be sealed.

Earth the power.

Open the circle.

Bury the poppet during a waning moon, far from your house, under a heavy rock.

Notes

1. Robert Duncan, "The Fire: Passages 13," in Hayden Carruth, ed., *The Voice that Is Great Within Us* (New York: Bantam Books, 1971).
2. Dion Fortune, *Moon Magic* (New York: Weiser, 1972), p. 117.
3. John C. Lilly, *The Center of the Cyclone* (New York: Julian Press, 1972), p. 218.
4. The word *hex* actually derives from the Latin word for "six," and became identified with spell casting because of the six-sided symbolic forms used in German and Pennsylvania Dutch magic. In those traditions, it does not have a negative connotation, but in general usage it is identified with cursing or sending negative energy and bad luck.

8 Energy: The Cone of Power

Between the Worlds

The chant begins as a low crooning, a deep vibration barely heard. One by one, voices take it up:

"Aaaaaaaah...."

"Ooooooooooh...."

"Eeeeeeeeee...."

It rises, an eerie nonharmony. The air seems to thicken, to dance with electric sparks that begin to fly, circle, spin, careen madly in the center of the circle.

"Eeeeeeeoooooooh...."

The air glows, a luminous cloud, that pulsates, burning with a black heat. The chant opens, full-throated, a ringing chord...

The light begins to spin, a shining wheel of breath, turning and turning. Voices rise higher. The light spirals upward, faster, faster, as it narrows toward the top. The sound is indescribable; the voices are the shrieking wind, the howling of wolves, the high cries of tropical birds, the swarming of bees, the sigh of receding waves. The cone builds and builds a pulsing spiral, a unicorn's horn, rare and marvelous. Its tip cannot be seen. It is flooded with color: red, blue, green, sunlight moonlight. It rises—

"Now!" A voice cries out. A final shriek. The cone flies off, an arrow *loosed to do its work, sucking the air clean. The coven collapses, limp dolls, sprawled on the floor. They smile, deliciously relaxed.*

They have sent the cone of power.

> "Four laws of ecology: (1) everything is connected to everything else, (2) everything must go somewhere, (3) nature knows best, and (4) there is no such thing as a free lunch."
>
> Barry Commoner[1]

The primary principle of magic is connection. The universe is a fluid, ever-changing energy pattern, not a collection of fixed and separate things. What affects one thing affects, in some way, all things: All is interwoven into the continous fabric of being. Its warp and weft are energy, which is the essence of magic.

Energy is ecstasy. When we drop the barriers and let power pour through, it floods the body, pulsing through every nerve, arousing every artery, coursing like a river that cleanses as it moves. In the eye of the storm, we rise on the winds that roar through mind and body, throbbing a liquid note as the voice pours out shimmering honey in waves of golden light, that as they pass, leave peace. No drug can take us so high; no thrill pierce us so deep because we have felt the essence of all delight, the heart of joy, the end of desire. Energy is love, and love is magic.

Of all the disciplines of magic, the art of moving energy is the simplest and most natural. It comes as easily as breathing, as making sound. Picture the power in motion, and it moves. Feel it flowing, and it flows, cleansing, healing, renewing, and revitalizing as it passes.

Witches conceive of the subtle energies as being, to a trained awareness, tangible, visible, and malleable. They are, as Dion Fortune says, "more tangible than emotion—less tangible than protoplasm." We can learn to sense them and mold them into form.

The laws of ecology are the laws of energy. Everything is interconnected; every action, every movement of forces, changes the universe. "You must not change one thing, one pebble, one grain of sand, until you know what good and evil will follow on that act. The world is in balance, in Equilibrium. A Wizard's power of changing and summoning can shake the balance of the world. It is dangerous, that power. It is most perilous. It must follow knowledge and serve need. To light a candle is to cast a shadow."[2]

Yet the equilibrium of the universe is not static, but dynamic. Energy is constantly in motion. It cannot be stopped. Again, using water as our metaphor, when we block its flow it becomes stagnant and foul. When it flows freely, it cleanses and purifies. The rituals, spells, and meditations of the Craft center on aiding energy to flow.

Energy flows in spirals. Its motion is always circular, cyclical, wave-like. The spiral motion is revealed in the shape of galaxies, shells, whirl-pools, DNA. Sound, light, and radiation travel in waves—which themselves are spirals viewed in a flat plane.[3] The moon waxes and wanes, as do the tides, the economy, and our own vitality.

The implications of the spiral model are many. Essentially, it means that no form of energy can be exerted indefinitely in one direction only. Always, it will reach a peak, a point of climax, and then turn. In personal terms, activity is balanced by passivity. Exertion must be followed by rest; creativity by quiescence. Men cannot live entirely in the active mode, nor women in the passive—as patriarchal culture expects—and be whole. No one can be constantly creative, constantly sexual, constantly angry—or constantly *anything* that requires energy. Recognizing this alternation can help us sustain a dynamic, healthy balance.

Socially and politically, movement toward greater freedom is usually followed by movement toward greater security. Expansion is followed by contraction. The wise can learn to take advantage of this alternation, instead of being buffeted by it and forfeiting gains during every period of reaction. Freedom and security are not mutually exclusive goals.

Political actions could be more effective if they were consciously understood to be energy workings. Power can move through a group as it does through an individual, renewing and revitalizing group energy. An important aspect of this movement is grounding the energy after it is raised, consciously recognizing its fall as well as its peak, and returning it to the earth, its elemental source. When energy is not grounded, the group remains "charged"—like a room full of static electricity, with what soon becomes felt as tension and anxiety. Instead of generating a useful current, such groups short-circuit themselves, and their members "burn out."

Rallies, meetings, conferences, and demonstrations raise power—but rarely do organizers think about grounding it afterward. Grounding does not have to be elaborate—simply remembering to formally end each working session will help earth the power. Group members might simply take hands in a circle and sit quietly for a moment. Recently, there has been a growing tendency in the feminist movement to incorporate ritual into conferences and demonstrations, for the express purpose of grounding and channeling the power raised. The following is an account of a ritual several women[4] and I created in November 1978, as part of a conference on violence and pornography, with the theme "Take Back the Night!" The climax of the weekend was a march through the North Beach section of San Francisco, the heart of the topless-bottomless and massage parlor scene. The ritual took place in Washington Square Park, at the end of the march.

The women pour in from the street. It takes so much longer than we expected. I had no conception of 3,000 women in a mass. . . .

Witches, at the front of the march, aspurge North Beach with salt water. They chant Laurel's couplet:

> Wipe the slate clean,
> Dream a new dream!

At Broadway and Columbus, the artists create a mini-ritual around their float. In the front, it is a giant, candle-lit Madonna; behind, slabs of dead meat and pornographic magazines. A strong symbol of images that squeeze women into narrow, hurtful roles. They bring out the float, chant, tear the pornography into confetti. Holly Near sings.

We wait at the park, too nervous to leave and risk not getting back in time. The Witches arrive at the entrance to the park, form a double line, a birth canal. They hold lighted candles and incense and sprinkle the women with salt water as they enter:

> From a woman you were born into this world,
> By women you are born into this circle.

We are onstage (the back of Anne's truck). Our backdrop is the lit façade of the church: an irony. Lennie Schwendinger of Lighten Up has created beautiful lighting for us—it is the first time I have done a ritual so theatrical, where the bright lights cut us off from the crowd, who become "audience." Our pool of light seems the only world—and I'm not sure I like it. Behind us, in the trees, a woman's acrobatic troupe, Fly By Night, perform a slow, aerial dance.

Nina leads the chant:

> We're taking back the night,
> The night is ours!

The women are not dancing, as we had hoped. The audience-performer image is too strong—they are watching us. I feel awkward, unsure of what to do. The chant dies away—still, crowds are flowing into the park. . . .

Toni Marcus begins to play her violin. The sound carries over the park, electric, magical. . . .

We can put off starting no longer. I take the microphone, and say that we should turn for a moment and look at each other, at how beautiful we are, how real we are. . . .

I say, "We have been taught that women's bodies are unclean, that our sexuality degrades us, that we must either be Virgins or whores. But we accept neither image! Instead we raise the banner of the naked Goddess, whose body is truth, who is within us, in the human spirit.

"We say that our bodies are sacred, because they bring forth life, because they are life, because they give *us* pleasure, because with them we make, build, think, laugh, create, and do. . . . "

Lee and I lead the responsive chant:

> "Our bodies are sacred,
> Our breasts are sacred,
> Our wombs are sacred,
> Our hands are sacred. . . ."

It builds and builds.

> "Our voices are sacred,
> Our voices carry power!
> The power to create!
> The power to change the world!
> Let go—let them become sound—
> Chant without words—let them be heard!"

The voices roar into the night. Not a cone—it is too strong, too amorphous —a tidal wave sweeping out of the park.

It stops. Quietly, I lead a soft, low chant. A humming—the buzz of two thousand bees, a deep throb. . . .

Over it, Hallie leads the meditation:

"Softly, softly now begin to feel the earth's energy beneath your feet as She dances with us. . . .

"Close your eyes . . . feel your strength sparkling through your body and women around you. This is the power generated by our marching, our chanting, our dancing, our destruction of the symbols of violence. . . . Know that each of us, and all of us together, have the power to change the world. Feel the effects of your action rippling out into the world . . . reflect on how your life will be different. . . .

"Open your eyes and look about you . . . see our strength in one another's face . . . know that we are strong. Know what the women of old knew . . . that the night must belong to us. Know that we are women who take back the night. Know that the night is ours!"

Cheers, laughter, screams, kisses. Some of us touch the earth. The women follow. The ritual is done.

Nature knows best. Magic is part of nature; it does not controvert natural laws. It is through study and observation of nature, of the visible, physical reality, that we can learn to understand the workings of the underlying reality.

Magic teaches us to tap sources of energy that are unlimited, infinite. Nevertheless, there is no "free lunch." To raise energy, we must expend energy. We cannot get without giving. In working magic, we expend our own physical and emotional energy and must take care to replenish it. Magic is an art and a discipline, that demands work, practice, and effort before it can be perfected. Every change brings consequences; some seen and some unforeseen.

In coven rituals, energy raised is most often molded into the form of a cone, the Cone of Power. The base of the cone is the circle of coveners; its apex can focus on an individual, an object, or a collectively visualized image. At times, the cone is allowed to rise and fall naturally, as in the power chant described in Chapter Three. It may also be sent off in a burst of force, directed by one person, who may be part of the circle, or may stand at its center. When a group is familiar with the exercises given in Chapter Three, the following will prepare members for more advanced energy workings:

EXERCISE 45: THE CONE OF POWER

All ground and center. Standing or sitting in a circle, take hands. Begin with a Group Breath, and gradually build a wordless Power Chant.

As the energy builds, visualize it swirling clockwise around the circle. *See* it as a blue-white light. It spirals up into a cone form—an upright shell, a cornucopia. Hold the visualization until it glows.

The High Priestess (or whoever directs the cone) senses the movement of energy. She holds the visualized image, the object of the working, clearly in mind. When the power reaches its peak, she cries out, "Now!"

(This requires great sensitivity and practice. It can only be learned by experience—which of necessity implies many mistakes along the way. If the High Priestess is afraid of power, she will ground the cone too quickly. If she is indecisive, she will let it go on too long, so that its full force is dissipated. The best course is to relax into the power and not think about when to ground it. When the right time comes, a sensitive High Priestess will find herself calling the drop, out of intuition, not conscious decision.) Coveners let the energy go, fall to the ground, and relax completely, seeing the cone fly off to its objective. They breathe deeply and let the residue of power drain into the earth. Generally, a trance state follows.

Rhythm, drums, hand claps, and dance movements may also be used in building the cone. Covens should experiment, and feel free to try many methods. Other words, names, Goddess or God names, or simple incantations can be used to raise power. The energy can also be molded into other forms: for example, a fountain, that rises and flows back on the coveners, a wave form, or a glowing sphere. Possibilities are infinite.

EXERCISE 46: WOMB CHANT

(Coveners lie in a wheel, with heads at center, on their backs.)

Stretch out your arms and touch the womb of the person next to you. If he is a man, place your hand on the spot where his womb would be, which is the womb center of his energy body. Clasp hands on each other's bellies.

Ground and center. Begin with a Group Breath and Power Chant. As you breathe, imagine that you breathe through the womb. See it glow white, like the moon, as you inhale power. See it glow red with blood, with creative fire. Feel the power of the womb to create—not the physical womb only, but the inner womb where ideas and visions are generated. Let your breath become a sound that resonates in the womb.

With each breath—feel its power—feel the woman or man next to you—feel her power—feel how we are linked—how strong we are when we are linked— breathe the power of vision—breathe the womb power of creation—and let your voice carry that power....

The chant will build and die naturally. Earth the power and end.

EXERCISE 47: FORMAL GROUNDING

(This is for use in rituals and group workings.)

All clasp hands. If you wish, all take hold of the coven wand. Raise them high, and visualize the power flowing downward through your hands. Ground and center, and Leader gives the line, and coveners repeat:

> Source to source
> Flow through me
> Above and below,
> Turn to return,
> Clearly
> Fade to grow.
> As I will,
> So it shall be.
> Spell make it so!

Lower hands as you speak, until they (the wand) touch the ground. Exhale, and feel the power flow down.

Witches conceive of subtle energy as being of three basic types. Again, this is meant as a conceptual model, not a doctrine. Each person is also seen as an energy field, with subtle bodies that surround and interpenetrate the physical body.

The first type of energy is "elemental" or *raith* energy, also called *etheric substance* and *ectoplasm* by some occultists. It is the subtle force of the elements; earth, air, water and fire, of plants, and animals. Elemental vitality sustains the physical body. We feed off of it, and its movement through our bodies "primes the pump," so to speak, drawing the higher forms of power.

The *raith,* the elemental energy body, is also called the etheric body and the vital body, because through it we receive our vitality, our physical and emotional energy. It is the body of Younger Self, and it perceives

through the starlight consciousness of the right hemisphere. Its perceptions are often more accurate than our conscious perceptions—but its
ability to express them in words is limited. The *raith* extends out from the
physical body for only about a centimeter, and appears to most psychics
as a blue-gray glow.

Animals, plants, clean air and water, physical exercise, and sex increase vital energy. When *raith*-energy is low, people become physically
ill, tired, and emotionally depressed. Magic uses a great deal of vital
energy, and anyone who practices magic regularly must take care not to
become depleted. Regular physical exercise is one of the best methods of
increasing vital energy. Being outdoors, consciously making contact with
nature and the elements, also restores vitality. Witches also traditionally
keep special pets, "familiars,"[5] in part as a source of elemental energy.

Grounding before every magical working or psychic exercise prevents
us from becoming depleted. Instead of draining our own vitality, we tap
directly into the unlimited sources of elemental energy in the earth. Power
flows through us, not out of us.

The second type of energy can be thought of as the energy of consciousness, of thoughts, dreams, fantasies, mind—auric or astral energy.
The astral body, as it is called by occultists, can be thought of as the body
of Talking Self. It is the force that makes up the "astral plane," the hidden
reality behind appearances, the dream realm, sometimes called the Over-
world, or the Other Side. The *raith* and astral body together make up a
person's aura,[6] or energy field. The astral body is less dense than the *raith*
and extends out about nine inches from the physical body. If the truth
were known, I believe that every psychic would see it somewhat differently. To me, it appears like a glowing, misty cloud, sometimes obscuring a
person's features. Colors, unlike any seen with the physical eyes, shift and
play within the aura. It is strongest about the head and easiest to see in
dim light, against a plain background, especially when either I or the
subject are in a light trance.

The astral body can be projected away from the physical body. Consciousness is not bound by the limitations of the physical senses. Out-of-
body experiences may be vividly sensual, or they may simply involve
awareness without sight or sound. The region of travel may be astral or
material; purely subjective, purely objective, or a mixture of both.

The third type of energy is that of the High Self, of the Gods. It is
the finest of vibrations, yet the most powerful. When we invoke the
Goddess and God in rituals, we connect with this energy. That connection
is the heart of the greater magic, of mystical ecstasy.

Generally, Younger Self is far more aware of subtle energy than Talking Self. We are all psychic, unconsciously. The difficulty is in finding
ways to translate that awareness into terms the conscious mind can understand. Yogis and Eastern occultists talk about opening "the third eye," the

pychic center located in the pineal gland, in the center of the forehead. For me, this is secondary to opening the energy centers in the womb and solar plexus, which connect directly with Younger Self. To put it less esoterically, when the conscious and unconscious minds can communicate freely, in a healthy, highly vital physical body, the higher consciousness will awaken naturally, in its own time. A useful tool in establishing this communication is a pendulum.

EXERCISE 48: PENDULUM EXERCISE

(A pendulum can be a necklace, a ring, key, watch, or crystal on a string or chain—anything that will swing freely and that is emotionally appealing.)

Ground and center, and breathe deeply, from the diaphragm and belly. Hold the pendulum lightly by the top of its chain, so that it hangs about two inches above the open palm of your other hand.

Relax, and tell yourself that the pendulum will begin to swing sunwise, reflecting the energy in your hand. Wait quietly. For most people, it will soon begin to circle. (While it seems to move of its own volition, actually involuntary movements of your own hand cause its motion. Don't attempt to control it consciously—the purpose is to let your unconscious speak to you through your own muscle movements, reflected in the pendulum.

If it does not move, deliberately make it circle a few times, showing Younger Self what you want. Wait. Some people will need several sessions before the pendulum will work.)

EXERCISE 49: SENSING THE AURA: PENDULUM METHOD

(Two people are needed for this exercise, a sender and a receiver. Both should be successful at Exercise 48.)

Sender sits in a relaxed position, breathing deeply from the belly. The receiver holds the pendulum so that it swings about two feet over the sender's head. Both ground and center.

Slowly, the receiver lowers the pendulum, telling herself that it will begin to swing when it hits the sender's aura. Practice until you can feel the edge or corona of the aura. When the pendulum reacts consistently, explore the outlines of the astral body. Search out areas of tension, and note vortexes of energy.

Exchange positions and repeat.

EXERCISE 50: SENSING THE AURA: DIRECT METHOD

Again, the sender sits in a relaxed position, breathing deeply. Both ground and center. The receiver lowers her hand, palm toward the sender, into the field of the aura. Stop when you can feel the outer, radiating edge of the astral body. The "feel" will at first be extremely subtle—a slight tingling, heat, an almost imperceptible difference; perhaps only a sudden urge to stop. Scan the astral body with your hands—again feeling for areas of tension, which may register as cold, as absence of energy, or simply as uneasiness. Sense the body's power centers, as well. Share your impressions with the sender, and compare results with the pendulum method.

Exchange positions and repeat.

EXERCISE 51: DAMPING AND PROJECTING ENERGY

(The sender sits in a relaxed position. The receiver can use either the pendulum or direct method of sensing the aura.)

Ground and center. The receiver locates the sender's aura, above the crown of her head. Ask the sender to do the Tree of Life Meditation, and, as the energy rises, to visualize and feel it as a strong stream of flowing water, bursting up from her head like a fountain. The receiver observes the pendulum's swing become stronger and faster as the energy increases—or feels the difference through her hand.

Ask the sender to damp the energy—visualize herself swathed in cotton wool or smothered in mashed potatoes. Feel the change—see the motion of the pendulum decrease.

Practice until the sender becomes adept at projecting and damping energy, and the receiver becomes adept at sensing the change. Test yourselves by having the sender either damp or project power without first telling the receiver, who should be able to feel which is happening. Exchange positions, and also practice projecting and damping energy through other power centers you have discovered.

EXERCISE 52: SEEING THE AURA

(This exercise is best practiced in a group. Each of the members can take turns being the subject. All should first be proficient at sensing the aura.)

Set up a plain background—a black cloth or a white sheet. The subject should stand against it or lie down on it, and if possible, be nude. Everyone should ground and center, and relax with one of the exercises in Chapter Three, which will produce a light state of trance. The lighting should be dim.

Breathe deeply, from your diaphragm, and let your eyes relax. Lightly scan the space around the subject. You may see a thin, glowing line around her body—the *raith*. Around it, look for the cloudlike astral body, which may appear to glow, or may seem like a shadow, oddly lighter than the background. To some, the astral body will simply appear as a subtle difference between foreground and background—a wavering, like heat waves over a radiator. It may appear and blank out, shift, move, and change, but will gradually become more stable as you accustom yourself to astral vision.

The colors in the aura have many interpretations. Rather than following a set rule, "feel-see" them for yourself. The quality of the color is most illuminating—is it clear and bright, or muddy and dull? What does it make you think of? Feel? Are you attracted or repelled by it? What associations does it have? Share perceptions and feedback, and with time and experience you will be able to interpret what you see.

The subject can practice projecting and damping energy, and the viewers can learn to see the energy move. In later sessions, subjects can also practice projecting colors and energy forms. The more group members practice, the more acute their perceptions will become.

When you have learned to sense or see energy on individuals, you will be more sensitive to the forms and levels of power in rituals. Inanimate objects also can store a charge of subtle power. (See Chapter Four.) Examine your magical tools, and sense the aura of power.

Awareness of energy is awareness of the great dance of the universe. Seemingly intangible, it underlies all that we can touch. It is the only constant, although it is constant change; eternal flux. Awareness of your own energy is the awareness that flesh and spirit are one, that thou art Goddess, eternally linked, connected, at one with the moving spirit of All.

Notes

1. Barry Commoner, *The Closing Circle* (New York: Knopf, 1971), p. 18.
2. Ursula K. LeGuin, *A Wizard of Earthsea* (New York: Bantam Books, 1975), p. 44.
3. An easy way to visualize this is to examine a child's Slinky toy: a spiral formed of thin metal coils. Stretch it out and look at it from the side: You will see wave forms.
4. Besides myself, Hallie Iglehart, Nina Wise, Ann Hershey, Lee Schwing, Helen Dannenberg, Diane Broadstreet, Lennie Schwendinger and Toni Marcus, as well as others, participated in planning & executing the ritual.
5. "Familiars" have many uses. They can divine; a cat can point out herbs for spells or Tarot cards with her paw, for example. They may "ground" negative energy; Cats are especially good at this, and it does not harm them. Dogs exude vitality, and you can no more drain them than you can outrun them. During rituals and magical workings, however, animals often will try to enter the circle and soak up the power. Animals often become nervous when people trance and leave their bodies, and will attempt to "bring them back" by leaping on their stomachs, nipping their feet, and licking their faces. Animals should either be extremely well trained, or excluded from the room during trance work.
6. Some occult systems postulate a further hierarchy of "mental" and "spiritual" bodies. I have attempted to present a conceptual system that is simple enough to be easily grasped and workable and consistent with both Craft tradition and my own experience. Again, this is an elaborate metaphor, not a Sacred Truth. If some other metaphor works better for you, use it!

9 *Trance*

Between the Worlds

I say, "Relax, breathe deep, and look into the well—the well beyond the world's end.... Call up the shadow you saw in the dream."

Valerie sinks deeper into trance. Her aura glows—the face disappears beneath it. She sighs; a shadow clouds the glow.

"She's here ... now I see it—the same shadow I saw months ago—it's the woman who appeared in my dream last night, and stole my work from me."

"What does she look like?"

"Tall, icy—her face is made of knives, clashing and revolving."

"How do you feel?"

"Afraid."

"What must you do?"

"Fight her—defeat her."

"Ask her name."

We wait. The shadow grows darker.

"She won't tell me."

"Demand it."

"I can't—can't get it."

"What do you need to get it?"

"Power."

"Where is power?"

"In—my wand."

Quietly I cross the room, take her wand from the altar, and place it in the limp hand. Her fingers close around it. Sparks from an inner battle dance around her head.

"Her name is anger," Valerie says softly.

"Who is she?"

"Me."

"What must you do?"

"Become her, take her in."

"How do you feel?"

"Afraid. The knives will cut me."

"Yes."

"I won't be strong enough."

"You are."

"How can I be sure?"

"Because you were able to learn her name."

She sucks in her breath. Her aura explodes in fireworks of red and violet. Her body shakes; she sobs, screams, gasps.

"She's choking me."

"Keep breathing—deep—relax."

She pants. Her face is sweating. Gently I wipe it off. There is a white flash over her head—she signs, relaxing. Her face is clear again.

"I've done it. I've taken her in. She is me."

"How do you feel?"

"Strong. At peace."

> "The seekers of new mind states—the mind control devotees, encounter group enthusiasts, the drug takers, the psychics, the meditators—all are on a journey into the interior universe trying to burst the limits of the socially conditioned mind. Whether acceptable or unacceptable, moral or immoral, wise or foolish, the mind of man is stirring toward a new evolution."
>
> Dr. Barbara Brown[1]

The universe is a dance of energy, a uni-verse, a single song of ever-changing rhythms and harmonies. Sustaining the melody of the physical world is a rich interplay of counter-point and descant. We see only a fraction of the band of radiation that makes up the spectrum; we hear only a small range of possible frequencies of sound. Ordinarily, we are conscious of only one, isolated melody; we listen to only the piccolo out of a infinite orchestra. To trance is to shift and expand our awareness: to pick out the beat of the drum, the throbbing violins, the cry of saxophones, to know the interwoven harmonies played in new keys, to thrill to the soaring symphony itself.

Trance states, states of nonordinary consciousness, have been called by many names: expanded awareness, meditation, hypnosis, "getting high." Trance techniques are found in every culture and religion—from the rhythmic chant of a Siberian shaman to free association on a Freudian analyst's couch. The pull to burst beyond the limits of the socially conditioned mind seems to be a deep-seated human need. There are an infinite variety of possible states of trance. We all experience light trance whenever we are daydreaming; concentrating deeply; watching a play, film, or television show; turning attention inward; and forgetting the sensory world. In deep states, we may have experiences such as John C. Lilly describes:

"I moved into a region of strange life forms, neither above nor below the human level, but strange beings, of strange shapes, metabolisms, thought forms, and so forth. These beings reminded me of some of the drawings I had seen of Tibetan gods and goddesses, of ancient Greek portrayals of their gods and of some of the bug-eyed monsters of science fiction."[2]

Deeper levels of trance may open up paranormal senses, psychic awareness, precognition. We may empathize and connect with other beings and life forms; in Balinese, the word for *trance* means "to become."

Occultists and metaphysicians delight in attempting to order, define, and rank the various states of consciousness, a process somewhat like attempting to measure a cloud with a ruler. I will not indulge in it here, because I feel it creates an erroneous impression that we know more than we do about these states. When we impose a left-brain, linear order on a right-brain, complex pattern, we tend to feel that we have gained control of the phenomenon—when we have done nothing more than point out a few stars with the beam of our flashlight. Classifying consciousness also encourages "higher than Thou" games of oneupmanship. People waste energy defining which state they are in, as if consciousness were a cosmic grammar school, in which third-graders were entitled to look down on kindergarteners. The point is not what level we are on, but what we are learning.

Sharing and comparing trance experiences, and reading descriptions of altered states of awareness, can, however, yield useful insights. One of the most important realizations is that trance states are both subjective and objective. There is a continuum of experience, part of which is relevant only to the individual's interior world, and part of which can be shared and agreed on by others. What begins in the imagination becomes real—even though that reality is of a different order than the reality of the physical senses. It is the reality of the underlying energy currents that shape the universe.

Ordinary perception is a process of the physical senses. What we see, hear, feel, smell, or taste is further conditioned by language, the set of cultural symbols that allows us to name what we have perceived. The name shapes an amorphous sensory stimulus into something recognizable and familiar—and guides our response. But perception in the trance state is not bound by the physical senses. "Astral colors" are not seen with the physical eyes; sounds are "heard" only in our minds. The currents of subtle energy fit no sensory modes. Our language does not name them or contain words that adequately describe them.

Trance perception must be translated into the modes we know. In essence, we construct an elaborate metaphor world, to represent the reality of what is called the *astral*. If we are adept enough, we create metaphor senses that "see," "hear," "feel," "smell," and "taste." Those pseudosensory perceptions are then further interpreted in a symbolic system that fits our expectations. For example, Lilly describes meeting two helpful "guides," who "may be two aspects of my own functioning at the supraself level. They may be entities in other spaces, other universes than our consensus reality. They may be helpful constructs, helpful concepts that I use for my own future evolution. They may be representatives of an esoteric hidden school. They may be concepts functioning in my own human biocomputer at the supraspecies level. They may be members of a civilization a hundred thousand years or so ahead of ours."[3] A devout Christian, however, might call the same entities "angels" or perhaps "Blessed saints," and "see" them with wings, harps, haloes, and all the appropriate trappings. A Witch might call them the two linked motes of consciousness within the High Self, and "see" them in female and male human forms, that glow blue.

Astral vision is always a mixture of the subjective and the objective. Sensory forms and symbolic interpretations are subjective, the cloak of objective energies and entities. Whether those entities are internal forces or external beings depends on how one defines the self. It is more romantic and exciting (and probably truer) to see them as at least partly external; it is psychologically healthier and probably wiser to see them as internal. A thing can be internal and still be objective, still be real. A neurosis or conflict, for example, may be verified as real by others even before it is perceived by the self. And nothing external can be admitted into the psyche unless a corresponding internal force admits it. No "entity" can possess a soul that denies it entrance.

Astral energies can be molded into forms that will last and be perceived by more than one person. Collective beliefs and images also shape astral energies and create "places" and beings. Heaven, hell, and the Land of Youth all exist in the astral. The energy forms we collectively create, in turn, shape us and the world we live in.

Astral forms can be "anchored" into physical objects. When ancient people held that idols *were* their gods, they meant that the astral form of the god was keyed into the statue. In *Moon Magic,* Dion Fortune describes the anchoring of an energy form into a place of magical working, which "has to have the astral temple built over it, and that is the really important part; and this is how we do it—we sit down and imagine it—nothing more—*but*—it is the imagination of a trained mind!

"So we sat down, my friend and I . . . and we pictured the temple of Isis as we had known it near the Valley of the Kings in the great days of the cult. We pictured it in its broad outline, and then we pictured it in all its detail, describing what we saw till we made each other see it more and more clearly. We pictured the approach through the avenue of ram-headed sphinxes; the great pylon gate in the temenos wall; the court with its lotus pool; shadowed colonnades, and the great hall with its pillars. . . . And as we did this, alternately watching and describing—the phantasied scenes began to take on the semblance of objective reality and we found ourselves in them—no longer looking at them with the mind's eye, but walking about in them. After that there was no more effort of concentration, for the astral vision took charge."[4]

Consciousness can travel in the astral in many different ways. "Astral projection," described by many occultists, involves the separation of the astral body from its physical housing, retaining only a cord of etheric energy as a connection. In other words, it is the creation of a complete, vivid, sensory metaphor state, through which all perceptions can be understood. The astral body may move through the physical universe, although with difficulty. Most often, it remains within the realm of energy and thought forms that is the astral.

It is also possible to project consciousness alone, without the construction of a "body." Physical "sensation" is lessened, and a great deal of practice may be required in order to achieve clarity and learn to interpret perceptions, but this method is less draining of vitality and less dangerous.

The astral body, when projected, "feeds" off of the *raith,* and the practice can be devitalizing if it is engaged in too often. It is common to return feeling extremely cold and ravenously hungry. When learning to enter trance states, it is important to protect the health of the physical body by eating well, sleeping sufficiently, and exercising regularly.

Trance work of any kind should be conducted only in a safe, private place, where you can remain undisturbed. As trance temporarily lessens your perceptions of the outer world and its dangers, city parks, public beaches, streets, and busses where you may be mugged, robbed, or molested are not suitable locations. Cast a protective circle around your body before leaving it, with either an elaborate ritual or a simple visualization. This will create an energy barrier, assuring safety on the astral as you have assured it in the physical realm.

Trance states offer many possibilities besides astral projection. Trance unlocks the tremendous potential inherent in our unused awareness. We can augment our sensitivity, growth, and creativity.

In trance, we are more suggestible—a fact that underlies the most common uses of hypnosis. Suggestibility can seem frightening if we see it as opening people to control and exploitation by others. Actually, the self overrides any suggestions that contradict deeply ingrained moral or ethical principles or personal desires. Suggestion alone will not make an honest person a thief, nor an unwilling person a murderer. The Craft teaches the use of suggestion to help us consciously direct our own minds, not the minds of others. As we increase our awareness of the functioning of suggestion and learn to use it deliberately on ourselves, our suggestibility to others seems to decrease. The unconscious is no longer split off, but is in constant communication with the conscious mind and can no longer be easily programmed without our conscious consent.

We can use our own suggestibility for both physical and emotional healing. Mind and body are linked, and our emotional state contributes to disease, whether it is purely physical or psychosomatic. Suggestion can aid learning, increase concentration, and further creativity. It can also open up new forms of awareness and awaken the psychic senses.

Trance stimulates vision and imagination and opens up new sources of creativity. When the barriers between the unconscious and the conscious are crossed, ideas, images, plans, and solutions to problems arise freely. As the right-hemisphere, holistic vision is awakened, it becomes a rich source of insight, of new and original approaches to situations.

The psychic abilities also increase under trance. We are all psychic, unconsciously. Younger Self is aware of energy flows, communicates without words, senses the currents of the future, and knows how to channel power. In trance, we can become aware of that awareness and can perceive and shape the currents that move our lives.

Finally, in trance we find revelation. We invoke and become Goddess and God, linked to all that is. We experience union, ecstasy, openness. The limits of our perception, the fixation on a single note of the song, dissolve: We not only hear the music, but we dance the whirling, exhilarating, spiral dance of existence.

Trance can be dangerous, however, for the same reason it can be valuable—because it opens the gates to the unconscious mind. To pass through the gates, we must confront what has been called by occultists the Guardian, or the Shadow on the Threshold: the embodiment of all the impulses and qualities we have thrust into the unconscious because the conscious mind finds them unacceptable. All that we are and feel we should not be—sexual, angry, hostile, vulnerable, masochistic, self-hating, guilty, and even, perhaps, powerful or creative—squats in the doorway between Younger Self and Talking Self, refusing to let us pass until we have looked it in the face and acknowledged our own essential humanness. No fear is stronger than our fear of our own Shadow, and nothing is more destructive than the defenses we adopt in order to avoid the confrontation.

The real dangers of magic stem not from the Guardian or Shadow itself, nor from external entities or forces. They stem from our own defense strategies, which can be intensified and rigidified by trance and magic as they can by drugs or fanaticism. Magic can also help us dissolve those strategies, confront the Guardian—a process that is never as frightening in actuality as it is in anticipation—and win clear. But unless people are willing to face fear, and confront their own negative qualities, they will be defeated by what Yaqui sorceror Don Juan calls "the first of his natural enemies: Fear! A terrible enemy—treacherous, and difficult to overcome. It remains concealed at every turn of the way, prowling, waiting."[5]

There are many ways of running from the Shadow. Some people simply deny it and never approach a confrontation. Others attempt to destroy the Shadow by destroying themselves with drugs or alchohol.

A defense strategy favored by many "spiritual" people is an elaborate form of denial, an assertion that the individual has "gone beyond" the shadow qualities of sexuality, anger, passion, desire, and self-interest. Many religions cater exclusively to this strategy. Priests, ministers, gurus, and "enlightened masters" who adopt a posture of transcendent superiority have great appeal to people with similar defense systems, who are able to escape their personal confrontations by identifying as members of an elite, "enlightened" group. Thus are cults born and perpetuated.

But this strategy of avoidance is accompanied by tremendous anxiety. However much we assert our transcendence and detachment, the Shadow remains. We may attempt to be more than human—even achieve great success, near miracles—but we remain fallible, vulnerable. That vulnerability becomes terrifying and fascinating. It may lead us to spurious acts of self-sacrifice and masochism, or self-embraced martyrdom, as a desperate attempt to ourselves control that shadow fear. The history of Jim Jones and the People's Temple is a classic example.

Victor Anderson, Faery Priest, tells the story that when he was a young man beginning to study the Craft, he met two shining, beautiful guides on the astral, who told him that he must make a choice. If he wanted great magical power, he must give up the hope of a lasting love in his life. His reply was, "Powers of evil, begone! Get you to the Outer Darkness! I will have both power and love."

"How did you know that they were evil?" I asked him.

"No truly helpful being will demand that you give up something that is natural and beautiful," he said.

"Evil spirits" are not necessarily outside entities: They may be elements of the unconscious mind. Groups that reinforce feelings of superiority, separation from the mainstream of human life, and removal from ordinary frailties and fallibilities, reinforce their members' defenses and stunt their personal growth.

The flip side of the strategy of superiority is that of sickness. Instead of denying or pretending to transcend the shadow qualities, this type of person admits them, but interprets them as physical or mental illness. The seduction of sickness is that it absolves the individual from responsibility and allows her or him to luxuriate in passivity. Too often, self-definition of illness is fostered by therapists and "helping professionals," who after all have a vested interest in seeing others as sick.

Sickness as a defense is characterized by guilt. Such people often feel responsible for things that are, in reality, not under their control. Their shadow is their own, feared power, which they perceive in inflated, omnipotent terms. This defense often masks, and can undermine, great creativity and intelligence. If the practice of magic is misused to reinforce feelings of omnipotence, it can be devastating to these people.

Projection is another favorite strategy. When the negative qualities of the Guardian are sensed, it is easy to simply propel them outward and assign them to some other person or group. The special appeal of this strategy is that projection creates conflict, which is dramatic, exciting, and distracting. At its most extreme, however, it degenerates into paranoia. Such people never feel completely safe or accepted. Because their own anger and hostility are projected outward, they sense hostility everywhere around them.

Of course, all of us use many strategies, but most of us favor a particular mode. No one can be forced into a confrontation with the Shadow, nor can the process be hurried. It must happen in its own good time. As an example, the trance confrontation that opens this chapter is the record of an actual session between myself and one of my coveners. It was, however, the culmination of several months of work and training. In earlier sessions, Valerie managed to call up the Shadow, but could not get its name. She was not yet ready to confront and absorb it. Had we tried to force the confrontation—it might have been extremely destructive or simply useless. But when the timing was right, she found herself capable of taking in the qualities that before had seemed so threatening. The process marked a deep integration in her personality, and a flowering of her personal and creative power, to such an extent that I was moved to "pass the wand" of the coven to her, and she is now High Priestess of Compost.

One of the functions of a coven is to support and guide each other through the confrontation/s with the Guardian. This is not always done so directly as in the preceding example; in fact, untrained coveners should not work with each other in this fashion, because it can be as harmful as amateur psychoanalysis. Coveners help each other best simply by not being seduced into each other's defense strategies. "Transcenders" should never be idolized or placed on a pedestal (even if they happen to be High Priestesses). What they most need is to be loved for their weaknesses, their mistakes, and their humanness as well as their strengths.

Projectors sometimes have to literally fight out their confrontation with another person. The process can shatter a coven unless it is perceived correctly. Other members of the group should avoid taking sides or focusing on the outward cause of the quarrel. It is equally important to resist the temptation to toss one or both of them out of the group, except as a last resort. In a true Shadow fight, emotions will run far deeper than events seem to warrant. It is characterized by statements such as "I can't stand the way she makes me feel" or "She brings out the worst in me." The group should not accept the projections of the embroiled parties. If they are committed to the group and to their own growth, they will eventually come to confront the shadow of their own anger. They need to be loved throughout the battle.

It is a great temptation to love, smother, and coddle those people who define themselves as sick. It is also a temptation to lose patience with them, urge them to "buck up," quit whining, and start off each day with a smile. Neither approach is helpful. Such people need to have their power recognized for what it is, and need to have its limits also recognized. They need support to struggle and function, not to retreat into illness or crippling guilt. They need to be loved for their power.

In learning to trance, we are indeed learning to "change consciousness at will," which implies control. Mind-altering drugs are *not* used in magic (at least, not by the wise), because they destroy that control. No drug can force a confrontation with the Guardian; it can at best strip away a defense that may be all that stands between the self and stark terror. More often, it simply reinforces existing defenses at a deeper and more destructive level. Superiority becomes a savior-complex; sickness may become psychosis; projection may become true paranoia. In traditional societies, where drugs are used to bring on mystical visions and religious ecstasy, the experience is controlled and firmly structured along mythological lines. Shamans and priestesses have a deep understanding of the many states the mind may reach, and they know how to guide people through those states. But we do not live in a traditional society. We live in a society based on commodities, in which even enlightenment can purportedly be encapsulated and bought and sold. But what is bought and ingested is not really enlightenment, not really magic. The work, training, and discipline of magic can lead to a sensual trance similar to that produced by marijuana, and the goal of ritual is the ecstatic vision and high sense of wonder like that found on the highest LSD trips. But magic also opens up infinitely more subtle, sublime states, and teaches us not only how to go forth through the gate but also how to return. Consciousness is not, as Timothy Leary proclaims, a chemical phenomenon. Chemistry is a phenomenon of consciousness.

The best protection, when learning to trance—or learning anything else—is a sense of humor. Nothing you can laugh at, whether it is a demon, spirit, UFO, angel, guide, guru, teacher, vision, discorporate entity, or aspect of yourself, can possess you. No one can be whole who is incapable of laughing at him- or herself.

Expanded awareness begins with dreams. "This we call the Door Without a Key, which is also the Door of Dreams; Freud found it, and he used it for the coming forth by day; but we who are initiates use it for going forth by night."[6] Volumes have been written about the "coming forth by day": the bringing into waking consciousness of dream material from the unconscious. Here, I will restrict myself to pointing out aspects of interpretation that pertain especially to magic.

Dreams, while our most direct line into the subjective processes of Younger Self, may also contain objective elements. Some dreams reflect in symbolic language a direct cognition of astral currents. They may give insights into other people's motives, plans, or emotions, or give information about external events. Dream figures are not always an aspect of the individual: sometimes they are the person or thing they seem to be, although generally there is something in the individual that resonates with the external force.

Once we begin consciously working with magical symbols and mythology, our dreams reflect those images and should be interpreted in that light. To a Witch, for example, a snake is far more than a Freudian phallic symbol: It is a symbol of the Goddess, of renewal and regeneration.

Keeping a dream log, remembering dreams, sharing them in the coven, and reentering them in trance or guided fantasy all are ways of opening the door without a key. Learning to take active charge of our dreams, to suggest subjects, to change dreams as they happen, to confront attackers and defeat enemies, are ways of "going forth by night."[7]

There are many methods of trance induction, but all seem to function on one or more of four related principles: relaxation, sensory restriction, rhythm, and boredom. Physical tension blocks the trance state. Most inductions begin with deliberate relaxation, as in Exercise 9. When trance follows exertion, as after raising the Cone of Power, relaxation may occur naturally.

Sensory restriction has been explored in research described by Robert

Ornstein in *The Psychology of Consciousness.* When subjects stared at a fixed image, after a time it seemed to disappear. At the same time, alpha waves showed on their electroencephalograms. The alpha rhythm has been shown to be characteristic of meditation and deep relaxation. Ornstein concludes that "one consequence of the way our central nervous system is structured seems to be that, if awareness is restricted to one unchanging source of stimulation, a 'turning off' of consciousness of the external world follows. The common instructions for concentrative meditation all underscore this."[8]

Not enough is known about the neurophysiology of awareness. But the ancient techniques of trance and scrying (crystal gazing) always involved restricting sensory awareness, often to one unchanging source of stimulation: a candle flame, a crystal ball, a black mirror, a dark bowl of water, or a bright sword.

Rhythm, whether experienced in motion, song, drumming, chanting, or poetic meter, also induces a state of heightened awareness. Afro-American religions depend heavily on rhythmic drumming and dancing to induce a trance state in which worshippers become "mounted" or possessed by the "loa," the Gods. The metrical rhythm of poetry, according to Robert Graves, induces a trance of heightened sensitivity. In Craft tradition, it was believed that certain rhythms could induce particular emotional states. Drummers originally accompanied armies because their rhythms could make men fighting mad. (This secret, as far as I can tell, has been lost to the military and Witch covens alike, only to be rediscovered by the producers of disco music.) Spoken trance inductions are always soft, singsong, and rhythmic.

Boredom can also bring on trance—as generations of daydreaming schoolchildren have discovered. When we are not stimulated, sensorily, emotionally, or mentally, awareness turns elsewhere. Repetition is important in inducing trance—it creates a state of security and familiarity. The mind "tunes out" the repeated stimulus and "tunes in" on another channel.

The trance state is most easily learned in a group, with help from others. Later, it is easy to lead yourself through the same exercises alone. I will present the following exercises as if a leader were speaking to a group. A circle should be cast before beginning, and cautions should be repeated after everyone is relaxed:

EXERCISE 53: CAUTIONS

"You are about to enter into a very deep, very comfortable state of mind, where you will be perfectly safe and perfectly protected.

"You will be aware of any danger in the outer world and will awaken immediately, perfectly alert, and able to react and function.

"You will remain lucid and conscious at all times, able to concentrate fully.

"You will remember everything you experience.[9]

"At any time you should need to or want to, you can awaken fully and completely.

"When you awake, you will feel refreshed, renewed, and filled with energy."

Inductions vary widely. Use any set of imagery that works for you: diving into water, descending in an elevator, going down Alice's rabbit hole, walking down a spiral staircase, or whatever you invent. Here is my favorite voice induction:

EXERCISE 54: THE RAINBOW: TRANCE INDUCTION

(Begin with the Exercise 9, Relaxation. Everyone should be lying down, comfortably relaxed.)

"Breathe deep—you are floating down . . . down . . . on a beautiful red cloud, and your whole body is red—as you go drifting and floating . . . rocking gently . . . deeper . . . and deeper . . . down . . .

(repeat, once each, with an orange
        yellow
        green
        blue
        and violet cloud).

"Land very gently . . . very softly . . . in the center of a round, white pearl. See it glowing, softly, gently . . .

"Now turn and face the East . . .
and then the South . . .
and then the West . . .
and now the North.

"Open all of your inner senses."

The first trance exercise is to create an internal Place of Power, a safe space that serves as 'home base' for all trance journeys. After the induction, continue:

EXERCISE 55: PLACE OF POWER

"In a moment, you will enter into a new space, a place in which you are completely safe and protected, where you are in complete control and in touch with your deepest sources of strength. It may seem to be indoors or outdoors—it may contain anything or anyone you like. It is completely yours. Wherever you may be, whatever state of consciousness you may be in, you can return to your Place of Power, simply by visualizing it.

"Now turn and face in the direction that feels most comfortable to you. On the pearl's wall, draw an invoking pentacle. If you like, you may use a symbol of your own, that will be your own secret key into your Place of Power. See the symbol glow with a deep blue flame. Take a deep breath—inhale—exhale. See the wall open, and walk through into your Place of Power.

"You are in your Place of Power. Turn and face the East. Notice what you see and hear and feel and sense. (Pause.)

"Turn and face the South. Notice what you see and hear and feel and sense. (Pause.)

"Turn and face the West. Notice what you see and hear and feel and sense. (Pause.)

"Turn and face the North. Notice what you see and hear and feel and sense. (Pause.)

"Now take time to explore your Place of Power. (Allow at least five minutes.)

"You are about ready to leave your Place of Power. Finish whatever you need to complete.

"Now turn and face the East, and say goodbye. (Pause.)

"Turn and face the South, and say goodbye. (Pause).

"Turn and face the West, and say goodbye. (Pause.)

"Turn and face the North, and say goodbye. (Pause.)

"Now look for your symbol. See it glow. See it open. Take a deep breath—inhale—exhale—and walk through back into the pearl."

Coming out of trance is equally as important as going in. Take time to emerge slowly and gently, reversing every process of the induction. Facing the directions is important because it forces you to orient yourself in inner space—to *be* in the scenes, not just watch them like movies. It also reinforces the protective circle, and the repetition, with each trance, reinforces the depth of the state.

EXERCISE 56: THE RAINBOW: EMERGING

"In the pearl, prepare to awaken. When you awake, you will feel refreshed, alert, renewed, and filled with energy. You will remember all that you have experienced. Now turn and face the East . . . then the South . . . then the West . . . then the North. Take a deep breath . . . inhale . . . exhale . . .

"You are floating up . . . up . . . on a beautiful violet cloud, and your whole body is violet as you drift gently upward . . .

"On a beautiful blue cloud . . . up . . . up . . . and your whole body is blue and you are beginning to awaken gently and you drift gently up . . .

"On a beautiful green cloud . . . and your whole body is green . . . as you drift gently . . . up . . . up . . .

"On a beautiful yellow cloud . . . getting more and more awake . . . and your whole body is yellow . . . as you drift gently . . . up . . . up . . .

"On a beautiful orange cloud . . . filled with energy and vitality . . . your whole body is orange . . . as you float up gently . . .

"On a beautiful red cloud . . . almost fully awake now . . . and your whole body is red as you float gently . . . remembering fully . . .

"And in a moment you will count to three and awaken fully and completely, feeling refreshed, renewed, and filled with energy . . . take a deep breath . . . inhale . . . and exhale . . . one . . . two . . . three . . .

"Open your eyes, and awake."

Occasionally subjects do not come out of trance. This is nothing to be alarmed about—it simply means they have drifted from trance into sleep. Awaken them gently by touching them or by calling their names.

Scrying involves concentrating on an object: a crystal ball, a bowl of ink or a dark bowl filled with water, or a mirror with a black-painted back, in order to see psychicly.

EXERCISE 57: SCRYING

Cast a circle. Ground and center. Sit in a comfortable position, and look at your crystal or focusing object. Some people prefer to have the room completely dark: others light a candle. Lighting should never be bright.

Relax, and wait peacefully. Do not force anything to come. Many people feel fear and insecurity—"It won't work for me"—"I'm not doing it right." Acknowledge the fears, relax into them, and let them dissolve.

After a time—and it may require regular practice over several sessions—the surface of the crystal may "cloud over" with *raith* energy. For some people, the clouds clear, and images appear in the crystal. Others find themselves closing their eyes, and seeing the images with the inner eye. Both methods are valuable— choose the one that comes most easily.

To end, let the clouds return, then disperse. See the crystal as the solid object it is. Cover it, and open the circle.

EXERCISE 58: SUGGESTION:

Because suggestion works through Younger Self, it is most effective in the language of symbols and imagery. Suggestion can be incorporated into any trance. Instead of verbal assertions, create a mental scene showing the results of what you want. If you want to overcome shyness, see yourself at a large party, behaving with poise and charm. If you want to be richer, see yourself enjoying money. If you want to be healed, see yourself healthy and active.

Cast a circle, go into trance, and go into your Place of Power. Orient yourself to the four directions.

Create your suggestion in your Place of Power. Make it as vivid, as real, as sensual, as you can. Take as much time as you need to do so.

Leave your suggestion in your Place of Power. It will take root and grow, and become your reality.

Bid farewell to the four directions, and come out of trance.

EXERCISE 59: MEMORY

Cast a circle, go into trance, and orient yourself in your Place of Power. Face in the direction that feels most comfortable to you.

In front of you, you see a path. Search for the path, and find it. Now follow it, looking around you, noticing what you see and hear and feel and sense. Follow it along, further and further.

The path leads over a ridge. Climb the ridge, and begin to descend, going down . . . down . . . down . . . circling down the hillside.

On your way down, you will see the entrance to a cave that leads deep . . . deep into the hill. Find the cave, and stand before the entrance.

Within the cave are all of your memories, from this life, and from all previous lifetimes. In a moment, you will enter the cave. You will be able to go as deep as you wish, to explore any branching tunnel, any cavern that you wish. If you have a particular memory you want to experience, hold it in your mind, and you will be led to the proper place. If there is a memory you are not ready to face, the path to it will be blocked.

Take a deep breath, inhale, exhale, and, as you count to three, enter the cave of your memories. Take as much time as you need to explore. (Allow at least ten minutes.)

Now prepare to come back from your memory. Take time to end it. Come back to the entrance of the cave.

Take a deep breath—inhale, and as you exhale count to three and come out of the cave. Exhale—count one, two, three.

Come out of the cave, and climb back up the hillside. Return up the hill, over the ridge, following the path back to your own Place of Power.

Bid farewell to the four directions, and come out of trance.

EXERCISE 60: TRANCE INTO A DREAM

Cast a circle, go into trance, and orient yourself in your Place of Power. Face in the direction that feels most comfortable to you.

You see a new path—a winding, secret path, that leads down to a river. Look for the path, and find it. Follow it. Look around you, noticing what you see and hear and feel and sense along the way.

Stop on the riverbank. Across the river is the dream realm. When you enter it, you can explore or change your dreams at will. You can confront and defeat your enemies, and can learn from your friends. Now picture the dream you wish to enter, and see its landscape form across the river.

Take a deep breath. Inhale. As you exhale, step down into the river. Feel the cold water on your feet, and notice it moving and sparkling.

Take another deep breath. Inhale. As you exhale, wade across the river. Feel the stones under your feet; hear the river.

Take another deep breath. Inhale. As you exhale, step up on the far shore, into the dream realm. Exhale. Feel the firm ground under your feet again.

You are now in the dream realm. Take as much time as you need to explore, change, and discover your dreams.

Now prepare to leave the dream realm. Say farewell to any beings you have met, and complete your exploration. Come back to the river.

Again, taking three deep breaths and three steps, cross the river. Step down into it, wade across, and emerge on the other side. Feel the stones under your feet; hear and see the water.

Follow the path back into your own Place of Power. Bid farewell to the four directions, and come out of trance.

Dreams can also be explored through scrying. A group can visualize a dream image in a crystal or water bowl and can explore it. For example, here is a partial record of a group trance into an image from Holly's dream, in which a group of old women were looking at a picture of a seal in a newspaper, and one said, "The seal will bring perpetual youth."

We are on a beach—waves—faint music plays from a carnival merry-go-round—Holly is in the lake—her father says she swims like a fish. . . .

Now there is a lighthouse—a foghorn, foam sprays on rocks—the sound of seals. . . .

Holly is in the water, her hair floating behind like a mermaid's hair—we are all swimming under the rocks, the water is crystal blue—the rocks are made of crystal. . . .

There is a cave under the rocks—Valerie recognizes it from a dream she had long ago—there were people who wanted to dive into the cave, she warned them not to go, but they did. They couldn't get out. The cave is filled with bones.

We move through it and emerge into a city of glass. Towers and turrets of shining crystal rise under the sea . . . colored fish swim in the clear glass walls . . . we move down a long corridor, through Gothic halls with clear arches. . . .

The city is spinning—we are flung with it, spun around, spun back into the cave.

In the cave is a seal. The seal guards a fountain. "The seal will bring perpetual youth." We drink from the fountain.

Once you become familiar with trance techniques, you can create your own imagery and use the trance state for many kinds of experience. You can call up a negative part of yourself, as Valerie did at the opening of this chapter, or you can call your High Self into your Place of Power and receive help, teaching, and advice. You can search for answers to questions, drink from the fountain of inspiration, die, and be reborn.

In rituals, all elements of trance induction (excepting, hopefully, boredom), are present. The release of energy with the Cone of Power creates relaxation. The space is dark, and attention can be focused on candle flames or a central cauldron. Chants, invocations, and movements are rhythmic and repetitive. Trance inductions are a natural and beautiful element of the ritual itself. Often they involve multiple voices, an effect difficult to reproduce on the printed page. In the following, imagine the grouped lines read simultaneously, like a musical score.

EXERCISE 61: RITUAL INDUCTION

1st Voice: Your fingers are dissolving into water, and your
2nd Voice: (Pause) Your fingers are dissolving into
3rd Voice: Sle-eee-ee-eep Dee-ee-eee-ee-eep, and

1st Voice: toes are dissolving into water, and your wrists
2nd Voice: water, and your toes are dissolving into water,
3rd Voice: drea—ea—ea—eam of becoming,

1st Voice: are dissolving into water, and your ankles are
2nd Voice: and your wrists are dissolving into water, and
3rd Voice: drea—ea—eam deee-ee-ee-ee-eep,

1st Voice: dissolving into water, and your hands are dissolving
2nd Voice: your ankles are dissolving into water, and your
3rd Voice: and slee-eee-ee-ee-eep,

1st Voice: into water, and your feet are dissolving into water,
2nd Voice: hands are dissolving into water, and your feet are
3rd Voice: Slee-eee-eeee-ee-p dee-ee-ee-eep, and

1st Voice: and your forearms are dissolving into water, and
2nd Voice: dissolving into water, and your forearms are dis-
3rd Voice: drea—ea-ea-eam of becoming,

1st Voice: your calves are dissolving into water, and your
2nd Voice: solving into water, and your calves are dissolving
3rd Voice: Brea—the dee-ee-ee-ee-p,

1st Voice: elbows are dissolving into water, and your knees
2nd Voice: into water, and your elbows are dissolving into
3rd Voice: and slee—ee—ee—ee—eep.

Continue on with this induction until the whole body is relaxed. Another voice may then pick up and continue to guide the trance and later reawaken members. When coveners are comfortable working together, the guiding can also be shared by several members, who may each create part of the imagery.

Mystery rituals, such as those of Witchcraft, follow a pattern of induction and revelation. The Mysteries are teachings that cannot be grasped by the intellect alone, but only by the deep mind made accessible in trance. They may be conveyed by an object—a shaft of wheat, as in the Eleusinian Mysteries—by a key phrase, or symbol. The secret itself may be meaningless when out of context: only within the framework of the ritual does it take on its illuminating power.

Divination, through palmistry, Tarot cards, astrology, and reading oracles, is another method of awakening the deep mind. I don't have space to even begin a discussion that would do justice to such a vast practice, except to point out that all divinatory techniques work essentially to focus awareness and engage the heightened intuition and perception that is possible in trance. Today, these techniques are used not for "fortunetelling," but as methods of spiritual and psychological counseling.

Cakes and Wine

After trance, the process of returning to the world and ending the ritual begins with the sharing of food, the "Cakes and Wine." These may actually be anything from red wine and barley-flour crescents to cookies and milk. Sometimes a full meal is shared; at other times a coven will prefer organic fruit and apple juice, or champagne and caviar. The tastes and resources of members are the only limitations.

The High Priestess and High Priest (or other members) hold up a plate of food and a goblet of wine, and say a blessing that is simple and often spontaneous:

BLESSING OVER CAKES AND WINE

All life is your own,
All fruits of the earth
Are fruits of your womb,
Your union, your dance.
Lady and Lord,
We thank you for blessings and abundance.
Join with us, Feast with us, Enjoy with us!
Blessed be.

A small libation may be poured into the fire or cauldron. The goblet is passed around the circle, and each member gives thanks for good things that have happened since the previous meeting. While eating, members relax, laugh, joke, and socialize, or talk about the ritual and plan future meetings. The social aspect of ritual is an integral part of strengthening and maintaining the group bond. Sharing food is sharing a tangible symbol of love and caring. It is important that this part of the ritual be fun—a reward to Younger Self for undergoing all the serious work of ritual and magic.

It is vitally important to formally end the meeting, and break the circle. Having stepped between the worlds when we began the ritual, we must deliberately and consciously step back out into ordinary space and time. Only thus can we preserve the integrity of the ritual space and time. People should never be allowed to drift away before the circle is opened, and the transition back to ordinary consciousness is complete.

Dismissal of the Goddess and God

The power of the ritual should be grounded, if this has not already been done. The High Priestess (or whoever performed the invocations) goes to the altar, and stands facing the coven in pentacle position. She says,

> Lady and Lord,
> We thank you
> For your presence,
> For your circle,
> For light and love,
> For night and change,
> We ask for your blessing
> As you depart.
> Hail and farewell! Blessed be.

Opening the Circle

The High Priestess goes to each of the four directions in turn, and draws a Banishing Pentacle (see illustration, page 51), saying,

Guardians of the East (South, West, North), Powers of Air (Fire, Water, Earth), we thank you
For joining in our circle

And we ask for your blessing
As you depart.
May there be peace between us
Now and forever. Blessed be.

She raises her *athame* to the sky and touches it to the earth, then opens her arms and says,

> The circle is open, but unbroken,
> May the peace of the Goddess
> Go in your hearts,
> Merry meet, and merry part.
> And merry meet again. Blessed be.

Notes

1. Barbara Brown, *New Mind, New Body* (New York: Bantam Books, 1975), p. 17.
2. John C. Lilly, *The Center of the Cyclone* (New York: Julian Press, 1972), p. 49.
3. Lilly, p. 39.
4. Dion Fortune, *Moon Magic* (New York: Weiser, 1972), pp. 81–82.
5. Carlos Castaneda, *The Teachings of Don Juan: A Yaqui Way of Knowledge* (New York: Ballantine Books, 1969), p. 79.
6. Fortune, p. 76.
7. For a further exploration of dreamwork, see Patricia Garfield, *Creative Dreaming* (New York: Simon & Schuster, 1975).
8. Robert Ornstein, *The Psychology of Consciousness* (San Francisco: W. H. Freeman, 1972), p. 126.
9. The traditional view of trance and hypnosis is that the subject forgets the experience, presumably so that the doctor or psychiatrist in charge can elicit information from the unconscious that the patient may not be ready to face. Trance work in the Craft, however, is aimed at teaching the subject to control her own state of consciousness, and so memory becomes vitally important. If she is not ready to face certain information, she will not contact it. It is considered a misuse of the trance state to pry into each other's secrets.

10 Initiation

Between the Worlds

THE GODDESS IN THE KINGDOM OF DEATH

In this world, the Goddess is seen in the moon, the light that shines in darkness, the rain bringer, mover of the tides, Mistress of mysteries. And as the moon waxes and wanes, and walks three nights of its cycle in darkness, so, it is said, the Goddess once spent three nights in the Kingdom of Death.

For in love She ever seeks her other Self, and once, in the winter of the year, when He had disappeared from the green earth, She followed Him and came at last to the gates beyond which the living do not go.

The Guardian of the Gate challenged Her, and She stripped Herself of her clothing and jewels, for nothing may be brought into that land. For love, She was bound as all who enter there must be and brought before Death Himself.

He loved Her, and knelt at her feet, laying before Her his sword and crown, and gave Her the fivefold kiss, and said,

"Do not return to the living world, but stay here with Me, and have peace and rest and comfort."

But She answered, "Why do you cause all things I love and delight in to die and wither away?"

"Lady," He said, "It is the fate of all that lives to die. Everything passes; all fades away. I bring comfort and consolation to those who pass the gates,

159

that they may grow young again. But You are my heart's desire—return not, but stay here with Me."

And She remained with him three days and three nights, and at the end of the third night She took up his crown, and it became a circlet that She placed around her neck, saying:

"Here is the circle of rebirth. Through You all passes out of life, but through Me all may be born again. Everything passes; everything changes. Even death is not eternal. Mine is the mystery of the womb, that is the cauldron of rebirth. Enter into Me and know Me, and You will be free of all fear. For as life is but a journey into death, so death is but a passage back to life, and in Me the circle is ever turning."

In love, He entered into Her, and so was reborn into life. Yet is He known as Lord of Shadows, the comforter and consoler, opener of the gates, King of the Land of Youth, the giver of peace and rest. But She is the gracious mother of all life; from Her all things proceed and to Her they return again. In Her are the mysteries of death and birth; in Her is the fulfillment of all love.

Traditional Craft Myth

An initiation is a symbolic death and rebirth, a rite of passage that transforms each person who experiences it. In the Craft, it marks acceptance into a coven, and a deep, personal commitment to the Goddess. It is a gift of power and love that coveners give each other: the experience of those inner secrets that cannot be told because they go beyond words. For the individual, it becomes a change that causes revelation and understanding and sparks further growth and change.

The timing of an initiation is important. Traditionally, apprentice Witches were required to study for "a year and a day" before they could be initiated. This rule is not always followed in present-day covens, but it is a good one. Magical training cannot take place overnight. It is, as we have said, a process of neurological repatterning, which requires time. Unless an initiate can, at least to some extent, channel energy and move into altered states of awareness, she will not benefit deeply from the ritual.

There is another, more subtle aspect to timing. Initiation also means "beginning," and what is begun is the process of confronting the Guardian of the Threshold. A new initiate may not yet have faced the Shadow, but she* must be committed to doing so. The Guardian's injunction—"Better to fall upon my blade and perish than to make the attempt with fear in thy heart"—does not mean she must be fearless, but that she is willing, in spite of fear, to go on, not to run away, to face her defenses even though

---

*An initiate may be female or male—in this and following chapters I use 'she' inclusively to simplify questions of grammar.

the process may be painful. "Are you willing to suffer to learn?" she is asked, because learning, and growth, always involve pain.

When an apprentice is able to confront other people in the group, face issues, take responsibility for her own feelings and actions, and both expects and desires to influence the course of the group, she is probably ready for initiation. She must ask for initiation, because she is not ready until she realizes that she, and no one else, controls the course of her progress in the Craft. An initiation creates a strong emotional bond and a deep, astral tie between coven members, so consider very carefully who you initiate.

Death and rebirth are the theme of initiation. Death is the root of our deepest fears, and the true face of the Shadow. It is the terror behind vulnerability; the horror of annihilation that we fear our anger or our power will provoke. As in the myth, what pulls us to risk that confrontation is desire and longing, for those split-off parts of ourselves that lie on the other side of the abyss, which alone can complete us and free us to love. Because where there is no courage, there is no love: Love demands honesty, which is frightening, or it is only pretense. It demands vulnerability, or it is hollow. It engages our deepest power, or it lacks force. It brings us to confront sorrow, loss, and death.

And so we learn the Mystery: the feared Shadow, the Guardian of the Threshold, is none other than the God, who is named Guardian of the Gates, in his aspect of Death.

We must strip ourselves of our defenses, pretensions, masks, roles, of our "clothing and jewels," all that we assume and put on, in order to cross that threshold and enter the inner kingdom. The door opens only to the naked body of truth, bound by the cords, our recognition of mortality.

Death is seductive, for once the frightening threshold is crossed there is no more fear. Fear and hope are both dissolved; all that is left is rest, repose, relief, blessed nothingness, the void. But just as the void, to physicists, is the "mother state," so the crown of death becomes the circlet of rebirth, and the cords of binding become the umbilical link to life. Death is subsumed to life, and we learn the Great Mystery—not as a doctrine, not as a philosophy, but as an experience: There is no annihilation.

Traditionally, initiation rituals are secret—if for no other reason than to preserve the element of surprise. I have somewhat mixed feelings about publishing one of our initiations, but I feel the book would not be complete without it. I have omitted secret Faery material and concentrated on many of the creative elements of the ritual, which we generally write anew for each new member. The following should not be seen as an unchangeable script, but as a blueprint for creating your own rituals.

An initiation begins with a death cycle—an enacted dissolution, symbolic annihilation and purification. An element of testing is sometimes involved. In the country, an apprentice might be taken to an unknown path and told to find her way along it. At intervals, guides will reveal secrets, or point out the direction. At the beach, a blindfolded apprentice might be asked to find her way by scent, by sound, and finally to let go of fear and walk trustingly into the waves, where protective hands will pull her back. Indoors, an apprentice might be told to keep solemn silence and lie quietly, while a plaster face-mask is made, and then left to meditate while it dries. At Paul's initiation, he was told to close his eyes and led into the garden. At intervals, he was allowed to open his eyes; a light was flashed and revelations were made; for example, he was shown an ear of corn, and told, "Behold Kore, the Maiden." He was shown a rose, and told, "Feel the blossom and the thorn." He was shown a lacy, insect-eaten leaf, and told "See how life feeds on life."

He was then left to meditate on the sky, while the rest of us went indoors, cast the circle, and prepared the ritual bath.

The ocean, or a running stream, are ideal locations for ritual baths, but most of them are held in an ordinary tub. Coveners perform their Salt-Water Purification; salt is added to the bath water and it is charged with the power to cleanse and make new. Appropriate herbs and oils are added: I use rose petals, bay leaves, mistletoe, vervain, rue, a few drops of High Priestess or Goddess oil, and Delphi water. Incense and candles are lit. The blindfolded apprentice is helped into the tub, washed by other coveners, and chanted over. She is told to meditate, purify herself, resolve any doubts, and look for a new name. She is then left alone.

Coveners finish any last preparations for the ritual, and invoke the Goddess, God, and Mighty Ones of the Craft. One covener, who acts as the sponsor for the apprentice, returns to her, dries her, and makes sure she is ready to enter the circle. She ties a thin cotton cord loosely around the apprentice's wrists, saying, "And She was bound as all living must be, who would enter the Kingdom of Death." She ties the cord also around one ankle, saying, "Feet neither bound nor free," recognizing that entrance into the Craft is a free choice, but that once a person steps on the path, they have set in motion currents that will impel them forward. The sponsor asks the apprentice her new name and leads her to the circle, where a gate has been cut in the east.

A covener chosen to be the Challenger steps forward with sword or *athame* and says, "Who comes to the gate?"

The apprentice, coached beforehand, answers, "It is I, _____ (her new name), child of earth and starry heaven."

Challenger: "Who speaks for you?"

Sponsor: "It is I, _____, who vouches for her." The Challenger holds the point of the blade up to the apprentice's heart, and says,

"You are about to enter a vortex of power, a place beyond imagining, where birth and death, dark and light, joy and pain, meet and make one.

You are about to step between the worlds, beyond time, outside the realm of your human life.

"You who stand on the threshold of the dread Mighty Ones, have you the courage to make the essay? For know that it is better to fall on my blade and perish than to make the attempt with fear in thy heart!"

The apprentice answers, "I enter the circle with perfect love and perfect trust."

The Challenger grounds the point of her blade to earth, kisses her, and draws her into the circle, saying "Thus are all first brought into the circle."

The High Priestess and/or High Priest now lead the apprentice to each of the four quarters, sunwise, saying:

"Hail, Guardians of the Watchtowers of the East (South, West, North) and all the Mighty Ones of the Craft. Behold _____ (new name), who will now be made Priestess and Witch."

The apprentice is brought back to the altar. The High Priestess kneels, and gives her the fivefold kiss, on the parts of the body named, saying:

> Blessed are your feet, that have brought you in these ways.
> Blessed are your knees, that kneel at the sacred altar.
> Blessed is your sex, without which we would not be.
> Blessed are your breasts, formed in strength and beauty.
> Blessed are your lips, which shall speak the sacred names.

The apprentice is then measured with thin cord, from head to toe. The cord is cut; she is measured around the head and chest. Knots are tied to mark the measurements. The High Priestess rolls up the cord, and asks the apprentice, "Are you willing to swear the oath?"

Apprentice: "I am."

High Priestess: "Are you willing to suffer to learn?"

Apprentice: "Yes."

The High Priestess takes the apprentice's hand, and, with a needle properly purified by fire and water (that is, sterilized), pricks her finger, squeezing a few drops of blood onto the measure.

High Priestess: "Repeat after me:

'I, _____, do of my own free will most solemnly swear to protect, help, and defend my sisters and brothers of the Art.

I always will keep secret all that must not be revealed.

This do I swear on my mother's womb and my hopes of future lives, mindful that my measure has been taken, and in the presence of the Mighty Ones.'"

The apprentice is then told to kneel, place one hand on her head and the other beneath her heel; she say,

"All between my two hands belongs to the Goddess."

Coven: "So mote it be!"

Coven members grab her suddenly, lift her up (if possible,) and carry her three times around the circle, laughing and shrieking. They lay her face down before the altar and press her into the ground. Gradually, the pressing changes to stroking. They chant her new name, raising a Cone of Power over her, giving her power to open her awareness and work magic. The blindfold is removed, and she is told,

"Know that the hands that have touched you are the hands of love."

The Charge of the Goddess is spoken, and other myths, mysteries, and secrets are revealed. Generally, the new initiate is given time to scry in a crystal, to find her own personal sources of power and inspiration. She is told the coven names of other members, the inner name and symbols of the coven.

The sponsor consecrates her on breasts and forehead with oil, with a coven symbol. The High Priestess returns her measure, saying:

"In the Burning Times, when each member of the coven held the lives of the others in her hand, this would have been kept, and used against you should you endanger others. But in these more fortunate times, love and trust prevail, so take this, keep it or burn it, and be free to go or stay as your heart leads you."

The new initiate is then given a set of tools—which other coveners have made or collected for her. One by one, they are handed to her, their use is explained, and they are consecrated and charged. (See Exercise 36—although the process is often shortened within the initiation ritual.)

Food and wine are shared, and coveners relax and party. An initiation is a joyful occasion.

Before the circle is opened, the new initiate is taken around to the four quarters for a final time. The High Priestess says,

"Guardians of the East (South, West, North), and Mighty Ones of the Craft, behold _____, who has now been made Priestess and Witch, and member of the _____ coven."

Goddess, God, and Guardians are thanked and dismissed, and the circle is opened.

11 *Moon Rituals*

Between the Worlds

ESBATS

The coven meets in moontime, new, full, or dark. The rituals are healing rituals, magical workings, times of growth, inspiration, insight. They change constantly, are never static. We make them anew, rewrite them, recreate them, but always on the same pattern: the creation of the sacred space, the invocations, the use of magical symbols, the raising of the cone of power, trance, sharing of food and wine and laughter, and the formal return to ordinary space and time. The ritual may be formal or informal; scripted or spontaneous; structured or loose—as long as it is alive. As long as it sings.

> "The first and most important effect of a living mythological symbol is to waken and give guidance to the energies of life."
> Joseph Campbell[1]

The rituals that follow in this chapter and the next are scripts meant to be changed, reworked, improved on, or used as they are. If you use written words, they should be memorized rather than read aloud. Speaking memorized words may itself create a trance state; reading entraps us in the left-brain, flashlight mind. If you cannot memorize, improvise.

Don't worry about literary quality—simply say what you feel. Or better yet—let your rituals be wordless.

WAXING MOON RITUAL

(To be performed after the first visible crescent has appeared.)

On the altar, place a bowl of seeds. Fill the central cauldron with earth, and place a candle in the center.

When the coven gathers, begin with a breathing meditation. A Priestess says,

"This is the time of beginning, the seed time of creation, the awakening after sleep. Now the moon emerges, a crescent out of the dark; the Birthgiver returns from Death. The tide turns; all is transformed. Tonight we are touched by the Maiden who yields to all and yet is penetrated by none. She changes everything She touches; may She open us to change and growth. Merry meet."

Purify, cast the circle, and invoke the Goddess and God.

A covener chosen to act as Seed Priestess takes the bowl of grain from the altar, saying,

"Blessed be, creature of earth, moon seed of change, bright beginning of a new circle of time. Power to start, power to grow, power to make new be in this seed. Blessed be."

Going sunwise around the circle, she offers the bowl to each person, asking, "What will you plant with the moon?" Each person replies with what she plans to begin, or hopes will grow, in the month to come. "The blessing of the new moon be it," the Priestess answers.

Each person visualizes a clear image of what they want to grow, charging the seeds with the image. One by one, they plant the seeds in the earth in the central cauldron.

Together, they raise a Cone of Power to charge the seeds and earth with energy, and empower the projects they represent. The Cone is grounded into the cauldron.

Trance work or scrying may focus on clarity of vision for the projects now begun.

Share cakes and wine, and open the circle.

FULL MOON RITUAL

(To be performed on the eve of the Full Moon.)

The circle gathers, does a breathing meditation, and a Priestess says,

"This is the time of fullness, the flood tide of power, when the Lady in full circle of brightness rides across the night sky, arising with the coming of dark. This is the time of the bearing of fruits, of change realized. The Great Mother, Nurturer of the world, which is Herself, pours out her love and her gifts in abundance. The Hunter draws near to the Brilliant One, She who awakens yearning in the heart and who is the end of desire. We who look on her shining face are filled with love. Merry meet."

Purify, cast the circle, and invoke the Goddess and God.

One covener moves into the center of the circle, and speaks her name. The others repeat it, and chant it, raising a Cone of Power as they touch her, earthing it into her and filling her with the power and light of the moon. She returns to the circle, and another covener takes her place, until each in turn has been the focus of the power. While chanting, other coveners come to recognize that each individual is, in truth, Goddess/God.

A final Cone can be raised for the coven as a whole. Earth the power, trance or scry, then share cakes and wine and open the circle.

DARK MOON RITUAL

(To be performed on the waning moon. A gazing crystal or scrying bowl should be placed in the center of the circle.)

Gather, and meditate on a group breath. A Priestess says,

"This is the ending before the beginning, the death before new life. Now on the ebb tide the secrets of the shoreline are uncovered by the retreating waves. The moon is hidden, but the faintest of stars are revealed and those who have eyes to see may read the fates and know the mysteries. The Goddess, whose name cannot be spoken, naked enters the Kingdom of Death. In the most vast silence and stillness, all is possible. We meet in the time of the Crone, to touch the deep power of the dark."

Purify and cast the circle, but do not light the altar candle. Invoke the Goddess and God.

The leader begins an *antiphon* chant: a repeated bass line, with spontaneous lines interjected between.

Leader: "She lies under all, She covers all."
All: "She lies under all, She covers all." (Repeat several times.)
Covener: "She is the teacher of mysteries."
All: "She lies under all, She covers all."
Covener: "She is the motion behind form."
All: "She lies under all, She covers all."
Covener: (Improvised line)
All: "She lies under all, She covers all."

Continue as long as there is energy and inspiration. (This type of chanting requires sensitivity and openness, both to personal inspiration and to others. While at first there may be some hesitations, silences, and collisions, in a cohesive group it will soon flow naturally. It is a powerful way of opening the inner voice.)

Build into a wordless power chant, and earth the cone into the scrying bowl or gazing crystal. Scry together, sharing what you see.

Share cakes and wine, and open the circle.

Note

1. Joseph Campbell, *Myths to Live by* (New York: Bantam Books: 1973), p. 89.

12 *The Wheel of the Year*

Between the Worlds:

THE SABBATS[1]

Winter, Spring, Summer, Autumn—birth, growth, fading, death—the Wheel turns, on and on. Ideas are born, projects are consummated, plans prove impractical and die. We fall in love; we suffer loss; we consummate relationships; we give birth; we grow old; we decay.

The Sabbats are the eight points at which we connect the inner and the outer cycles: the interstices where the seasonal, the celestial, the communal, the creative, and the personal all meet. As we enact each drama in its time, we transform ourselves. We are renewed, we are reborn even as we decay and die. We are not separate from each other, from the broader world around us; we are one with the Goddess, with the God. As the Cone of Power rises, as the season changes, we arouse the power from within, the power to heal, the power to change our society, the power to renew the earth.

Yule (Winter Solstice, December 20–23)[2]

The altar is decorated with mistletoe and holly. A fire of oak roots is laid, but not lit. The room is dark.

169

The circle gathers. All meditate together, linking breaths. The High Priestess* says,

"This is the night of Solstice, the longest night of the year. Now darkness triumphs; and yet, gives way and changes into light. The breath of nature is suspended: all waits while within the Cauldron, the Dark King is transformed into the Infant Light. We watch for the coming of dawn, when the Great Mother again gives birth to the Divine Child Sun, who is bringer of hope and the promise of summer. This is the stillness behind motion, when time itself stops; the center which is also the circumference of all. We are awake in the night. We turn the Wheel to bring the light. We call the sun from the womb of night. Blessed be!"

Purify, cast the circle, but do not light the candles. Invoke the Goddess and God. All sit down, and begin an antiphonal chant.

All:

> To die and be reborn,
> The Wheel is turning,
> What must you lose to the night? (Repeat.)

Covener: "Fear."

All:

> Fear is lost to the night.
> Fear is lost to the night.
> To die and be reborn,
> The Wheel is turning,
> What must you lose to the night?

Continue interjecting lines and echoing each other, until the energy dies away. Stand up, and link hands. The High Priest* stands before the altar, holding an animal skull filled with salt. The High Priestess leads a slow, spiral procession, that first snakes outward so that each member is brought to face the High Priest. They are chanting,

> The light was born,
> And the light has died. (Continue repeating.)

Another Priestess whispers,

> Everything passes,
> All fades away.

The High Priest places a pinch of salt on each member's tongue, saying,

---

*Parts may be taken by any coveners: High Priestess and High Priest are given here for simplicity.

My body is salt,
Taste the breath of death.

The High Priestess leads the spiral inward, until the members are huddled together. She leads an improvised trance induction, slowly suggesting that they crumble to the earth and sleep. As all lie down, they are sent into a deeper trance with a multivoiced induction. As it fades out, they are told,

"You are entering a space of perfect freedom."

Time is allowed for trance in the state of suspension before birth.

The High Priestess approaches one of the coveners, stands by her head with her legs apart, and pulls her through, symbolically giving her birth. She becomes part of the birth canal; they continue the process with the other coveners, the birth canal growing longer. The men of the coven take the newborns one by one and lay them back down to sleep, telling them,

"Sleep the sleep of the newborn."

As all sink back into trance, they are guided into a visualization of their hopes for their new life to come. Priestesses smear honey on their tongues, one by one, saying,

"Taste the sweetness of life."

A new chant begins softly, builds in power as it gradually wakes the sleepers, who join in on repeating lines:

Set sail, set sail,
    Follow the twilight to the West,
Where you may rest, where you may rest.

Set sail, set sail,
    Turn your face where the sun grows dim,
Beyond the rim, beyond the rim.

Set sail, set sail,
    One thing becomes another,
In the Mother, in the Mother.

Set sail, set sail,
    Make of your heart a burning fire,
Build it higher, build it higher.

Set sail, set sail,
    Pass in an instant through the open gate,
It will not wait, it will not wait.

Set sail, set sail,
    Over the dark of the sunless sea,
You are free, you are free.

Set sail, set sail,
Guiding the ship of the rising sun,
You are the one, you are the one.

Set sail, set sail,
Into the raging wind and storm,
To be reborn, to be reborn.

Set sail, set sail,
Over the waves where the spray blows white,
To bring the light, to bring the light.

All:

We are awake in the night!
We turn the Wheel, to bring the light!
We call the sun from the womb of night!

High Priestess:

He sets his face to the West, but in the East arises!
All: Who is that?
Priestess: Who goes down in darkness?
All: Who is that?
P: Who sails?
A: Who is that?
P: The Renewer.
A: Who is that?
P: Who brings the golden fruit.
A: Who is that?
P: Unstained.
A: Who is that?
P: Whose hands are open?
A: Who is that?
P: Whose eyes are bright!
A: Who is that?
P: Whose face is shining?
A: Who is that?
P: Morning's hope!
A: Who is that?
P: Who passes the gate?
A: Who is that?
P: Who returns in light?
A: Who is that?
P: A glow between twin pillars.
A: Who is that?
P: A cry between thighs!

All: "Io! Evohe! Io! Evohe! Io! Evohe!"
High Priestess: (leading, repeated by all):

Queen of the sun!
Queen of the Moon!
Queen of the horns!
Queen of the fires!
Bring to us the Child of promise!

It is the Great Mother
Who gives birth to Him,
It is the Lord of Life,
Who is born again!
Darkness and tears
Are set aside,
When the sun comes up again!

Golden sun,
Of hill and field,
Light the earth!
Light the skies!
Light the waters!
Light the fires!

All: "Io! Evohe! Io! Evohe! Io! Evohe!"
The High Priest lights the fire and point candles, and all begin chanting:

I who have died am alive again today,
And this is the sun's birthday! (Repeat.)

This is the birthday of life and love and wings,
And the gay great happening illimitably earth.[3]

We are born again, we shall live again![4] (Repeat).

The Sun Child, the Winter-born King!

Build a Power Chant, focused on reawakening life. Share feasting, and friendship, ideally, until dawn. Before ending, the High Priestess says,

The Dark God has passed the Gate,
He has been reborn through the Mother,
With Him we are each reborn!

All:

The tide has turned!
The light will come again!
In a new dawn, in a new day,
The sun is rising!
Io! Evohe! Blessed be!

Open the circle.

Brigid (Candlemas, February 2)

This ritual is dedicated to Brigid, the Goddess of fire and inspiration; in Ireland, the Triple Goddess of poetry, smithcraft, and healing.

The central cauldron is filled with earth. Unlit candles—one for each covener and guest, are piled beside it. One candle stands upright in the center.

The circle gathers and does the breath meditation. The High Priestess says,

"This is the feast of the waxing light. What was born at the Solstice begins to manifest, and we who were midwives to the infant year now see the Child Sun grow strong as the days grow visibly longer. This is the time of individuation: within the measures of the spiral, we each light our own light, and become uniquely ourselves. It is the time of initiation, of beginning, when seeds that will later sprout and grow begin to stir from their dark sleep. We meet to share the light of inspiration, that will grow with the growing year."

Purify, cast the circle, and invoke the Goddess and God. The High Priestess leads a call and response chant:

> Fire of the heart,
> Fire of the mind,
> Fire of the hearth,
> Fire of the wind,
> Fire of the Art,
> Fire out of time!

All: "She shines for all, She burns in all!"
(Repeat. Spontaneous lines can be interjected.)

When power has been raised, light the central candle. Begin the Spiral Dance, singing,

> I circle around, I circle around,
> The boundaries of the earth.
> Wearing my long wing feathers as I fly.[5]

(The Spiral Dance: All face out. The leader begins moving counter-clockwise, with a simple grapevine step. As the circle unwinds, she whips around, facing the person next to her, and leads the spiral inward, clockwise. As coveners pass, face to face, they kiss.)

When the dance unwinds back into a circle, drummers break away and begin a stronger, wilder beat. One by one, each covener breaks out of the circle, takes a candle and lights it from the center, and then dances with the lit candle, raising power and focusing on the inspiration and creativity they wish in the coming season. Then, one by one, they place their candles in the central cauldron of earth. A Cone of Power is raised, and grounded into the cauldron.

Allow time for trance, opening to inspiration.

Share cakes and wine. Coveners share their creative work—poetry, songs, art works, stories, crafts. Those who are not artistic might share something about their work—a plan that materialized, a good idea, a special accomplishment. The Goddess is thanked for her inspiration.

Open the circle.

Each covener takes home some earth to sprinkle on her garden or keep on her altar for grounding.

Eostar Ritual (Spring Equinox, March 20–23)

Decorate the altar with spring flowers. Place the appropriate element at each of the four points: earth at the North, smoking incense at the East, fire at the South, and a bowl of water at the West. Also place flowers of an appropriate color at each point.

Gather and do a breath meditation. The High Priestess says,

"This is the time of spring's return; the joyful time, the seed time, when life bursts forth from the earth and the chains of winter are broken. Light and dark are equal; it is a time of balance, when all the elements within us must be brought into a new harmony. The Prince of the Sun stretches out his hand, and Kore, the Dark Maiden, returns from the Land of the Dead, cloaked in the fresh rain, with the sweet scent of desire on her breath. Where They step, the wild flowers appear; as They dance, despair turns to hope, sorrow to joy, want to abundance. May our hearts open with the spring! Blessed be!"

Purify, cast the circle, and invoke the Goddess and the God.

The High Priest takes a skein of black wool and goes to each covener in turn. He asks them: "What binds you?"

When they reply—saying, for example, "guilt"—he binds their wrists lightly, repeating, "Guilt binds you; guilt binds you."

Other initiates begin the Kore Chant.* All softly repeat:

> She changes everything She touches,
> And everything She touches, changes.

The High Priestess, following the High Priest, asks each bound covener "Where must you go to be free?" Each replies with one of the four

*See page 88.

directions—which embodies the quality she feels she most lacks: for example, the East. The High Priestess replies: "Go to the East, and free your mind." (Continue, using spirit for the South, emotions for the West, body for the North.)

Each covener goes to the appropriate direction, meditates on its quality (still chanting softly), and passes the bindings through smoke, flame, water, or earth.

The chant slowly builds into a wordless Cone of Power. At its peak, the High Priestess cries out "Now!" All break the bindings, shouting out, and begin dancing freely, singing, chanting, or whatever they are inspired to do.

When all is quiet, and the circle has formed again, time is allowed for trance and meditation. High Priest and High Priestess gather the flowers from the points and go around to each covener, saying, "Take what you need."

Each takes the color or colors of the direction they feel most in need of.

Share cakes and wine, and open the circle.

Beltane: May Eve

A Maypole, crowned with flowers and hung with multicolored ribbons, is set up in an outdoor clearing. Fruits, flowers, round breads, cookies, and doughnuts are hung from bushes and tree branches. A fire is built in the South, well within the boundaries of the circle.

Gather, and breathe together. The High Priestess says,

"This is the time when sweet desire weds wild delight. The Maiden of Spring and the Lord of the Waxing Year meet in the greening fields and rejoice together under the warm sun. The shaft of life is twined in a spiral web and all of nature is renewed. We meet in the time of flowering, to dance the dance of life."

Purify, cast the circle, and invoke the God and Goddess.

One by one, each covener chooses a ribbon of the appropriate color, saying aloud what it is for:

"I choose the red of blood, for my health."

"I choose the sky-blue, for flights of imagination."

"I choose green, for growth." (Etc.)

The music begins (if you don't have musicians in the coven, teach the group a simple folk tune they can all sing together.) Coveners dance the Maypole dance, weaving in and out, concentrating on weaving what they have chosen into their lives. As the ribbons wind tighter, the power grows, until it becomes a wordless Cone of Power. When the cone is released, coveners may continue dancing, and leap over the bonfire, calling out loudly their particular wish each time they leap. Jumping the flames is an act of purification and brings luck. Lovers can leap the bonfire together, to cleanse their relationship of petty disharmonies. Those who want to get rid of something—insecurity, for example—can jump, calling out "I leave my insecurity in the flames!"

When the excitement dies down, raise a quieter, more solemn cone for healing, for members, or for friends not present. Bless cakes and wine, and open the circle.

Feast on the fruits and food that have been hung in the trees.

Litha (Summer Solstice, June 20–23)

The altar and circle are decorated with roses and other summer flowers. A bonfire is lit in the center of the circle. The High Priest carries a God figure made of woven sticks. A loaf of bread (carefully wrapped in many layers of tin foil) is concealed in its center. A wreath of roses and wildflowers lies on the altar. Coveners and guests also wear flowers.

Gather, do a breathing meditation, and light the fire. The High Priestess says,

"This is the time of the rose, blossom and thorn, fragrance and blood. Now on this longest day, light triumphs, and yet begins the decline into dark. The Sun King grown embraces the Queen of Summer in the love that is death because it is so complete that all dissolves into the single song of ecstasy that moves the worlds. So the Lord of Light dies to Himself, and sets sail across the dark seas of time, searching for the isle of light that is rebirth. We turn the Wheel and share his fate, for we have planted the seeds of our own changes, and to grow we must accept even the passing of the sun."

Purify, cast the circle, and invoke the Goddess and God.

Dance the Spiral Dance, singing,

> She is luminous
> She is white
> She is shining
> Crowned with light!
> He is radiant
> He is bright
> He is rising
> He takes flight!

As power is raised, the chant gradually changes. (The following lines are chanted over and over again; different coveners chant different lines simultaneously):

SHE who is at CENter, SHE WHO BLOOMS!
The LEAFy One The GREEN One The LEAFy One The GREEN One ...
She who is CROWNED, She who EmBRACes!

The High Priest dances with the God figure in the center of the circle. Still chanting, coveners place flowers on the figure, twining them into the sticks, until, as the power grows, the figure is covered with blossoms. The circle opens out; the chant becomes a wordless Cone of Power, as High Priest and High Priestess dance closer to the fire. As the Cone peaks, the High Priestess opens her arms and calls out: "To me! To me!"

The High Priest tosses the figure onto the flames. All are silent, meditating on the withering and burning blossoms.

As the blossoms die away, coveners may softly chant "Set Sail" (see the ritual for the Winter Solstice). A Priestess carries the wreath around the circle, holding it up to each person's face so that they can see the flames through it. She says, "See with clear sight."

She holds the wreath aloft, and says, "And know the mystery of the unbroken circle!"

High Priest and High Priestess remove the bread from the fire and break it open. The Priestess holds it up.

High Priestess: "Behold, the God has gone into the grain!"
All: "He will feed us!"
High Priestess: "The sun is on the water!"
All: "He will quench our thirst!"
High Priestess: "The God is in the corn!"
All: "It will grow high!"
High Priestess: "The God is on tree and vine!"
All: "He will ripen in season!"
High Priestess: "The sun is not lost!"
All: "It will rise again!"
High Priestess: "The sun is within us!"
All: "See how we shine!"

All chant "See how we shine!" as bread and wine are passed around the circle.

Share food, and open the circle.

Lughnasad (August 1)

Decorate the altar with sheafs of wheat and grain. A large cornbread God figure lies on the altar, and small bread men and women are piled in baskets. Other baskets hold star-shaped cakes or cookies. A fire is lit in the center of the circle.

Gather, meditate, and breathe together. The High Priestess says,

"This is the wake of Lugh, the Sun King who dies with the waning year, the Corn King who dies when the grain is reaped. We stand now between hope and fear, in the time of waiting. In the fields, the grain is ripe but not yet harvested. We have worked hard to bring many things to fruition, but the rewards are not yet certain. Now the Mother becomes the Reaper, the Implacable One who feeds on life that new life may grow. Light diminishes, the days shorten, summer passes. We gather to turn the Wheel, knowing that to harvest we must sacrifice, and warmth and light must pass into winter."

Purify, cast the circle, and invoke the Goddess and God.

The High Priestess carries the baskets of bread figures to each covener, asking, "What do you fear?" The covener answers, saying, for example, "Failure." The High Priestess repeats the answer, encouraging the covener to chant it: "Failure, failure, failure. . . ." A chant emerges out of all the collective fears, as they are channeled into the bread figures.

As the chant grows stronger, the High Priestess leads a chain-procession dance in a snake, going against the sun, and passing the fire. Each person tosses their bread figure into the fire, concentrating on freeing themselves from their fear. The High Priestess chants,

> "In this fire, may it pass from me and mine!
> May it pass, May it pass,
> May it pass on the outflowing tide
> And burn with the red sun
> As the year dies
> And fade
> As everything fades,
> As everything passes,
> All fades away. . . ." (Repeat the last 2 lines.)

When all have passed the fire, a wordless Cone is raised to purify the group of their fears. Priestesses now carry around the baskets of stars, giving one to each person and asking,

"What do you hope to harvest?"

A chant is built from the responses, and a new Cone is raised to charge the stars with the power to make hope manifest. When the power is earthed, the High Priestess holds up a star, saying,

"May the star of hope be in us always."

All eat the stars.

The High Priest holds up the bread God, saying, "Behold the grain of life!"

He carries it to each person, and, as each breaks off a piece and eats it, he says, "Eat of the life that ever dies and is reborn."

Share cakes and wine, and open the circle.

Mabon (Fall Equinox, September 20–23)

Decorate the altar with fall fruits, flowers, and grain. Coveners should bring thank offerings of sprouts, grain or cloth. Baskets of yarn, seed pods, shells, feathers, and small pine cones are set by the altar. A fire is lit.

Gather, do a breathing meditation. The High Priestess says,

"This is the time of harvest, of thanksgiving and joy, of leave taking and sorrow. Now day and night are equal, in perfect balance, and we give thought to the balance and flow within our own lives. The Sun King has become the Lord of Shadows, sailing West: we follow Him into the dark. Life declines; the season of barrenness is on us, yet we give thanks for that which we have reaped and gathered. We meet to turn the Wheel and weave the cord of life that will sustain us through the dark."

Purify and cast the circle. Invoke the Goddess and God.

Begin with a Banishing Dance, moving counterclockwise. One person shouts out a phrase, something that has hurt her or held her back, kept her from being less than she could be. The others take it up and echo it until its power dies away. Then someone else shouts out a phrase, which is picked up by the rest. Continue until a banishing, purifying Cone can be raised and earthed.

All sit in the circle, and baskets of cord, seeds, shells, and so on are passed around. Each person braids or weaves a cord, twined with natural symbols, concentrating on what she wants to weave into her life. While the work goes on, all chant the Kore Chant.*

When the cords are woven, the High Priestess knots each around the neck of its creator, saying,

> Behold the circle of rebirth,
> The cord of life.
> You will never fade away.

A Cone is raised to charge the cords. Time is allowed for trance and meditation. Then the High Priest steps forward, holds up a sheaf of wheat, and says,

"Autumn's grain is spring's seed."

*See page 88.

He tosses it into the fire and pours out a libation of wine, saying,

> Blessed be the Mother of all life.
> Blessed be the life that comes from Her and returns to Her.

He gives the cup to the High Priestess, who says,

> We have sown, We have tended,
> We have grown, We have gathered,
> We have reaped a good harvest.
> Lady, we thank you for your gifts.
> Lord, we thank you for your bounty.
> I thank you for _____. (Something personal.)

She pours a libation and tosses her offering into the fire. As the cup goes around, each person gives thanks for something and burns her offering.

Share food and wine, and open the circle.

Samhain (Halloween, October 31)

(The ending of the year at Halloween is the Witches' New Year. And so we end in the beginning, as we should, and the Wheel turns on.)

Before leaving home for the ritual, each covener sets out a plate with cakes and wine and a lighted candle, as an offering to their own beloved dead, and spends some time recalling the memory of friends and relatives who are gone.

The altar is decorated with fall leaves. An apple and pomegranate sit on the altar, and in the center of the circle is a gazing crystal or scrying bowl.

The circle gathers, does a breathing meditation, and the High Priestess says,

"This is the night when the veil is thin that divides the worlds. It is the New Year in the time of the year's death, when the harvest is gathered and the fields lie fallow. For tonight the King of the Waning Year has sailed over the sunless sea that is the womb of the Mother, and steps ashore on the Shining Isle, the luminous world egg, becoming the seed of his own rebirth. The gates of life and death are opened; the Sun Child is conceived; the dead walk, and to the living is revealed the Mystery: that every ending is but a new beginning. We meet in time out of time, everywhere and nowhere, here and there, to greet the Lord of Death who is Lord of Life, and the Triple Goddess who is the circle of rebirth."

Purify, cast the circle, and invoke the Goddess and God.

All take hands, and begin an antiphonal chant:

It is the great cold of the night, it is the dark.[6] (Repeat.)
The woman lives, she passes, she dies.
It is the great cold of the night, it is the dark.
Fear lives, it passes, it dies.
It is the great cold of the night, it is the dark.
(Continue with improvised lines.)

As the chanting goes on the High Priest and High Priestess blindfold each member. One by one, they are taken out of the circle, spun around, and formed into a "ship"—aligned in a long triangle, with hands on each other's shoulders, swaying and rocking back and forth. The High Priest winds a cord around their wrists, binding them together. Priestesses are softly chanting,

Weaving the silver ship's thread
of the milk-white
sail the waves
of the sunless sea are
weaving (Etc.; repeat.)

As each person boards the "ship," they are given one word or phrase to repeat: "weaving, weaving, weaving," or "Sail the waves, sail the waves," for example, so that a complex, hypnotic rhythm is built up. Continue until coveners begin to trance—then the chant changes to:

Pearl-gray warrior, ghostly quest;
Prince of twilight, sailing West!

Build power, wait for silence. The High Priest steps forward, and says,

We are in sight of the far shore.
See the light on the waves, a shroud,
A track to follow.
Step into the surf, step ashore.
Cast off your bonds, and be free!

Coveners break bindings.

For here there is no binding.
Cast off the veils that cloud your sight!

Coveners remove blindfolds.

For here all eyes are opened!
You warriors—here your battles are over.
You workers—here your tasks are done!
You who have been hurt, here find healing!
You who are weary, here find rest.
You who are old, here grow young again!
For this is the Land of Youth,

The Shining Land, the Isle of Apples.
Here woods never fail; here there is a tree, the heart of light,
And a well of silence.
Sink down, sink to sleep, beside that deep, green well.

Coveners lie down, looking at the gazing crystal. Priestesses begin a multivoiced trance induction while the High Priest continues:

And follow Him—He is here—
The Comforter, the Consoler,
Heart's Ease, and Sorrow's End.
He is the Guide: the Gate is open.
He is the Guide: the way is clear.
He is the Guide: Death is no barrier—
For He is Lord of the Dance of Shadows—
King in the realm of dreams.

All scry together, either silently, or saying what they see. Allow a long time: This is the best night for scrying in the year.

When all have returned, the High Priest and Priestess go to the altar. She takes the pomegranate and holds it up, saying, "Behold the fruit of life ..."

He plunges his *athame* into it and splits it open, saying, "Which is death!"

They feed each other and the coveners seeds, saying, "Taste the seeds of death."

He holds up the apple, saying, "Behold the fruit of death ..."

She cuts it crosswise, saying, "Which is life!" She holds it up to show the pentacle formed by the seeds, and says, "Behold the five-fold star of rebirth!"

Everyone is given a taste of apple and a sip of wine, as they say, "Taste the fruit of rebirth, and sip the cup of wine of life."

All take hands, and hold them up. The High Priestess says,

"Here is the circle of rebirth. Through you (to the High Priest) all passes out of life, but through Me all may be born again. Everything passes, changes. Seed becomes fruit; fruit becomes seed. In birth, we die; on death, we feed. Know Me, and be free of all fear. For My womb is the cauldron of rebirth, in Me, the circle is ever turning."

All: "Blessed be!"

Share food and wine, and open the circle.

Notes

1. The rituals of our tradition are constantly changing and evolving. We rewrite them and recreate them every year, keeping the elements we like the best and adding new aspects

that grow out of the underlying myth and season. Some festivals seem to evoke words, chanting, and liturgy; others cry out for action and concrete symbolism. The rituals given here are necessarily condensed, a skeletal framework on which new ceremonies can be built. Readers may be moved to enact the rituals as written, but should also feel free to change them, discard parts of them, and add to them.

Generally, people are present who are unfamiliar with the structure of the ritual and the responses to be made. We run through the outline of the ritual with guests and coveners first. In a complicated ritual such as that for the Winter Solstice, we teach them simple responses linked to cue words: for example, "Follow!" might mean "Repeat the lines after me"; "Now!" might be the cue to shout "Io! Evohe!" etc. Initiates may memorize the more complicated responses beforehand, and others join in as they pick it up. For the antiphonal chants, we generally prepare some "spontaneous" lines ahead, enough to get the process started, so that genuine spontaneity can take over.

Some people dislike "wordy" rituals and memorization—they should feel free to ignore the "set" chants and speeches and should improvise their own. Although the rituals are written, for the sake of simplicity, as being performed by the High Priestess and High Priest, different coveners may each lead a section of the ritual—which cuts down considerably on the amount of memorization necessary.

2. The dates of solstices and equinoxes vary from year to year. Check them with an ephemeris or astrological calendar.
3. E. E. Cummings, from "i thank you God", *Poems 1923–1954* (New York: Harcourt, Brace, Jovanovich, 1954).
4. Native American Ghost Dance song. Jerome Rothenburg, ed. *Technicians of the Sacred*, (New York: Doubleday & Co. 1969), p. 99.
5. Native American Ghost Dance song. Rothenburg, p. 99
6. Adapted from the Gabon Pygmy, "Death Rites II," in Rothenburg, p. 171.

13 *Creating Religion: Toward the Future*

Between the Worlds

SAMHAIN, DAWN:

The women climb Twin Peaks, which rise like uplifted breasts above San Francisco Bay. They form circles. Their voices ride the wind. On the summit, they leave gifts for the Goddess: a feather, a shell, a bird's nest.

They are reclaiming the heights.

NIGHT:

The speakers at the Conference on Violence and Pornography stand before an image of the Goddess of Night, with her hands upraised and her hair streaming.

Three thousand women march through the streets where the topless bars and sex shows blare a constant, neon assault. At the park where they finish, they chant, dance, sprinkle each other with purifying salt water:

"Wipe the slate clean; Dream your own dream!"

"Our bodies are sacred; our breasts are sacred."

"Take back the night; the night is ours!"

They are reclaiming the night.

NOVEMBER 1978:

It is the ebb tide of the year, the waning moon before the winter solstice. I am writing this final chapter. The newspapers are filled with corpses; mass "suicides," sudden death. Murder at City Hall—the gun held to the back of the head, fired deliberately. In Guyana, we hear, mothers held the cup of poison to their children's lips. Horror follows horror. One by one, species abandon the earth. The sacred places are strip-mined. Consider: pesticides in breast milk; the neutron bomb. Consider: I am trying to write about things for which there are no longer words in the language, and the meanings of the words I use have been twisted, and may twist my *meanings. Religion has come to mean placing our trust outside of ourselves, remaining like children following a long succession of father figures, teachers, preachers, politicians. And how do we know, once we have ceased to trust ourselves, whether they are Gods or psychopaths?*

Are we, as a species, lined up to drink a poisoned brew?

Witch—Wicca—*from* wic—*"to bend." Can we bend the meanings of the words back? Can we make "religion" mean "re-linking"? And can we make "spirituality" refer to the* human *spirit?*

"The Goddess is reawakening," I say to Laurel, in a moment of probably lunatic optimism. "What do you mean by that?" she asks.

I say, "A mode of consciousness that has been dormant for thousands of years is now coming to the fore; we are beginning to see holistically; our model of the cosmos has been changed; we are beginning to value the feminine, the life-generative principle, to value humanness, and the existing world."

I look at what I have written,

"In circles, in cities, in groves, in streams, in waking and sleeping dreams, in words, in motion, in a flow of music, in poetry, in an opening art, in a day and a night, in struggle, in hunger, in joy, in quickening, in milk, in wine, in the blink of an eye, in a breath, in love, a seed is planted."

But I am forced to consider the question, "Will it have time to take root and grow?"

At first I think of it in terms of faith—that the credo qui absurdum, *the 'I believe because it is absurd,' of Witchcraft is belief in the continuance of life, and the possibility of a truly life-serving culture.*

The dogs scratch to go out. I take them across the street to the empty lot, and watch them play fight, rolling in the mud belly-up, their teeth clicking together like glasses of champagne. I realize suddenly that it is not a question of faith, but of will. I will *life to go on.*

We have collectively created the death cults. We can collectively create a culture of life.

But to do so, we must be willing to step out of line, to forgo the comfort of leaving decisions up to somebody else. To will *is to make our own decisions,*

*guide our own lives, commit ourselves, our time, our work, our energy, to act
in the service of life.*

To will *is to reclaim our power, our power to reclaim the future.*

From my Book of Shadows

"We tell you this: We are doing the impossible. We are teaching ourselves to be human."

Susan Courtot[1]

and when we have won clear
we must return to the circle

Return
the hunt
to the measure of the dance.

Diane Di Prima[2]

Kevyn, one of my coveners, recently had a dream in which a powerful
woman figure appeared to her and said "When a Witch acquires the
acrostic eye, she changes." We both thought a lot about the meaning of
"the acrostic eye." An acrostic, of course, is a form of crossword puzzle,
in which everything has many meanings. Looked at as we normally do,
horizontally, the letters form certain words—but if we shift our vision to
right angles, it all changes. The essence of Witchcraft, and of political
feminism, is acrostic vision: We look at our culture and our conditioning
from another angle, and read an entirely different message. Acrostic vision
is uncomfortable; it sets us at odds with everything we have been taught.
We are forced to validate our own experience, since no external authority
will do it for us.

In thinking about the future of religion and of culture, we need to look
at the present through the acrostic eye. That slightly skewed vision reveals
those underlying mind sets I think of as the scabies of consciousness—
because they cause us extreme discomfort and yet we can't ordinarily see
them. They are embedded in us, under the skin. In this chapter, I want to
examine the destructive forces, as well as the creative forces that are
influencing the direction of our evolution as a society. Only when we
understand the currents of the present can we clearly envision the future.

If we accept the responsibility of claiming the future for life, than we
must engage in the demanding task of recreating culture. A deep and
profound change is needed in our attitude toward the world and the life
on it, toward each other, and in our conceptions of what is human. Somehow, we must win clear of the roles we have been taught, of strictures on
mind and self that are learned before speech and are buried so deep that

they cannot be seen. Today women are creating new myths, singing a new liturgy, painting our own icons, and drawing strength from the new-old symbols of the Goddess, of the "legitimacy and beneficence of female power."[3]

A change in symbols, however, is not enough. We must also change the context in which we respond to symbols and the ways in which they are used. If female images are merely plugged into old structures, they too will function as agents of oppression, and this prospect is doubly frightening because they would then be robbed of the liberating power with which they are imbued today.

Witchcraft is indeed the Old Religion, but it is undergoing so much change and development at present that, in essence, it is being recreated rather than revived. The feminist religion of the future is presently being formed. Those of us who are involved in this re-formation must look closely at the cultural context in which our own ideas about religion were formed, and examine the many regressive tendencies present in society today. Otherwise, the new incarnation of the Goddess will be subtly molded on the very forms we are working to transcend.

One regressive tendency is what I call *absolutism,* which stems from an intolerance of ambiguity. Our culture is highly symbol-bound, and we carry the unconscious assumption that symbolic systems *are* the realities they describe. If the description *is* the reality, and descriptions differ, only one can be true. *Either* God created Adam and Eve, *or* they evolved a la Darwin. *Either* unresolved unconscious conflicts are the final cause of our unhappiness, *or* economic and material conditions. We may change ideologies, but we do not examine the underlying idea that there is One Right, True, and Only Way—Ours!—and everybody else is wrong.

Absolutism is divisive. It sets up false conflicts; for example, between politics and spirituality. In an article entitled "Radical Feminism and Women's Spirituality: Look Before You Leap," Marsha Lichtenstein writes, "the contradiction which is the seed of the distance and distrust between spirituality and politics is that each perceives consciousness in *antithetical* [italics mine] ways... An analysis of consciousness growing from spirituality seeks final causes in a priori categories of thought, as in the discovery of archetypes, as in the mythology of Eve as the repository of evil ... processes of change emphasize an inward journey.... Radical feminism analyzes the historical material conditions under which women's consciousness has developed ... the orientation toward social change is outer-directed, directed at transforming those societal conditions which shape our lives."[4]

The key word in this passage is *antithetical.* A feminist spirituality based on the Goddess immanent in the world will see these analyses as complementary, rather than in opposition. They are both true. *Of course,* a priori categories of thought influence consciousness—and, *of course,* material conditions affect our ability to be whole. We need both inner and outer change—either one alone is not enough.

The Judeo-Christian heritage has left us with the view of a universe composed of warring opposites, which are valued as either good or evil. They cannot coexist. A valuable insight of Witchcraft, shared by many Eastern religions, is that polarities are in balance, not at war. Energy moves in cycles. At times, it flows outward, pushing us to change the world; at other times, it flows inward, transforming ourselves. It cannot be indefinitely exerted exclusively in one direction; it must always turn and return, push and pull, and so be renewed. If we label either end of the cycle as "wrong" or unnecessary, we cut ourselves off from any possibility for renewal or for the exercise of sustained power. We must win clear of the tendency to associate religion and spirituality with withdrawal from the world and the field of action. The Goddess is ourselves *and* the world—to link with Her is to engage actively with the world and all its problems.

Dualism slides over into what I call the "Chosen People Syndrome." When there is One Right True and Only Way—Ours!—and everybody else is wrong, then those who are wrong are damned, and the damned are evil. We are excused from recognizing their humanness and from treating them according to the ethics with which we treat each other. Generally, the Chosen People set about the task of purifying themselves from any contact with the carriers of evil. When they are in power, they institute inquisitions, Witchhunts, pogroms, executions, censorship, and concentration camps.

Oppressed and powerless groups also tend to see themselves as the Chosen People. Since they are not in a position to weed out undesirables from society, they can be "pure" only by removing themselves from the larger community. In the women's movement, this has given birth to separatism.

I distinguish between separation and separatism. Women need women's spaces, especially at this point in history when many of us are recovering from hurts inflicted by men. There is a special intensity in women's mysteries and an unequaled intimacy in women's covens. Women who love other women, or who live Virgin, belonging to themselves alone, attain a very special power. But it is not the *only* form of power inherent in feminist spirituality, nor is it the best form for everyone. The Goddess is Mother, Crone, Lover, as well as Virgin; She is bound up with the birth, love, and death of men as well as of women. If She is immanent in women, and in the world, then She is also immanent in men.

A matrifocal culture, based on nature, celebrates diversity, because diversity assures survival and continuing evolution. Nature creates thousands of species, not just one; and each is different, fitted for a different ecological niche. When a species becomes overspecialized, too narrow in its range of adaptations, it is more likely to become extinct. When political and spiritual movements become too narrow, they are also likely to die out. The strength of the women's movement lies in its diversity, as old and young women, gay and straight, welfare mothers and aspiring bank presidents discover common interests, common needs, and common sisterhood. If our culture as a whole is to evolve toward life, we need to foster diversity, to create and maintain a wide range of differences in lifestyle, theory, and tactics. We need to win clear of the self-righteousness that comes from seeing ourselves as Chosen People, and need to create a religion of heretics, who refuse to toe any ideological lines or give their allegiance to any doctrines of exclusivity.

Another spurious conflict created by absolutism is that between religion and science. When God is felt to be separate from the physical world, religion can be split off from science, and limited to the realm of things having to do with God. But the Goddess is manifest in the physical world, and the more we understand its workings, the better we know Her. Science and religion are both quests for truth—they differ only in their methodology and the set of symbols they use to describe their findings. The field of inquiry is the same.

"Understanding a thing is to arrive at a metaphor for that thing by substituting something more familiar to us,"[5] writes Julian Jaynes (in *The Origin of Consciousness in the Breakdown of the Bicameral Mind*); "We say we understand an aspect of nature when we can say it is similar to some familiar theoretical model."[6] Scientific knowledge, like religious knowledge, is a set of metaphors for a reality that can never be completely described or comprehended. Religion becomes dogmatic when it confuses the metaphor with the thing itself. Metaphors themselves are not contradictory or antithetical; many can be true at once. They point to something beyond themselves; they are separate lights beaming at the same spot.

Scientific metaphors strive to be consistant and testable. They are expected to conform to objective reality. The myths and symbols of nature-oriented religions also began as metaphors for observed reality: for the movement of sun and moon, plant growth and decay, animal behavior and seasonal changes. They resonate on many levels, engaging both our verbal-analytical awareness and our holistic-imagistic awareness. They touch our emotions, determining not only what we know but also how we feel about nature. If we describe the vagina as a flower, we feel differently about it than if we call it "a piece of meat" or a "genital orifice." If we call the ocean "our Mother, the womb of life," we may take more care not to pump Her full of poisons than if we see the ocean merely as "a mass of H_2O."

I would like to see the Goddess religion of the future be firmly grounded in science, in what we can observe in the physical world. Observation is meditation, as the builders of Stonehenge—temple, astronomical observatory, calendar, and calculator—knew well. Witchcraft has always been an empirical religion; Herbs, spells and practices were constantly tested, and results compared at gatherings of the covens. Today, when we introduce a new ritual, exercise, or invocation, the question is always "does it work?" The tests are more subjective than those of science: Did we feel anything? Were we changed? Did we get the results we expected? Were we excited? Ecstatic? Anxious? Bored? Why?

The old symbols were drawn from observation of recurring patterns in nature. Some have merely been deepened by our expanded knowledge of those patterns. For example, the spiral was the ancient symbol of death and rebirth. We now recognize it as the shape of the DNA molecule, which sets the pattern for an organism's growth, and so it takes on another level of meaning. The galaxy is a spiral; "As above, so below."

Other myths and symbols may change to reflect new knowledge. Many of the old seasonal myths are based on the experiential perception that the sun moves around the earth. Even our language reflects this misconception; we say, "the sun rises," although we know intellectually that it does not and never has; instead, the earth turns. Because our physiology and psychology evolved under the apparently-rising-and-setting sun, the old myths "work" to connect our internal cycles with those of the outer world and cannot just be discarded. Yet perhaps there is an esoteric meaning in the earth's motion, too: We do not just await the light; we journey toward it.

In future or contemporary Goddess religion, a photograph of the earth as seen from space might be our mandala. We might meditate on the structure of the atom as well as icons of ancient Goddesses; and see the years Jane Goodall spent observing chimpanzees in the light of a spiritual discipline. Physics, mathematics, ecology, and biochemistry more and more approach the mystical. New myths can take their concepts and make them numinous, so that they infuse our attitudes and actions with wonder at the richness of life.

Spirituality leaps where science cannot yet follow, because science must always test and measure, and much of reality and human experience is immeasurable. Without discarding science, we can recognize its limitations. There are many modes of consciousness that have not been validated by Western scientific rationalism, in particular what I call "starlight awareness," the holistic, intuitive mode of perception of the right hemisphere of our brains. As a culture, we are experiencing a turn toward the intuitive, the psychic, which have been denied for so long. Astrology, Tarot, palmistry—all the ancient forms of divination are undergoing a revival. People seek for expanded consciousness in everything from yoga to drugs to expensive weekend seminars, and they see no value in a religion that is merely a set of doctrines or a dull Sunday morning's entertainment. Any viable religion developing today will inevitably be concerned with some form of magic, defined as "the art of changing consciousness at will."

Magic has always been an element of Witchcraft, but in the Craft its techniques were practiced within a context of community and connection. They were means of ecstatic union with the Goddess Self—not ends in themselves. Fascination with the psychic—or the psychological—can be a dangerous sidetrack on any spiritual path. When inner visions become a way of escaping contact with others, we are better off simply watching television. When "expanded consciousness" does not deepen our bonds with people and with life, it is worse than useless: It is spiritual self-destruction.

If Goddess religion is not to become mindless idiocy, we must win clear of the tendency of magic to become superstition. Magic—and among its branches I include psychology as it purports to describe and change consciousness—is an art. Like other arts, its efficacy depends far more on who is practicing it than on what theory they base their practice. Egyptian tomb painting is organized on quite different structural principles than twentieth-century Surrealism—yet both schools produced powerful paintings. Balinese music has a different scale and rhythmic structure from Western music, but it is no less beautiful. The concepts of Freud, Jung, Melanie Klein, and Siberian shamanism can all aid healing or perpetuate sickness, depending on how they are applied,

Magical systems are highly elaborate metaphors, not truths. When we say "There are twelve signs in the Zodiac," what we really mean is "we will view the infinite variety of human characteristics through this mental screen, because with it we can gain insights"; just as when we say "there are eight notes in the musical scale," we mean that out of all the possible range and variations of sounds, we will focus on those that fall into these particular relationships, because by doing so we can make music. But when we forget that the signs are arbitrary groupings of stars, and start believing that there are large lions, scorpions, and crabs up in the sky, we are in trouble. The value of magical metaphors is that through them we identify ourselves and connect with larger forces; we partake of the elements, the cosmic process, the movements of the stars. But if we use them for glib explanations and cheap categorizations, they narrow the mind instead of expanding it and reduce experience to a set of formulas that separate us from each other and our own power.

The longing for expanded consciousness has taken many of us on a spiritual "journey to the East," and Hindu, Taoist, and Buddhist concepts are infusing Western culture with new understandings. The East-West dialogue has become a major influence on the evolution of a new world view. Eastern religions offer a radically different approach to spirituality than Judeo-Christian traditions. They are experiential rather than intellectual; they offer exercises, practices, and meditations, rather than catechisms. The image of God is not the anthropomorphic, bearded God-Father in the sky—but the abstract, unknowable ground of consciousness itself, the void, the Tao, the flow. Their goal is not to *know* God, but to *be* God. In many ways, their philosophies are very close to that of Witchcraft.

As women, however, we need to look very closely at these philosophies and ask ourselves the hard-headed, critical question, "What's in it for *me*? What does this spiritual system do for women?" Of course, the gurus, teachers, and ascended masters will tell us that, even by asking such a question, we are merely continuing in our enslavement to the Lords of Mind; that it is simply another dodge of the ego as it resists dissolution in the All. The truth is that while men, in our society, are encouraged to have strong egos and to function in competitive, aggressive, intellectualized modes that may indeed cause them pain, for most women the ego is like a fragile African violet, grown in secret from a seed, carefully nursed and fertilized and sheltered from too much sun. Before I toss mine out into the collective garbage heap, I want to be sure I'm getting something in return. I don't feel qualified to discuss the way Eastern religions function within their own cultures. But if we look at women in the West who have embraced these cults, by and large we find them in bondage. An ecstatic bondage, perhaps; but bondage nevertheless.

Eastern religions may help men become more whole, in touch with the intuitive, receptive, gentle feelings they have been conditioned to ignore. But women cannot become whole by being yet more passive, gentle, and submissive than we already are. We become whole through knowing our strength and creativity, our aggression, our sexuality, by affirming the Self, not by denying it. We cannot achieve enlightenment through identifying with Buddha's wife or Krishna's gopi groupies. While India has strong Goddess traditions—of tantra, of Kali worship—these are less easily popularized in the West, because they do not fit our cultural expectation that truth is purveyed through male images, by charismatic males. If we look closely at the symbols, the hierarchical structure, the denial of sexuality and emotion purveyed by the gurus who do attract popular cults in the West, we can only conclude that, while they may be using different instruments, they are playing the same old song.

Another dimension of absolutism is our tendency to think that truth is somehow more true if it is expressed in extremes; that a theory to be valid must explain everything. For example, a psychologist discovers that rats can be conditioned to respond to certain stimuli in predictable ways and concludes that all learning is nothing more than conditioned responses. This makes for ringing pronouncements and endless arguments in professional journals—after all, how do we *prove* what we innately feel—that somewhere in the gap between the rat in its maze, and Makarova learning to dance, some other factor enters in? But were the psychologist to say simply "*Some* learning is a matter of conditioning," who would listen? A statement like that is not impressive, it doesn't sound new or original; it furnishes no grounds for starting experimental utopian communities, and leads to no international recognition or lucrative lecture tours. It sounds flat, obvious. Its sole virtue is that it is true, which the fine-sounding generalization is not.

Absolutist statements are often extremely appealing. Something in us wants life to be neatly organized around clear principles, with no loose ends left hanging. We desperately wish all problems in long division would work out to whole numbers, not fractions. But if we are interested in solving problems rather than manipulating pretty patterns, we have to accept that they don't. Only when we are ready to confront the muddiness and unclarity of reality can we hope to transform it.

In the past few years, a spate of secular gurus have traded heavily on our cultural longing for simple organizing principles around which to base our lives. The basis of many of the "growth" movements and human potential movements is the absolutist concept, "I create my own reality." It is in some ways comforting to believe this; in other ways, it is a terrifying thought. It seems to be true that we do create more of our lives, our opportunities, our physical health, than we ordinarily take responsibility for. If I blame my unhappiness on my mother, on the "system," on bad luck, I will continue being unhappy rather than taking action to change my situation. It is up to no one but me to create for myself meaningful work, money to live on, and important relationships, and nothing outside of myself stops me from having them all. I am, of course, like most members of these movements, white and middle class. If my skin was another color, if I were mentally retarded because of early malnutrition, or disabled, I doubt that I would be quite so sublime about my ability to create reality. Does the rape victim create the assault? Did the children of Vietnam create napalm? Obviously, no.

Much of reality—the welfare system, war, the social roles ordained for women and men—are created collectively and can only be changed collectively. One of the clearest insights of feminism is that our struggles are *not* just individual, and our pain is not private pain; it is created by ways in which our culture treats women as a class. Sexism, racism, poverty, and blind accident do shape people's lives, and they are not created by their victims. If spirituality is to be truly life serving, it must stress that we are all responsible for each other. Its focus should not be individual enlightenment, but recognition of our interconnectedness and commitment to each other.

Feminist religion does not make false promises. It does not set people up for the pain and disillusionment that comes when the growth groupie bumps up against a reality that can't be changed. Night will follow day, and there's not a damn thing you or I or Werner can do about it.

The paradox, of course, is that we are the Goddess: We are each a part of the interpenetrating, interconnecting reality that is All. And, while we can't stop the earth from turning, we can choose to experience each revolution so deeply and completely that even the dark becomes luminous. To *will* does not mean that the world will conform to our desires—it means that *we* will: We will make our own choices and act so as to bring them about, even knowing we may fail. Feminist spirituality values the courage to take risks, to make mistakes, to be our own authorities.

We need to win clear of the belief that only a few individuals in history have had a direct line on truth; that Jesus or Buddha or Mohammed or Moses or Freud or Werner Erhard know more about our souls than we do. Certainly, we can learn from teachers, but we cannot afford to give over our power to direct our lives. A feminist religion needs no messiahs, no martyrs, no saints to lead the way. Instead, it must validate us in discovering and sharing our experiences, inner and outer. Its goal should be that impossible task of teaching ourselves—because we have no models and no teachers who can show us the way—to become human, fully alive with all the human passions and desires, faults and limitations, and infinite possibilities.

Many forces today are shaping the genesis of new myths. I have discussed the changes science has brought to religion, and the impact of the East-West dialogue. Our growing awareness of ecology, the impending environmental apocalypse, has forced on us a realization of our interconnectedness with all forms of life, which is the basis of Goddess religion. Our changing cultural attitude toward sexuality is also influencing our spirituality.

Feminists have quite rightly pointed out that the so-called sexual revolution has too often meant the open marketing of women's bodies and the objectification of women. But this is because we are not yet sexually free. Pornography, rape, prostitution, sadomasochism simply bring out into the open the theme that underlies asceticism, celibacy, and Christian chastity—that sex is dirty and evil, and by extension, so are women. Under patriarchy, sexuality provides the rationale for violence against women—the stoning of adultresses, the burning of Witches, the snickering probe into the conduct of rape victims.

Goddess religion identifies sexuality as the expression of the creative life force of the universe. It is not dirty, nor is it merely "normal"; it is sacred, the manifestation of the Goddess. Fortunately, this does not mean you have to be ordained before you can do it. In feminist spirituality, a thing that is sacred can also be affectionate, joyful, pleasurable, passionate, funny, or purely animal. "All acts of love and pleasure are My rituals," says the Goddess. Sexuality is sacred because it is a sharing of energy, in passionate surrender to the power of the Goddess, immanent in our desire. In orgasm, we share in the force that moves the stars.

The strongest mythogenic force at work today, however, is feminism. Women have dared to look through the acrostic eye, and the molds have shattered. The process of cultural change is a long and difficult one. The laws, the language, the economic and social system do not yet reflect our vision. We are discovering and creating myths and symbols and rituals that do. We need images that move us beyond language, law, and custom; that hurl us beyond the boundaries of our lives to that space between the worlds, where we can see clear.

The feminist movement is a magicospiritual movement as well as a political movement. It is spiritual because it is addressed to the liberation of the human spirit, to healing our fragmentation, to becoming whole. It is magical because it changes consciousness, it expands our awareness and gives us a new vision. It is also magic by another definition: "the art of causing change in accordance with will."

If we are to reclaim our culture, we cannot afford narrow definitions.

And when we have won clear, "we must return to the circle." The circle is the ecological circle, the circle of the interdependence of all living organisms. Civilization must return to harmony with nature.

The circle is also the circle of community. The old family structures, the networks of support and caring are breaking down. Religion has always been a prime source of community, and a vital function of feminist spirituality is to create new networks of involvement. Community also implies broader issues of how equitably power, wealth, and opportunities are shared among different groups, and the issues of who cares for children, the aged, the sick, and the disabled. When the Divine becomes immanent in the world, these are all areas of spiritual concern.

The circle is also the circle of Self. Our view of the Self—what it is, how it perceives, in what modes it functions—has changed greatly. Feminist spirituality is also an inner journey, a personal vision quest, a process of self-healing and self-exploration.

To return to the circle does not necessarily mean to embrace Witchcraft specifically. I hope the religion of the future will be multifaceted, growing out of many traditions. Perhaps we will see a new cult of the Virgin Mary and a revival of the ancient Hebrew Goddess. Native American traditions and Afro-American traditions may flourish in an atmosphere in which they are given the respect they deserve. Eastern religions will inevitably change as they grow in the West—and part of that change may be in the roles they assign women.

But there are valuable underlying concepts in Witchcraft, on which other feminist traditions can draw. The most important is the understanding of the Goddess, the divine, as immanent in the world, manifest in nature, in human beings, in human community. The All-That-Is-One is not now and never has been separate from this existing physical world. She is here, now, *is* each of us in the eternal changing present; is no one but you, is nowhere but where you are—and yet is everyone. To worship Her is to assert, even in the face of suffering and often against all reason that life is good, a great gift, a constant opportunity for ecstasy. If we see it become a burden of misery for others, we have the responsibility to change it.

Because the Goddess is manifest in human beings, we do not try to escape our humanness, but seek to become fully human. The task of feminist religion is to help us learn those things that seem so simple, yet are far more demanding than the most extreme patriarchal disciplines. It is easier to be celibate than to fully alive sexually. It is easier to withdraw from the world than to live in it; easier to be a hermit than to raise a child; easier to repress emotions than to feel them and express them; easier to meditate in solitude than to communicate in a group; easier to submit to another's authority than place trust in oneself. It is not easy to be a Witch, a bender, a shaper, one of the Wise; nor is it safe, comfortable, "laid back," mellow, uplifting, or a guarantee of peace of mind. It requires openness, vulnerability, courage, and work. It gives no answers: only tasks to be done, and questions to consider. In order to truly transform our culture, we need that orientation toward life, toward the body, toward sexuality, ego, will, toward all the muckiness and adventure of being human.

Witchcraft offers the model of a religion of poetry, not theology. It presents metaphors, not doctrines, and leaves open the possibility of reconciliation of science and religion, of many ways of knowing. It functions in those deeper ways of knowing which our culture has denied and for which we hunger.

The world view of Witchcraft is cyclical, spiral. It dissolves dualities and sees opposites as complements. Diversity is valued; both poles of any duality are always valued because between them flows the on-off pulse of polar energy that sustains life. That cycle is the rhythm of the dance, to which the Hunter, the seeker, is always drawn back.

Finally, the Craft provides a structural model: the coven, the circle of friends, in which there is leadership, but no hierarchy, small enough to create community without loss of individuality. The form of ritual is circular: We face each other, not an altar or a podium or a sacred shrine, because it is in each other that the Goddess is found. Every Witch is Priestess or Priest: there are no hierophants, no messiahs, no avatars, no gurus. The Goddess says, "If that which you seek, you find not within yourself, you will never find it without. For I have been with you from the beginning."

When we return to the circle, when we win clear, what will we be? I have snatches of visions; perhaps they are the memories of future lives:

The children awaken in the middle of the night, to watch the moon rise. They are taught nothing about the moon until they have lived with her for a cycle, arising with her rising, sleeping when she sets. They are not taught about the sun until they have watched it for a year, following its movements along the horizon. Their teachers encourage them to make pictures, stories, and songs about the moon and sun.

When they are older, they are shown a model of the solar system. They are not told about it, they are simply left with it for a time each day, to observe it, with an open mind. For some of them, understanding will come in a moment's illumination. For others, it will not. It doesn't matter. After a time, they are encouraged to ask questions. After a time, they are answered.

When they are older yet, they may make a pilgrimage to the moon. Some may live for a time in the Shrine of the Bright Face, watching the earth wax and wane. Some may prefer the Dark Shrine, which always faces the stars.

The path is sometimes steep, but not hard to follow. Aradia knows her uneasiness comes only from being alone. Like all the other children, she has hiked and camped in these mountains many times. But never before alone.

She stops for a moment in a high meadow, to soak up the sun. Three days. She will live off the land, or fast. Already the Feast of First Blood, the celebration, the ceremonial dishes of red food, the gifts wrapped in red paper that she will not use for a year, are memories of a past life. Now she is passing. She has given away her dolls and toys. Along the high ridge, she follows the trail to the Lake of Women.

Anna waits by the lake. It lies cupped in the hollow of the mountains like a teardrop in the hand. She drinks the slience: after all the years of noise, children, work, demands. After years of drawing plans for buildings, it is good to look at trees and rocks, to take her Year of Repose. When the young girls come, she and the other women teach them things about their bodies, about wind and rock, fire and water. They learn to spin and weave, to bring flame without matches, to understand the speech of animals. At night, they are taught the mysteries and songs that women remember. And they work magic. . . .

It is the night of the Winter Solstice. In San Francisco, there are bonfires everywhere: strung along the beaches, blazing on Twin Peaks, on all the high places. In the parks and on rooftops, small groups gather around cauldrons. There are no mass meetings, only circles.

They begin with a very old custom: walking the land and searching for papers or foreign objects. The Elders have debated discontinuing the custom:

It is outdated. There is never any trash to find. Nothing is made to be idly tossed away; nothing is wasted.

From the hilltops, the city is a colored mosaic set in green. Everywhere are gardens. The last rays of the sun gleam rose in a thousand solar collectors.

The Witches take hands around the fire. The wind rises, rattling the eucalyptus branches. Across the city, thousands of gaily painted windmills spin to life, flashing the colored lights with which they are decorated at Midwinter. Candles are blown out; altars topple over. No one minds. They have all they need to make magic: their voices, their breath, each other.

Through the long night, they chant each other's names. They sing hymns to the newborn sun, to the eternally revolving Goddess. They pour libations and give thanks—especially the very old ones, who remember when it was different:

"I am thankful that in this city, no one goes hungry."

"I am thankful that in this city, no one is left to die alone."

"I give thanks that I can walk the dark streets without fearing violence."

"I give thanks that the air is clean, that life has returned to the waters of the bay, that we are at peace."

"I give thanks that everyone has work to do."

In the morning, there are parades down Market Street, and the neighborhood groups and unions present their elaborate floats, the creation of the city's finest artists. Gorgeously arrayed figures of the Virgin arrive from the Mission District, followed by a glittering Wheel of Lights from the Electrical Worker's Union, and a Sun Child made of yellow flowers from the Midwives' Guild. There are clowns, jugglers, marching bands—people pour out of their houses to dance in the streets. Later, there will be concerts, parties, masquerade balls, and special theater performances.

The last day of celebration is quiet and peaceful. People visit in each other's homes, exchanging food and simple gifts. Families and covens eat together.

At night, they return to the hillsides and rekindle the fires. They join together to earth the power of the season, and slip between the worlds. Beyond time, in touch with past and future both, with all possibilities, they speak to us. We can hear them. They say to each one of us,

"Wake up! You are it. You are a part of the circle of the Wise. There is no mystery that has not already been revealed to you. There is no power you do not already have. You share in all the love that is."

"When we return to the circle
we have won clear.
Return the dance to the pulses of the Hunt."[7]

The Goddess awakens in infinite forms and a thousand disguises. She is found where She is least expected, appears out of nowhere and everywhere to illumine the open heart. She is singing, crying, moaning, wailing, shrieking, crooning to us: to be awake, to commit ourselves to life, to be a lover in the world and of the world, to join our voices in the single song of constant change and creation. For Her law is love unto all beings, and She is the cup of wine of life.

May life thrive, now and always!
The circle is ever open, ever unbroken.
May the Goddess awaken in each of our hearts.
Merry meet, and merry part. And blessed be.

Notes

1. Martha Courtot, "Tribes," *Lady-Unique-Inclination-of-the-Night,* Cycle 2, Summer 1977, p. 13.
2. Diane Di Prima, "Now born in uniqueness, join the Common Quest," *Loba* (Berkeley: Wingbow Press, 1978), p. 188.
3. Carol P. Christ, "Why Women Need The Goddess", in Carol P. Christ and Judith Plaskow, eds. *Womanspirit Rising,* (San Francisco: Harper & Row, 1979) p. 278.
4. Marsha Lichtenstein, "Radical Feminism and Women's Spirituality: Looking Before You Leap," *Lady-Unique,* Cycle 2, Summer 1977, pp. 37–38.
5. Julian Jaynes, *The Origin of Consciousness in the Breakdown of the Bicameral Mind* (Boston: Houghton Mifflin, 1976), p. 52.
6. Jaynes, p. 53.
7. Di Prima, p. 189.

Tables of Correspondences

The Elements

AIR

Direction: East

Rules: The mind, all mental, intuitive and psychic work, knowledge, abstract learning, theory, windswept hills, plains, windy beaches, high mountain peaks, high towers, wind and breath

Time: Dawn

Season: Spring

Colors: White, bright yellow, crimson, blue-white

Signs of the Zodiac: Gemini, Libra, Aquarius

Tools: Athame, sword, censer

Spirits: Sylphs, ruled by their King Paralda (many of these systems are extremely male oriented; again, I include them for interest and reference—don't use them if you don't like them);

Angel: Michael

Name of the East Wind: Eurus

Sense: Smell

Jewel: Topaz

Incense: Galbanum

Plants: Frankincense, myrrh, pansy, primrose, vervain, violet, yarrow

Tree: Aspen

Animals: Birds, especially the eagle and the hawk

Godesses: Aradia, Arianrhod, Cardea, Nuit, Urania

Gods: Enlil, Khephera, Mercury, Shu, Thoth

FIRE

Direction: South

Rules: Energy, spirit, heat, flame, blood, sap, life, will, healing and destroying, purification, bonfires, hearth fires, candle flames, sun, deserts, volcanoes, eruptions, explosions

Time: Noon

Season: Summer

Colors: Red, gold, crimson, orange, white (the sun's noon light)

Signs of the Zodiac: Aries, Leo, Sagittarius

Tools: Censer, wand

Spirits: Salamanders, ruled by their King Djin

Angel: Ariel

Name of the South Wind: Notus

Sense: Sight

Jewel: Fire opal

Incense: Olibanum

Plants: Garlic, hibiscus, mustard, nettle, onion, red peppers, red poppies

Tree: Almond, in flower

Animals: Fire-breathing dragons; lions; horses, when their hooves strike sparks

Goddesses: Brigit, Hestia, Pele, Vesta

Gods: Agni, Hephaestus, Horus, Vulcan

WATER

Direction: West

Rules: Emotions, feelings, love, courage, daring, sorrow, the ocean, the tides, lakes, pools, streams, and rivers, springs and wells, intuition, the unconscious mind, the womb, generation, fertility

Time: Twilight

Season: Autumn

Colors: Blue, blue-green, green, gray, indigo, black

Signs of the Zodiac: Cancer, Scorpio, Pisces
Tools: Cup
Spirits: Undines, ruled by their King Niksa
Angel: Raphael
Name of the West Wind: Zephyrus
Sense: Taste
Jewel: Aquamarine
Incense: Myrrh
Plants: Ferns, lotus, mosses, rushes, seaweeds, water lilies, and all water plants
Tree: Willow
Animals: Dragons as serpents, dolphins and porpoises, fish, seals and sea mammals, water-dwelling snakes, all water creatures and sea birds
Goddesses: Arhrodite, Isis, Mariamne, Mari, Tiamat
Gods: Dylan, Ea, Llyr, Manannan, Osiris, Neptune, Poseidon

EARTH

Direction: North
Rules: The body, growth, nature, sustenance, material gain, money, creativity, birth, death, silence, chasms, caves, caverns, groves, fields, rocks, standing stones, mountains, crystal, jewels, metal
Time: Midnight
Season: Winter
Colors: Black, brown, green, white
Signs of the Zodiac: Taurus, Virgo, Capricorn
Tools: Pentacle
Spirits: Gnomes, ruled by their King Ghob
Angel: Gabriel
Name of the North Wind: Boreas, Ophion
Sense: Touch
Jewel: Rock crystal, salt
Incense: Storax
Plants: Comfrey; ivy; grains: barley, oats, corn, rice, rye, wheat
Tree: Oak
Animal: Cow or bull, bison, snakes (earth-dwelling), stag
Goddesses: Ceres, Demeter, Gaea, Mah, Nephthys, Persephone, Prithivi, Rhea, Rhiannon
Gods: Adonis, Athos, Arawn, Cernunnos, Dionysus, Marduk, Pan, Tammuz

SPIRIT/ETHER

Direction: Center and circumference, throughout and about
Rules: Transcendence, transformation, change, everywhere and nowhere, within and without, the void, immanence
Time: Beyond time, all time is one
Season: The turning wheel
Colors: Clear, white, black
Tools: Cauldron
Sense: Hearing
Plant: Mistletoe
Tree: The flowering almond
Animal: Sphinx
Goddesses: Isis, the Secret Name of the Goddess, Shekinah
Gods: Akasha, Iao, JHVH

The Heavenly Bodies

THE MOON

Rules: Woman; cycles; birth; generation; inspiration; poetry; emotions; travel, especially by water; the sea and tides; fertility; rain; intuition; psychic ability; secrets
  New or Crescent Moon—the Maiden, birth and initiation, virginity, beginnings, the hunt
  Full Moon—the Mother, growth, fulfillment, sexuality, maturation, nurturing, love
  Waning or Dark Moon—the Crone, the woman past menopause, old age, deep secrets, wisdom, divination, prophecy, death and resurrection, endings
Day: Monday
Element: Water
Color:
  New—white or silver
  Full— red or green
  Waning—black
Signs of the Zodiac: Cancer
Tone: Ti
Letter: S
Number: 3 or 9
Jewel: Moonstone, pearl, quartz, rock crystal
Cabalistic sphere: 9 Yesod—Foundation
Angel: Gabriel

Incense: Bay leaf, ginseng, jasmine, myrtle, or poppy

Plants: Banana, cabbage, chickweed, cucumber, leafy vegetables, lotus, melons, mushrooms, myrtle, opium poppy, pumpkin, purslane, sea holly, seaweed, watercress, wild rose, wintergreen

Tree: Willow

Animal: Hare, elephant, cat

Goddesses: Artemis, Brigit, Brizo, Ceridwen, Diana, Hathor, Isis, Hecate, Levanah, Lunah, Mari, Nimuë, Pasiphaë, Phoebe, Selene, Anna

   New—Artemis, Nimuë

   Full—Diana, Mari

   Waning—Hecate, Anna

Gods: Atlas, Khonsu, Sin

THE SUN

Rules: Joy, success, advancement, leadership, natural power, friendship, growth, healing, light

Day: Sunday

Element: Fire

Color: Gold, yellow

Signs: Leo

Tone: Re, D

Letter: B

Number: 1, 6, or 21

Metal: Gold

Jewel: Topaz, yellow diamond

Cabalistic sphere: 6 Tiphereth—Beauty

Angel: Raphael

Incense: Cloves, cinnamon, frankincense, laurel, olibanum

Plants: Acacia, angelica, bay laurel, chamomile, citrus fruits, heliotrope, honey, juniper, lovage, marigold, mistletoe, rosemary, rue, saffron, St. Joan's (or St. John's) Wort, sunflower, vine

Tree: Acacia, bay laurel, ash, birch, broom

Animal: Child, eagle, lion, phoenix, sparrowhawk

Goddesses: Amaterasu, Bast, Ilat, Sekhmet, Theia

Gods: Apollo, Helios, Hyperion, Legba, Lugh, Ra, Semesh, Vishnu-Krishna-Rama

MERCURY

Rules: Communications, intelligence, cleverness, creativity, science, memory, business transactions, thievery

Day: Wednesday
Element: Air, Water
Color: Violet, mixtures of colors
Signs of the Zodiac: Gemini, Virgo
Tone: Mi, B
Letter: C
Number: 1, 4, or 8
Metal: Quicksilver, alloys
Jewel: Opal, agate
Cabalistic sphere: 8 Chod—Glory
Angel: Michael
Incense: Storax, mace, or sandalwood
Plants: Caraway, carrots, cascara sagrada, dill, elecampane, fennel,
fenugreek, horehound, lavender, licorice, mandrake, marjoram, myrtle,
parsley, pomegranate, valerian
Tree: Hazel, ash, or almond
Animal: Hermaphrodite, jackal, or twin serpents.
Goddesses: Athena, Maat, Metis
Gods: Coeus, Anubis, Hermes, Lug, Nabu, Mercury, Thoth, Woden

VENUS

Rules: Love, harmony, attraction, friendship, pleasure, sexuality
Day: Friday
Element: Earth, Water
Color: Green, indigo, rose
Signs: Taurus, Libra.
Tone: La, E
Letter: Q
Number: 5, 6, or 7
Metal: Copper
Jewel: Amber, emerald
Cabalistic sphere: 7 Netzach—Splendor
Angel: Haniel
Incense: Benzoin, jasmine, rose
Plants: Acacia flowers, almond oil, aloes, apple, birch, daffodil,
damask rose, elder, elderberry, feverfew, fig, geranium, mint, mugwort,
olive oil, pennyroyal, plantain, raspberry, rose, strawberry, tansy,
thyme, verbena, vervain, violet
Tree: Apple, quince
Animal: Dove, lynx

Goddesses: Aphrodite, Beltis, Asherah, Astarte, Freia, Hathor, Inanna, Isis, Ishtar, Mari, Mariamne, Tethys, Venus
Gods: Eros, Oceanus, Robin Hood, Pan

MARS

Rules: Strength, struggle, war, anger, conflict, aggression
Day: Tuesday
Element: Fire
Color: Red
Signs of the Zodiac: Aries, some authorities give Scorpio also.
Tone: Do, C
Letter: T
Number: 2, 3 or 16, possibly 5
Metal: Iron, Steel
Jewel: Bloodstone, garnet or ruby
Cabalistic sphere: 5 Gevurah—Strength, severity
Angel: Kamael
Incense: Cypress, pine or tobacco
Plants: All-Heal, aloes, asafoetida, basil, betony, capers, chiles, coriander, dragon's blood, gentian, ginger, garlic, mustard, onion, pepper, radish, sarsaparilla, tarragon
Tree: Holly, Kerm-oak
Animal: Basilisk
Goddesses: Anath, Brigit, Dione, Morrigan
Gods: Ares, Crius, Heracles, Mars, Nergal

JUPITER

Rules: Leadership, politics, power, honor, royalty, public acclaim, responsibility, wealth, business, success
Day: Thursday
Element: Air, Fire
Color: Deep blue, royal purple
Signs: Sagittarius
Tone: So, A
Letter: D
Number: 5 or 4
Metal: Tin
Jewel: Amethyst, chrysolite, sapphire, or turquoise
Cabalistic sphere: 4 Chesed—Mercy

Angel: Tzadkiel

Incense: Cedar, nutmeg

Plants: Agrimony, anise, ash, balm, betony, blood root, borage, cinquefoil, clover, dandelion, hyssop, linden, mint, mistletoe, nutmeg, sage

Tree: Oak, olive, or terebinth

Animal: Unicorn

Goddesses: Isis, Hera, Juno, Themis

Gods: Bel, Eurymedon, Jupiter, Marduk, Thor, Zeus

SATURN

Rules: Obstacles, limitations, binding, knowledge, death, buildings, history, time

Day: Saturday

Element: Water, Earth

Color: Black, blue

Signs: Capricorn

Tone: Fa, G

Letter: F

Number: 7 or 3

Metal: Lead

Jewel: Pearl, onyx, or star sapphire

Sphere: 3 Binah—Understanding

Angel: Tzaphkiel

Incense: Civet, ironwood, myrrh

Plants: Aconite (monkshood or wolfbane), beets, bistort (dragonwort), comfrey, cypress, hellebore, hemlock, horsetail, hemp, henbane, mandrake, marijuana, opium poppy, nightshade, Solomon's Seal, thyme, yew

Tree: Alder, pomegranate

Animal: Crow, raven

Goddesses: Cybele, Demeter, Hecate, Hera, Isis, Kali, Nephthys, Rhea

Gods: Bran, Cronos, Ninib, Saturn, YHVH

Aspects of Life

LOVE

Element: Water, Earth

Planet: Venus

Best times:

Friday or Monday
New to Full Moon in
Taurus—earthy and sensual love
Cancer—home and family
Libra—idealistic
Scorpio—sexual!

Colors: Deep rose, green, orange for attraction
Metal: Copper or silver
Number: 5 or 7
Incense/Perfume: Benzoin, jasmine, rose; for sensual passion, civet, musk, patchouli, rose ava
Plants: All herbs of Venus, especially acacia flowers, aloes, Balm of Gilead (buds carried on your person will mend a broken heart!), cyclamen (if a potted plant is kept in the bedroom, the union will be long and happy), elecampane, jasmine, lavender, meadowsweet, mistletoe, myrrh, myrtle, rose, tansy, valerian, vervain, violet

Aphrodisiacs (reputed): Beth root, coriander, clover, damiana, dulse, fo-ti-tieng, ginseng, nasturtium, periwinkle, yohimbe
Goddesses: Aphrodite, Asherah, Astarte, Beltis, Branwen (can grant either union with true love or cure for the passion), Diana, Freia, Hathor, Ishtar, Isis, Maia, Mari, Mariamne, Venus
Gods: Cernunnos, Eros, Adonis, Robin Hood, Pan

MONEY AND BUSINESS

Element: Earth, Air
Planet: Jupiter, Mercury, the Sun
Best times:

Thursday, Wednesday, or Sunday
Waxing to full moon for increase in
an earth sign—for material gain
an air sign—for ideas, plans
a fire sign—for energy, growth
Virgo—for work involving detail
Capricorn—for caution, or to overcome obstacles
Leo—for solar power
Sagittarius—for expansion, travel
Aries—for beginning a new project

Colors: Green, gold, silver
Number: 1, 4, 8, or 7
Incense: Cedar, cinnamon, laurel, mace, nutmeg, or storax

Plants: Balm, borage, lavender, High Joan the Conqueress (or John the Conqueror) root, mandrake, oak leaves, saffron, sage, St. Joan's (John's) Wort, sunflower seeds, valerian
Goddesses: Earth Goddesses, Demeter, Hera, Juno
Gods: Earth Gods, Hermes, Lugh, Jupiter, Mercury, Zeus

CREATIVE WORK

Element: All
Planets: Earth, the Moon (for inspiration), Mercury (for communication), the Sun
Best times:
  Monday, Wednesday, or Sunday
  Moon waxing—for beginning
  Near the full—for inspiration
  Waning—for self-criticism, reworking
  an air sign—for mental work, especially involving words
  an earth sign—for crafts and work with the hands
  a fire sign—for creative energy
  a water sign—for emotional expressions
Colors: Gold, silver, violet, yellow, mixtures of colors
Number: 1, 3, 4, 6, or 9
Incense: Bay laurel, cinnamon, ginseng, mace, storax
Plants: Laurel, lavender, myrtle, skullcap, valerian
Goddesses: Brigit (Triple Goddess of poetry, healing, and smithcraft), Ceridwen (Keeper of the Cauldron of Inspiration), Athena or Minerva (for knowledge, wisdom), Mnemosyne (Mother of the Triple Muse)
  The Triple Muse:
    Calliope—"beautiful face"
    Erato—"beloved one"
    Urania—"heavenly one"
  The Ninefold Muse:
    Calliope—Epic poetry
    Clio—History
    Euterpe—Lyric poetry
    Melpomene—Tragedy
    Terpsichore—Choral dancing
    Erato—Erotic poetry and mime
    Polyhymnia—Sacred poetry
    Urania—Astronomy

Thaleia—Comedy
Any form of the Triple Goddess
Gods: Apollo (music and poetry); Orpheus (music); Ogma (poetry)
Hermes, Mercury, and Thoth (knowledge and communication); Credne,
Gobniu, and Hephaestus (all for crafts, smithcraft)

HEALING

Element: All
Planet: Sun, Moon, Earth
Best times:
Sunday or Monday
  Moon waxing to full—for increased health
  Moon waning or dark—to banish, drive away disease
  In earth or water sign
Colors: Blue, green, gold, orange
Number: 1, 3, 7, or 9
Incense: Bay, frankincense, sandalwood, eucalyptus
Plants: All healing herbs
Goddesses: Moon and Earth Goddesses, Artemis, Hebe, Hygeia
Gods: Asclepius, Apollo, Diancecht

LAW AND JUSTICE

Element: Earth, Air
Planet: Jupiter, Sun, Mercury, Saturn, Mars
Best times:
  Thursday—for success, securing justice
  Sunday—for freedom
  Saturday—to bind a criminal, to limit someone's freedom or
bring them to justice, for prosecution
  Tuesday—for strength in conflict
Colors: Deep blue, royal purple, red, black
Number: 4 or 8
Incense: Cedar, cypress, frankincense, pine, or sandalwood
Plants: herbs of the appropriate planetary powers, nettles (for
binding), garlic (for protection), High Joan the Conqueress root and St.
Joan's Wort (for invincibility)
Goddesses: Athena (for mercy, especially), Maat, Nemesis (to bring
justice against an offender), Themis, Aradia (to protect the poor)
Gods: The Dagda, Jupiter, Zeus, Osiris, Thoth

PROTECTION

Element: All
Planet: Moon, Sun
Best times:
  Monday or Sunday
  Waxing to full moon—to establish protection
  Waning Moon—banishing evil
Colors: Silver, white, blue
Number: 4, 5, 3, 9, 8
Metal: Silver
Incense: Bay laurel, rosemary
Plants: Asafoetida, avens (Star of the Earth), basil (wards off evil), blood root, broom tops (to put in water used for aspurging and purification), burdock, cinquefoil, feverfew (protects against sickness and accidents), garlic (wear the cloves or hang on the threshold to keep evil away), hyssop, High Joan the Conqueress root, laurel, mandrake, motherwort, nettles (for binding), purslane, rosemary (plant by your threshold to protect the home), rowan (especially against evil psychic forces), Solomon's Seal (used in exorcism), St. Joan's Wort, unicorn root, vervain (gathered with the left hand at the rise of the Dog Star, Sirius)
  Goddesses: Moon Goddesses, especially Artemis (protects young children), and Hera, Aradia
  Gods: Cuchulain, the Dagda, Jupiter, Thor

PSYCHIC WORK

Element: Air, water, fire
Planet: Moon
Best times:
  Full moon—for the height of psychic power
  Dark moon—for deep, hidden secrets and mysteries
Colors: Silver, white, black
Number: 3 or 9
Incense: Cinnamon, saffron, wormwood, other appropriate plants
Plants:
  Relaxation: Anise, catnip, chamomile, dandelion, hops, lavender, linden, mint, parsley, red clover, sage, savory, tarragon, thyme (wild), nutmeg (rub the oil on temples), valerian (stuff a pillow with it), vervain
  Visualization: Ginseng, gota cola, mugwort, skullcap
  Sleep pillow: Lavender and linden

Concentration and memory: All Heal, Eyebright, lemon balm, marjoram, nutmeg, parsley, petitgrain oil, rosemary, sage

Mental steadiness: Chamomile, celery, and rosemary together

Energy: Gota cola, ginseng, lovage (a bath in this herb refreshes psychic powers), yerba mate

Dreams: Ash leaves, mugwort, artemisia; chamomile, mugwort, and skullcap (together in a tea, drink before sleep)

To prevent nightmares and fearful visions: Chamomile, rosemary, wood betony (place some under your pillow)

Divination and trance work: Acacia flowers, bistort (dragonwort), ginseng, mugwort (drink a tea for clear vision), nutmeg, saffron (tea or incense), wormwood (incense, burned on Halloween to enable one to see the returning spirits of the Mighty Dead), laurel leaves (chewed by the Priestesses of Delphi)

Psychedelics: are better left alone when you are beginning to open up psychicly. They tend to wrench the psychic centers open too quickly and in an uncontrolled way—sometimes with destructive results.

Goddesses: All Moon Goddesses, Cybele, Hecate (for divination and spells), Ceridwen, Hera (for prophecy), Nephthys, Pasiphaë (for dream oracles)

Gods: Gwydion, Hermes, Math, Merddin, Thoth, Asclepius (for dream oracles that have to do with healing)

Selected Bibliography

Anderson, Victor. *Thorns of the Blood Rose* (San Leandro, Calif.: Cora Anderson, 1970).

Anima, An Experimental Journal, 1975, *1*(2).

Bartlett, Lee. "Interview—Gary Snyder." *California Quarterly* 9 (Spring 1975): 43–50.

Besant, Annie, and Leadbeater, C. W. *Thought-Forms* (Wheaton, Ill.: Theosophical Publishing, 1969).

Blanc, Alberto C. "Some evidence for the Ideologies of Early Man" in Washburn, Sherwood L., ed., *The Social Life of Early Man* (Chicago: Aldine Publishing Co., 1961) p. 124.

Bonewitz, P. E. I. *Real Magic* (Berkeley, Calif.: Creative Arts Books, 1979).

Braidwood, Robert J. "The Agricultural Revolution." *Scientific American,* 203, no. 48 (September 1960): 130–134.

Braidwood, Robert J. *Prehistoric Men* (Glenview, Ill.: Scott, Foresman, 1964).

Breuil, Henri, and Lantier, Raymond. *The Men of the Old Stone Age.* Trans., B. B. Rafter (London: Harrap, 1965).

Brown, Barbara. *New Mind, New Body* (New York: Harper & Row, 1974).

Buckland, Raymond. *Witchcraft from the Inside.* (St. Paul: Llewellyn, 1971).

Budapest, Z. *The Feminist Book of Lights and Shadows* (Venice, Calif.: Luna Publications, 1976).

Campbell, Joseph. *The Masks of God: Creative Mythology* (New York: Viking Press, 1970).

Campbell, Joseph. *The Masks of God: Oriental Mythology* (New York: Penguin Books, 1977).

Campbell, Joseph. *The Masks of God: Primitive Mythology* (New York: Penguin Books, 1977).

Campbell, Joseph. *Myths to Live by* (New York: Bantam Books, 1973).

Carruth, Hayden, ed. *The Voice That is Great Within Us: American Poetry of the Twentieth Century* (New York: Bantam Books, 1971).

Castaneda, Carlos. *The Teachings of Don Juan: A Yaqui Way of Knowledge* (New York: Ballantine Books, 1968).

Castaneda, Carlos. *A Separate Reality: Further Conversations with Don Juan* (New York: Simon & Schuster, 1971).

Castaneda, Carlos. *Tales of Power* (New York: Simon & Schuster, 1974).

Chadwick, Nora K. *Celtic Britain* (New York: Praeger, 1963).

Chicago, Judy. *The Dinner Party: A Symbol of Our Heritage* (Garden City, N.Y.: Anchor Press/Doubleday, 1979)

Christ, Carol P., and Plaskow, Judith, eds. *Womanspirit Rising* (San Francisco: Harper & Row, 1979).

Chrysalis, A Magazine of Women's Culture (Los Angeles: Winter Solstice, 1978).

Claiborne, Robert. *Climate, Man and History* (New York: Norton, 1970).

Clark, Grahame and Piggott, Stuart, *Prehistoric Societies* (London: Hutchinson & Co., 1967).

The CoEvolution Quarterly 12 (Summer 1976).

Commoner, Barry. *The Closing Circle* (New York: Knopf, 1971).

Courtot, Martha, "Tribes", *Lady-Unique-Inclination-Of-The-Night* (New Brunswick, N.J.: Sowing Circle Press, 1977) Cycle 2, pp.12–13.

Crawford, O. G. S. *The Eye Goddess* (New York: Macmillan, 1958).

Crowley, Aleister. *Magick in Theory & Practice* (New York: Dover, 1976).

Cummings, E. E., "i thank you God", *Poems 1923–1954,* (New York: Harcourt, Brace & Jovanovich, 1954)

Daly, Mary. *Beyond God the Father: Toward a Philosophy of Women's Liberation* (Boston: Beacon Press, 1973).

Daly, Mary. *Gyn/Ecology: The Meta-Ethics of Radical Feminism* (Boston: Beacon Press, 1978).

Davis, Elizabeth Gould. *The First Sex* (New York: Putnam's, 1971).

Diner, Helen. *Mothers and Amazons* (New York: Anchor Press, 1973).

Dinnerstein, Dorothy. *The Mermaid & The Minotaur; Sexual Arrangements and Human Malaise* (New York: Harper & Row, 1976).

Di Prima, Diane. *Loba* (Berkeley: Wingbow Press, 1978).

Ehrenreich, Barbara and English, Deirdre. *Witches, Midwives, and Nurses: A History of Women Healers* (Old Westbury, N.Y.: The Feminist Press, 1973)

Ehrenzweig, Anton. *The Hidden Order of Art* (London: Paladin, 1967).

Eliade, Mircea. *Rites & Symbols of Initiation.* Trans. William R. Trask. (New York: Harper & Row, 1958).

Eliot, T. S. *The Waste Land and Other Poems* (New York: Harcourt Brace Jovanovich, 1958).

Eogan, George. "The Knowth Excavations," *Antiquity* 41 (December 1967): 302–304.

Evans, Arthur. *Witchcraft and the Gay Counterculture* (Boston: Fag Rag Books, 1978)

Evans-Wentz, W. Y. *The Fairy Faith in Celtic Countries* (Secaucus, New Jersey: University Books, 1966).

Forfreedom, Anne, ed. *Women out of History: A Herstory Anthology* (Venice, Calif.: Anne Forfreedom, 1972).

Fortune, Dion. *Moon Magic* (New York: Weiser, 1972).

Frazer, Sir James. *The New Golden Bough.* (Ed. Theodor H. Gaster) (New York: Criterion Books, 1959).

Freund, Phillip. *Myths of Creation* (New York: Washington Square Press, 1965).

Gardner, Gerald B. *Witchcraft Today* (Cavendish, Suffolk, G.B., Great Britain: Ryder, 1954)

Gardner, Gerald. *High Magic's Aid* (New York: Weiser, 1975).

Garfield, Patricia. *Creative Dreaming* (New York: Simon & Schuster, 1975).

Glass, Justine. *Witchcraft, The Sixth Sense* (North Hollywood, Calif.: Wilshire, 1965).

Goldberg, Herb. *The Hazards of Being Male* (New York: Signet, 1977).

Goldenburg, Naomi. *The Changing of the Gods* (Boston: Beacon Press, 1979).

Graves, Robert. *The Greek Myths.* Vols. 1 and 2. (London: Hazell Watson & Viney, 1955).

Graves, Robert. *Food for Centaurs* (New York: Doubleday, 1960).

Graves, Robert. *The White Goddess* (New York: Farrar, Straus & Giroux, 1966).

Gray, Louis Herbert, and Moore, George F. *The Mythology of All Races,* Vols. 1, 3, 8, and 10 (New York: Cooper Square, 1964).

Grieve, M. *A Modern Herbal.* Vols 1 and 2. (New York: Dover, 1971).

Griffin, Susan. *Woman and Nature; The Roaring Inside Her* (San Francisco: Harper & Row, 1978).

Gurdjieff, G. I. *Meetings with Remarkable Men* (New York: Dutton, 1969).

Harding, M. Esther. *Women's Mysteries: Ancient and Modern* (New York: Pantheon, 1955).

Harding, M. Esther. *The Way of All Women* (New York: Harper & Row, 1975).

Harris, Marvin. *Cows, Pigs, Wars, and Witches: The Riddles of Culture* (New York: Random House, 1974).

Harrison, Jane Ellen. *Prolegomena to the Study of Greek Religion* (Cambridge, England: Cambridge University Press, 1922).

Hartley, Christine. *The Western Mystery Tradition* (London: Aquarian Press, 1968).

Hawkes, Jaquetta. *The First Great Civilizations* (New York: Knopf, 1973).

Hawkins, Gerald S. *Beyond Stonehenge* (New York: Harper & Row, 1973).

Heresies. "The Great Goddess Issue," Spring 1978 (New York).

Hitching, Francis. *Earth Magic* (New York: Morrow, 1977).

Hoyle, Fred. "Stonehenge, An Eclipse Predictor," *Nature,* 1966, *211,* 456–458.

Ingalls, John D. *Human Energy: The Critical Factor for Individuals and Organizations* (Reading, Mass.: Addison-Wesley, 1976)

Jaynes, Julian. *The Origins of Consciousness in the Breakdown of the Bicameral Mind* (Boston: Houghton Mifflin, 1976).

Kenyon, Kathleen. "Ancient Jericho," *Scientific American,* 190, no. 22 (April, 1968): 76–82.

Krippner, Stanley, and Rubin, Daniel. *The Kirlian Aura: Photographing The Galaxies of Life* (New York: Doubleday, 1974).

Lady-Unique-Inclination-of-the-Night. Cycle 1. (New Brunswick, N.J.: Sowing Circle Press, 1976).

Lady-Unique-Inclination-of-the-Night. Cycle 2. (New Brunswick, N.J.: Sowing Circle Press, 1977).

Laming, Annette. *Lascaux.* Trans. Eleanore Frances Armstrong. (Harmondworth, Middlesex: Penguin Books, 1959).

Leadbeater, C. W. *Man Visible and Invisible* (Wheaton, Ill.: Theosophical Publishing, 1971).

Leek, Sybil. *Diary of a Witch* (New York: Signet, 1968).

LeGuin, Ursula K. *A Wizard of Earthsea* (New York, Bantam Books, 1975).

Leland, Charles. *Aradia, Gospel of the Witches* (New York: Weiser, 1974).

Leroi-Gourhan, Andre, "The Evolution of Paleolithic Art", *Scientific American* 218, No. 17 (1968): 58–68.

Lichtenstein, Marsha, "Radical Feminism and Women's Spirituality: Looking Before You Leap", *Lady-Unique-Inclination-Of-The-Night*, (New Brunswick, N.J.: Sowing Circle Press, 1977) Cycle 2, pp. 36–43.

Lilly, John C. *The Center of the Cyclone* (New York: Julian Press, 1972).

Long, Max Freedom. *The Secret Science Behind Miracles* (Santa Monica, Calif.: Devorss, 1954).

Mander, Anica Vesel, and Rush, Anne Kent. *Feminism as Therapy* (Berkeley, Calif.: Bookworks, 1974).

Maringer, Johannes and Bandi, Hans-George, *Art In The Ice Age* (New York: Frederick A. Praeger, 1953).

Maringer, Johannes. *The Gods of Prehistoric Man* Trans. Mary Ilford. (New York: Knopf, 1960).

Maslow, Abraham H. *Toward a Psychology of Being* (Princeton, N.J.: D. Van Nostrand, 1962).

Mathers, S. L. MacGregor. *The Greater Key of Solomon* (Chicago: De Lawrence, 1914).

Mellaart, James. "Hacilar, a Neolithic Village Site," *Scientific American 205,* no. 27 (August 1961): 86–97.

Mellaart, James. *Catal Hüyük, a Neolithic Town In Anatolia* (New York: MacGraw-Hill, 1967).

Millet, Kate. *Flying* (New York: Ballantine Books, 1974).

Monroe, Robert A. *Journeys out of the Body* (New York: Doubleday, 1973).

Morgan, Robin. *Going Too Far* (New York: Random House, 1977).

Murray, Margaret A. *The God of the Witches* (New York: Oxford University Press, 1970).

Murray, Margaret A. *The Witch-Cult in Western Europe* (New York: Oxford University Press, 1971).

Noteskin, Wallace. *A History of Witchcraft in England,* (New York: Crowell, 1968).

Ornstein, Robert E., *The Psychology of Consciousness* (San Francisco: W. H. Freeman, 1972).

Ostrander, Sheila, and Schroeder, Lynn. *Psychic Discoveries Behind the Iron Curtain* (New York: Bantam Books, 1970).

Quest: A Feminist Quarterly (Washington, D.C.), 1975, *1* (4).

Patai, Raphael. *The Hebrew Goddess* (Philadelphia: Ktav, 1967)

Rainer, Tristine. *The New Diary* (Los Angeles: Tarcher, 1978).

Renfrew, Colin. "Carbon 14 and the Prehistory of Europe," *Scientific American* 225, no. 12 (October 1971): 63–70.

Reuther, Rosemary R. *New Woman/New Earth: Sexist Ideologies and Human Liberation* (New York: Seabury Press, 1975).

Ringgren, Helmer. *Religions of the Ancient Near East* Trans. John Sturdy. (Philadelphia: Westminster Press, 1973).

Rose, Jeanne. *Herbs & Things: Jeanne Rose's Herbal* (New York: Grosset & Dunlap, 1973).

Rothenberg, Jerome, ed. *Technicians of the Sacred* (New York: Doubleday, 1969).

Rothovius, Andrew E. "The Adams Family and the Grail Tradition: The Untold Story of the Dragon Persecution," *East-West* 7, no. 5 (May 1977): 24–30.

Rothovius, Andrew E. "The Dragon Tradition in the New World," *East-West* 7, no. 8, (August 1977): 42–54.

Rush, Anne Kent. *Moon, Moon* (Berkeley, Calif.: Moon Books/Random House, 1976).

Scholem, Gershom G. *Major Trends in Jewish Mysticism* (New York: Schocken Books, 1971).

Scot, Reginald. *The Discoverie of Witchcraft* (New York: Dover, 1972).

Sheba, Lady. *The Book of Shadows* (St. Paul, Minn.: Llewellyn, 1973).

Showerman, Grant. *The Great Mother of the Gods* (Chicago: Argonaut, 1969).

Simos, Bertha. *A Time to Grieve: Loss as a Universal Human Experience* (New York: Family Service Association Press, 1979).

Spretnak, Charlene. *Lost Goddesses of Early Greece* (Berkeley: Moon Books, 1978).

Squire, Charles. *Celtic Myth & Legend* (North Hollywood, Calif.: Newcastle, 1975).

Stern, Philip Van Doren, *Prehistoric Europe: From Stone Age Man to the Early Greeks,* (New York: W. W. Norton & Co. 1969).

Stone, Merlin. *When God Was a Woman* (New York: Dial Press, 1976).

Thom, Alexander. "Megaliths and Mathematics," *Antiquity* 40 (1966): 121–128.

Torrey, E. Fuller. *The Mind Game, Witchdoctors and Psychiatrists* (New York: Bantam Books, 1973).

Valiente, Doreen. *An ABC of Witchcraft, Past and Present* (New York: St. Martin's Press, 1973).

Von Cles-Reden, Sibylle. *The Realm of the Great Goddess* (Englewood Cliffs, N.J.: Prentice-Hall, 1962).

Waldo-Schwartz, Paul. *Art and The Occult* (New York: Braziller, 1975).

Watkins, Alfred. *The Old Straight Track* (New York: Ballantine Books, 1973).

Wedeck, Harry E. *A Treasury of Witchcraft* (Secaucus, N.J.: Stuart, 1972).

Womanspirit Magazine (Wolf Creek, Oregon).